Pepper Martin: A Baseball Biography

Pepper Martin
A Baseball Biography

by THOMAS BARTHEL

McFarland & Company, Inc., Publishers
Jefferson, North Carolina, and London

LIBRARY OF CONGRESS CATALOGUING-IN-PUBLICATION DATA

Barthel, Thomas.
    Pepper Martin : a baseball biography / by Thomas Barthel.
      p.   cm.
    Includes bibliographical references and index.

    ISBN 0-7864-1602-5 (softcover : 50# alkaline paper) ∞

    1. Martin, John Leonard Roosevelt, 1904–1965. 2. Baseball players—United States—Biography. I. Title.
GV865.M354B37   2003
796.357'092 — dc21   2003009928

British Library cataloguing data are available

©2003 Thomas Barthel. All rights reserved

No part of this book may be reproduced or transmitted in any form or by any means, electronic or mechanical, including photocopying or recording, or by any information storage and retrieval system, without permission in writing from the publisher.

Manufactured in the United States of America

Cover photograph: Pepper Martin at bat *(National Baseball Hall of Fame Library, Cooperstown, NY)*

McFarland & Company, Inc., Publishers
   Box 611, Jefferson, North Carolina 28640
   www.mcfarlandpub.com

This book is for my three best teachers:

George Herndl:
"One good schoolmaster is worth a thousand priests."

Judy Angaleen Lewis Barthel

Michael Lewis Barthel

Acknowledgments

The Martin family: Ruby, Alice, Jennie Lee, and Aleyne

In Oklahoma: Alan Cherry, Joe Crowl, Dee Sanders, Clyde Woolridge, Mac Creamer, Len Morton, Dr. Thurman Sheller

Bob McDonnell, for the very thorough Tomato Belt information

Jim Koreas

Don Gutteridge, for his generous talk

Wayne Macomb, author of the excellent book on Tulsa baseball and a great conversationalist

Gordon White, for specifications of the midget racer

Tim Wiles, at the National Baseball Hall of Fame, for the way he pays attention and for his boundless help

Valerie Prescott, of a certain upstate New York library, for her brilliant spirit and her extraordinary librarian skills

Contents

Acknowledgments	vii
Preface	1

PART ONE

1. Young Johnnie	5
2. 1919–1923: $5 a Game	10
3. 1924–1925: In the Low Minors	15
4. 1926–1927: Climbing and Stumbling	22
5. 1928–1930: A Cardinal, a Buffalo, a Red Wing	31
6. 1931: An Old Rookie	40

PART TWO

7. The 1931 World Series Nears	47
8. Thursday, October 1, 1931: Before Game One	53
9. Thursday, October 1, 1931: Game One	57
10. Friday, October 2, 1931: Game Two	60
11. Saturday, October 3, 1931: Travel to Philadelphia	65
12. Sunday, October 4, 1931: Practice Day	68
13. Monday, October 5, 1931: Game Three	71
14. Tuesday, October 6, 1931: Game Four	75

15.	Wednesday, October 7, 1931: Game Five	78
16.	Wednesday, October 7, 1931: After Game Five	83
17.	Thursday, October 8, 1931: The Train Home	86
18.	Friday, October 9, 1931: Game Six	90
19.	Saturday, October 10, 1931: Game Seven	94
20.	Saturday, October 10, 1931: After Game Seven	98
21.	The Last of 1931	102

PART THREE

22.	1932–1934: The Gas House Gang	105
23.	1935–1937: Maestro of the Mudcats	120
24.	1938–1940: A Captain of Cardinals	145

PART FOUR

25.	1941–1946: War's Needs	165
26.	1947–1948: Jack of All Trades	185
27.	1949–1952: A Florida League	189
28.	1953–1956: Five Teams in the Minors; One in the Majors	195
29.	1957–1964: At Home in Oklahoma	206
30.	1965: Death of a Baseball Man	216

Bibliography	221
Index	223

Preface

One writer, Lee Allen, described Pepper Martin this way: "A chunky, unshaven hobo who ran bases like a berserk locomotive, slept in the raw, and swore at pitchers in his sleep" (Chieger, 90).

Before the 1931 World Series was over, Martin's manager said, "Watch that kid. A couple of years from now he'll be filling your stadiums the way Babe Ruth does. He's a natural, ball-playing marvel" (Isaminger, *Inquirer*, Oct. 10, 1931).

The kind of baseball Pepper Martin exemplified was a game, he said, that "was more than just another ball game. It was a regular three-ring circus and everybody was wide awake and enjoying being alive."

In October 1931, Pepper Martin seemed to be a return to the kind of baseball that practiced daring during a period of national despondency. In a time when the country felt diminished and fearful, Pepper grew in stature with every at bat. Four inches shorter than Babe Ruth, forty-five pounds lighter, it seemed that all he had was his confidence, his nerve, his hard-trying to get him through. That he accomplished so much more than just getting through made fans want to touch him as if he had magical powers.

When Pepper Martin died, Joe King of the New York *World-Telegram* wrote this: "To a whole generation, John Leonard Martin was the red blood of baseball, the spirit of the game.... 'He gave us all the urge and daring to take the chance and get the extra base,' Johnny Keane said. Martin was a symbol of hope for all young men in the Great Depression, when there were no jobs, and for many, little to eat.... Martin was the hope of the finer future. He was the ordinary guy who thumbed his nose at VIP's and made them all seem stuffed shirts. He was a guy who could bounce fallen spirits sky high...."

Part I

1

Young Johnnie

It was in Temple, in the Oklahoma territory, that John Leonard Roosevelt (after president Teddy) Martin was born on February 29, 1904, the last of seven children born to Celia Spears Martin. The family needed to be strong to survive through hard times, and not all of them had that strength. Sister Mable died before John was born, sister Cora died in 1919, and then sister Mary followed her in death in 1926.

The Martin family had first begun its Oklahoma life after a pistol shot start, during a get-in-line-and-race land grant giveaway. When the official gun fired, Pepper's father, George Washington Martin, raced on foot into the Cherokee Strip to a claim of forty acres near Enid, Oklahoma. There, Pepper's father built a sod house for his family.

Those forty acres were given up, or traded, for a 160-acre farm near Temple, Oklahoma, a farming and ranching hamlet now with a population of about 1,200. Martin grew up with two Mormon parents when the population of his home state was eleven people per square mile. An "Indian Territory" was still listed on the census, and it was said that in addition to his Irish background, Martin had some Cherokee blood as well. But there is no evidence of that, simply the appearance of high cheekbones.

Martin's father was a painter or a carpenter, but here in Temple the entire family farmed; the major crop was cotton. Many times as an infant baby Johnnie was carried out to the harvesting by his mother and left to sleep on a cotton sack (Wilbur Adams, Sacramento *Bee*, Feb. 20, 1944: 15). We know that, as a boy, Pepper worked hard in the family's red barn and that he learned how to milk a cow, how to calculate the feed for the livestock, how to nurse sick calves, and how to tend to a 600-pound Poland-China sow and her fourteen piglets. Sister Letha and brothers Charley and George helped Johnnie out, since these animals were the source of the family's food.

In lean times the family ate cornmeal mush and fried mush, too. Beans

Pepper as an infant. (Copyright, *The Sacramento Bee*, 1941.)

and cabbage, bought by the hundred pound sack, supplied much of the family diet. His parents, in Martin's memory, were frugal to the extreme. Ice cream, which Pepper badly wanted, was, in his memory, an affordable pleasure denied him by his father. The memory of that ice cream privation would stay with Johnnie his whole life.

The hard life on the farm was softened partly by the fun the children had with the family horses. "I dubbed around just like any other kid," Martin told the Philadelphia *Inquirer*, "took my share of licking behind the old barn and probably learned to run fast escaping angry farmers and shopkeepers who objected when us kids broke down their fences or snitched their food" (Baumgartner, Philadelphia *Inquirer*, Oct. 4, 1931).

But when drought erased the farm — some claim a cyclone blew the farm down — George Martin found work as a carpenter in the state house in Oklahoma City. The family moved to 2448 North West 11th Street in Oklahoma City in 1910 when Johnnie was six. One odd feature of the house was a working oil well in the backyard, which provided income for the family.

The young boy was enrolled first in the Washington Grammar School and then at the Edgemere School, two miles from his house down by a creek. He spent much of his playtime at a game called Hare And Hounds. The hare would tear up bits of paper and scatter them in a trail across the schoolyard, down side streets and into the nearby woods; then the hounds would take out after him. Martin claimed that he "sure learned to run and if I was the hare I was seldom caught and when I was one of the pack of hounds, I usually caught the hare" (Brundidge, St. Louis *Star* July 21, 1931: 1). Later he was recalled as "one of the most likable fellows in school, a

Pepper entertaining childhood friends with his singing. (Copyright, *The Sacramento Bee*, 1941.)

flash at any kind of athletics, he was practically a total loss in the classroom ... but in order to get to play baseball and football he worked hard enough to be graduated."

These were troublesome times for the family, times which forced Martin to withdraw from school many times and to help bring some money into the house, as the family fought to survive. "When I was nine, I delivered morning newspapers in Oklahoma City.... I knew by heart the averages of pretty near every big leaguer. I saved enough money out of my earning as a newsboy to buy my first glove and I had it stuck in my back pocket wherever I went and whatever I did. Not so many kids in my neighborhood had gloves and owning that mitten gave me almost as much happiness as would a couple of home runs in a World's Series game" (Martin, *Philadelphia Inquirer*, Oct. 12, 1931). We can imagine Pepper circling the bases, one overall strap off, flapping, as he runs.

When Martin talked about the early morning job, he described another benefit to him, though he had to "get up at 3:30 every morning to get the Daily *Oklahoman* to the homes of my readers. But before I delivered a single paper, I used to sit down under a street corner lamp and study the box scores of the major leagues. In winter I'd read the gossip of the hot stove league. I delivered *The News* in the afternoons and my two jobs kept me busy" (Brundidge, St. Louis *Star*, July 21, 1931: 2).

One day when John was twelve, he came home in time to see the dog catcher tossing his dog into the truck's cage full of others. (No doubt the boy fed his dog with his newspaper earnings as well.) The dog catcher started off, but when he heard a loud crash, he stopped and found Johnnie in the cage with the dogs, grabbing his own. Johnnie snuggled the dog under his arm, leaped from the truck, and ran off.

Pepper pitching for his team at about age ten. (Copyright, *The Sacramento Bee*, 1941.)

He ran also on the soccer field, and pitched on the Edgemere team, "dream[ing] of the days when I would put on a uniform of the Boston Red Sox. I liked baseball and had ambitions to be a professional player, and Babe Ruth and 'Dutch' Leonard, then pitchers on the Boston Red Sox, were my heroes…" (Brundidge, St. Louis *Star*, July 21, 1931: 2). Pepper told the story many times, to Wilbur Adams of the Sacramento *Bee*, for one, of how he "never will forget playing another school for the soccer championship of the district. We would have won the game but there was a squabble over a goal and our captain gave it to the opponents and we lost the game and the title. I never forgave that kid for that. I don't believe in giving away anything that rightfully belongs to your side. That is the way I play everything. I don't want to cheat or take unfair advantage of a foe, but I do believe in battling for your rights. That little soccer argument is very minor, but I still remember it vividly" (Wilbur Adams, Sacramento *Bee*, Feb. 20, 1944: 15).

Arguments, Martin remembered, were often resolved between schoolboys by holding a wrestling match. As a student, Martin recalled that he was skilled at spelling and history, but did not like arithmetic or English (Wilbur Adams, Sacramento *Bee*, Feb. 21, 1944: 15).

Since he did like the money, he loaded up a home-made cart with soda pop and pulled the wagon to the sandlots where he would sell it to the players. That being done, Johnnie shagged flies when the soda was sold (Heinz, 101).

Johnnie found time to develop a reputation as a good hunter of quails and rabbits. Stories of his rabbit hunting would come back to him in a most colorful way. Martin's jobs kept him very busy and the parents were unwilling to dress their children for school as they needed to be dressed. Especially remembered by Martin was their refusal to provide shoes or

Young Johnnie

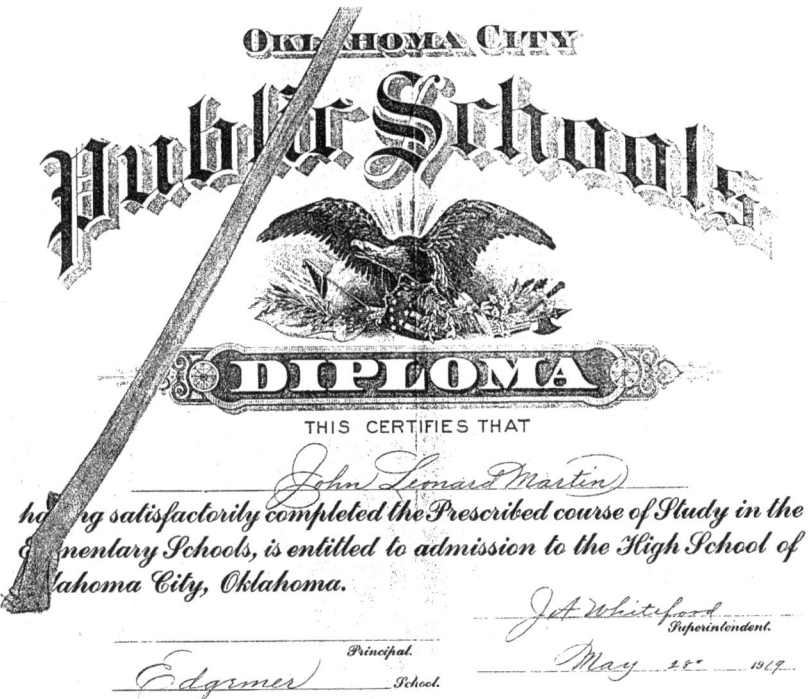

Pepper's Diploma: the date is 1919, when Pepper was 15. His schooling, as was often the case in those days, was irregular. (National Baseball Hall of Fame Library, Cooperstown, N.Y.)

more importantly, the turtle neck sweater that was so popular in those days. This lack of proper clothing caused Johnnie to be in and out of school so much that it was not until the age of fifteen, on May 18, 1919, that he was handed his elementary school diploma by the principal, Mrs. Dora Frye.

2

1919–1923:
$5 a Game

In the fall of 1919 in Oklahoma City, Martin played halfback on the Irving Junior High School football team through an undefeated season. Known by now for his speed, Martin later said, "Football is a game where, if you are fast, and can hit a line hard and aren't easily hurt, you get to going good." At Classen High School the next year, after one winning football game, Martin quit school to take work delivering on a bicycle for the Mistletoe Shoe Company for $12 per week. The choice of a company to work for may have been due to the fact that he had to quit high school for lack of shoes. Johnnie worked throughout the winter and thought about going back to school. Up until then, he did not play baseball in a school affair, since the school had neither a baseball team nor a track team, both of which Martin would have liked. Yet, as he said later, "The only playing I had done up to that time was with some picked teams in my neighborhood" (Martin, *Philadelphia Inquirer*, Oct. 12, 1931).

After returning to school briefly in March 1921, Johnnie got his job back at the shoe store and worked again "to earn money instead of fiddling around and getting an education."

Another kind of schooling was going on in the sandlots around Oklahoma City, and teams began to notice him. "Along in 1921 ... the first regularly uniformed club I was with was the Second Presbyterian Church team. I am a Baptist but that didn't make any difference with those boys. I nearly lost my voice trying to make sure they heard my 'yes'.... I finally pitched for the Second Presbyterian Church in the City League but got canned because I didn't go to Sunday school.... Most fellows aiming to be ball players ... want to be a pitcher because the pitcher gets his name in the papers plenty and ... the pitchers got the most money ... but I was

Pepper playing football in high school. (Copyright, *The Sacramento Bee*, 1941.)

different. I just couldn't make up my mind so I played every position in baseball and kept on doing that..." (Martin, Philadelphia *Inquirer*, Oct. 12, 1931). Then, too, as Martin would admit later, he did not feel a lot of confidence about his baseball abilities, but was eager to catch on somewhere.

After the season, he found a job at a filling station at Twenty-third and Robinson avenues and "many a good citizen of Oklahoma City has heard me ask: 'How many, please? Shall I fill it up? Shall I look at your oil? Do you need a grease job? Can I wash the car for you? How about your springs? Do your brakes need tightening?' ... But all the time I wanted to play ball. Oh! man how I wanted to play ball..." (Brundidge, St. Louis *Star*, July 21, 1931: 2).

Pepper still played sandlot ball but he needed cash and so he decided to learn a trade finding work as a helper for a tinsmith, with the three Nelson Brothers. Of his time there, he said, "My boss asked me if I could drive an automobile and I told him I knew how, although I had never had any actual experience. He told me to deliver some stuff and I started the car and drove away" down a one-way street (Brundidge, St. Louis *Star*, July 21, 1931: 2). Three minutes and five blocks later, Martin crashed into a street car. "What I needed, I explained to my boss later, was some experience inside the shop, so he put me to cutting galvanized iron and tin. I worked at that until my machine slipped and I sliced the end from the middle finger of my left hand" (Brundidge, St. Louis *Star*, July 21, 1931: 2).

That accident was enough to make him leave that job, and he decided that if he wasn't playing professional baseball he could at least get close to it. So for the home games in the Oklahoma City ballpark in 1922, Martin hustled soda and peanuts. One day a practice pitcher was needed and Martin, early on the job as usual, volunteered to throw. In those days, the second line players were the ones to throw batting practice, which was not a job they looked forward to. But for Martin it was wonderful, and his enthusiasm and infectious spirit did not go unnoticed. Soon he was hired as the bat boy and he was seen shagging flies in the outfield before games. "I was a pretty good pitcher in batting practice and, while no big-league scouts rushed to me with a contract, a bird from the Brooks Hardware Company offered me a chance to pitch for their team in the city league and I grabbed it. I went good," though without pay, even while filling in the outfield and infield" (Brundidge, St. Louis *Star*, July 21, 1931: 2). "... Later on I heard that the Kelley Jewelry team of Oklahoma City was going on tour and needed a player.... I ... was recommended to them. It was rough getting a place because they thought I was too young and I wasn't so big either. But finally they said 'Yes.' We went on a tour through the state" (Martin, Philadelphia *Inquirer*, Oct. 12, 1931). There is a photo of Johnnie Martin with his team in the summer of 1922 with the caption "Pepper Martin's first ball club" and the uniforms say "KELLEY JLRY CO." The team "would slip me $5 a game sometimes.... We got back in time to get into the series for the city championship.... I made three errors in seven chances in the infield and five hits in eight times up.... I finished up the year playing with the Oklahoma National Guard team which had games scheduled after the season had ended for the Kelley Jewelry club" (Martin, Philadelphia *Inquirer*, Oct. 12, 1931).

In the fall of 1922 (and in 1923 and 1929), Pepper Martin played football with the "terrors of the Midwest," a Native American professional football team named the Hominy Indians. A powerful team, "in December 1927, the Hominy Indians defeated the newly crowned champions of the National Football League, the New York Giants, 13–6, in a game played at Pawhuska, Oklahoma. The Hominy Indians remained undefeated until 1928 when they lost to the NFL All-Stars" (Ray Thurmond. *Journal of Sport History*, 1975, Vol. 2, No. 1, p. 51–78 [pdf]).

By June of 1923, Johnnie had played shortstop and pitched with a National Guard team for a while, but that affiliation didn't last because the Guard expected Martin to join the service. Until the next baseball season, Martin "caught on as a grease monkey at the Greenlese-Moore Cadillac Company." It seems like from time to time Martin would drift back to school for a while, play some football and then quit. He said that in the summer of 1923 the Oklahoma Gas & Electric Co. "offered me a job as a grunter if I'd pitch for the company team.... A grunter? He's the bird that helps the lineman. The helper grunts because the lineman makes him do

Pepper in about 1922, when he first played in the Oklahoma State League. (Copyright, *The Sacramento Bee*, 1941.)

all the work" (Brundidge, St. Louis *Star,* July 21, 1931: 2). That means, Martin said, "I worked on the ground and held up fellows that had to be lifted up to do some work and then you're a 'grunt man.' I tell you, you grunt" (Philadelphia *Inquirer*, Oct. 12, 1931). It meant that Martin grunted in blizzards at times. And dreamed of baseball out on the lonely Oklahoma roads. Baseball was played by the company team on Sunday only, but it was for those games that Martin lived.

"With them ... I was always trying too hard to make good. And not doing so good. I'd be so anxious to make putouts that no matter where I'd be playing I'd go running after the ball. Just not much good sense. If a hit was made to right and I was playing second or short, I'd be out in that field trying to make the catch. I had enough speed to get into the outfield lots of times before the ball came down. These players would pan me plenty for trying to patrol their beats and tangling up with them sometimes. But I just couldn't get over the habit. Anytime I'd see one of the other guys hitting the ball I'd get the fool notion that I was the man that had to make the play on it. And I'd be on my way after that ball" (Martin, Philadelphia *Inquirer*, Oct. 12, 1931).

Then, in the fall of 1923, Johnnie's boss sent him to the Western League Park where he had played in 1922, except now the park was flooded up to the fourth row, when the North Canadian River overflowed. "My boss sent a boat out there and told me to guard it because if some emergency might arise we might need it to go places and make repairs. While I was guarding the boat a policeman came along and tried to rush off with it.... The O. G. and E. had told me to protect that boat and that's what I meant to do. So I grabbed it back. The cop grabbed and I grabbed and we were scuffling around plenty. The law was against me and so was the cop's club and I landed in jail charged with being too rough. The O. G. and E.

people explained the next day and that saved me" (Martin, Philadelphia *Inquirer*, Oct. 12, 1931).

Martin's eagerness to succeed in baseball was clear to him and he later faced his discouragement, saying, "I pitched a mean ball for the gas company, but once again a season passed by without that scout showing up, and I decided it was about time I forgot all about baseball and went into business for myself. I looked about for a business" (Brundidge, St. Louis *Star*, July 21, 1931).

3

1924–1925: In the Low Minors

To put some money in his pocket, Martin fished golf balls out of the muddy ponds on the Oklahoma City golf courses and then re-painted and sold the found balls. When Martin went looking for a new line of work, he found the most humble employment, a job so low that it was given comical anti-heroic names like "crumb boss." Pepper told the Philadelphia Inquirer that this was: "the oil workers' title for Rockefeller valets.... I cleaned out the bunk houses and pitched when I wasn't catching for the outfit: There were plenty of oil men loafing about the country then, and as I grew up I began to bum around with them, that is between playing baseball.... I got a job with a pipe laying outfit and I guess that is what gave me the big forearms. Sure was hard work yanking those things around and plying the big wrenches. My arms ached so much I thought they would drop off—gee, that was tough work. A bat feels like a feather compared to those big sledges I used to swing. When work was slack I used to bum from one town to another. I guess you could call it hoboing." During that "hoboing" period, "there were many times when my one shirt would get its only bath in the creek" (Baumgartner, Philadelphia *Inquirer*, Oct. 4, 1931).

This seems to be a time, in Martin's life, probably in the winter of 1923–24, when he may have played for a team in the "Tomato Belt" in Mississippi, an area south of Jackson. The Copiah County League was probably semi-pro, or even industrial, comprising the four towns of McComb, Brookhaven, Hazlehurst and Crystal Springs. It may have been the last town that Martin played for, a team managed by Roscoe Miles, and a story has come to us about Pepper: "... From around the grandstand he appeared running with a bat in one hand, his shoes in the other, yelling at manager Miles, 'I couldn't run with them durn spikes on my feet.'"

This was clearly a low point in his life. Johnnie learned that confidence must always be a very important part of a ballplayer's life. Later, he said, "I'm old enough now to know that you have to convince yourself that you're good enough to advance before you can advance, but that is something I didn't know years ago. Harold Lee, who I always call 'Burr,' and who is thirteen years older than I, has been my pal since I was 18 and he always put in a good word for me that got me places on teams" (Martin, Philadelphia *Inquirer*, Oct. 13, 1931).

An even more important friend came along. "In March 1924, I met Cliff Campbell who was also my friend and of course I got right down to talking baseball with him. I never did talk anything much except baseball. He's the fellow who thought I was a ball player when all the time I was sort of sure in my heart I wasn't but trying all the time to improve my game. I kept saying to Cliff that I wished I could get on a real professional club and Cliff said: 'Trouble with you is that you are a better player than you think you are. But you're afraid to go and ask for a job. So I'll do the asking for you. After that you do the playing and if you don't play as good as I'll tell this fellow you can play, I'll rattle your ears right off your head....' It wasn't until 1924 that I started a sure-enough professional career.... Later on he rounded me up and said: 'I've got a job for you with Guthrie ... and you'll play anywhere they tell you'" (Martin, Philadelphia *Inquirer*, Oct. 13, 1931). Martin said, "I took an extra shirt rolled up in a newspaper and I went there" (Heinz, 102).

Of the spring of 1924, Martin said, "I reported to Manager M. H. Robertson at Guthrie in the Oklahoma State League and my professional career got started with me as a pitcher.... I was hoping I'd maybe get good enough to advance to a higher league, but, folks, I sure never did think I'd get into the big leagues, no sir, I never did think that. Those big leaguers, Cobb, Ruth, Hornsby, Frisch and others seem to be way, way up in the places where I was sure I'd never even get close to.... I guess the $125 a month the folks paid me at Guthrie was wages about as low as they ever did pay anybody (a paycheck of $94.68 was the average monthly wage in 1924), but I tell you it seemed sort of like I was stealing when I took that kind of big money from them for doing nothing but having a million dollars worth of fun playing baseball" (Martin, Philadelphia *Inquirer*, Oct. 14, 1931).

The league's season was scheduled to run from May 24 to September 7 and for that time Martin was paid a relatively low salary; the highest salary of the fourteen team members was $500 per month. "I certainly made up my mind that I wasn't going to flim the folks in Guthrie. I was sure out to give them a fair deal and I was trying all the time to help them win. But, like before, I was so blamed anxious to put out the other side all by myself that I kept the other infielders and some of the outfielders cussing me plenty for getting mixed up in their plays" (Martin, Philadelphia *Inquirer*, Oct. 13, 1931).

Martin said, of his days at shortstop, "Often my throws to first base were so high I was endangering the lives of the fans in the grandstand.... The club was about to release me so I told the manager I was really a pitcher and they held onto me" (Wilbur Adams, Sacramento *Bee*, Feb. 22, 1944: 15). Pepper said he pitched against the Cushing's team pitcher, a twenty-one year old Missourian named Carl Hubbell. In fact, Johnnie pitched two shutouts against the Bristow team, losses that prevented them from winning the first half pennant, something that the Bristow club would remember.

"We didn't have such a bad club at Guthrie, but the town didn't seem to go very much for baseball that year and the club dropped out of the league" (Martin, Philadelphia *Inquirer*, Oct. 13, 1931). Other teams disbanded or moved; Guthrie moved to McAlester on May 24, and then moved to Wewoka on June 8.

In this chaos, the story became muddled. One story had Martin say, after Guthrie folded, "Our boys figured out what was best to do and at least we decided to go barnstorming, but the pickings weren't much good and we were hardly able to pay expenses, so we gave up that tour" (Martin Philadelphia *Inquirer*, Oct. 13, 1931). As teams changed towns and names, another story said Martin's contract was bought by Bristow. Martin himself said, "It seemed like as if I just was all through as a league ball player when the Bristow team in the Oklahoma League decided it would take a chance on me and I was loaned to them for the rest of the season of 1924" (Martin, Philadelphia *Inquirer*, Oct. 12, 1931).

However, the league disbanded July 8. What seems to be the truth was that Martin traveled to a Cardinal tryout camp in Greenville, Texas, and then Guthrie sold him to Greenville for $300. "... Some of the men that had seen me play for Guthrie and Bristol told somebody at Greenville, Tex., which was in the Texas State League, that I was a fair sort of player and so before the 1925 season began I was sold for $300 to Greenville" (Martin, Philadelphia *Inquirer*, Oct. 13, 1931). Years later Martin recalled his selling price of $300 and remarked that, "Whoever got that $300 ... must have thought that he put a fast one over on Greenville because I was thinking that way too. I didn't figure I was worth $300 to anybody, but so long as Greenville paid that much for me I said to myself that I'd bust a leg if I had to, to prove to them that they weren't cheated too bad" (Martin, Philadelphia *Inquirer*, Oct. 13, 1931).

This is closer to the facts since there exists a copy of a contract dated July 10, 1924 (two days after the Oklahoma State League folded), with the signatures of J. L. Martin and President C. P. Nevill of the Greenville Hunters managed by Bernie Brownlaw. Martin was now in the East Texas League, a "D" level league. Greenville, a town of 12,384, had a player's salary at the Guthrie level of pay: $2000 per season. The team had played .620 ball for the first half of the season, good enough for second place in the league, and played almost as well in the second half to finish third.

Martin played competently, if erratically. In twenty-seven games with sixty-two at bats, he hit .274. In ten games playing center, he had eighteen put outs, two assists and a .974 fielding average. He pitched thirty-three innings in nine games, ending with a 1–1 record. He was, more importantly, a professional baseball player.

Martin came back to Greenville in 1925, signing with team president James P. Turner for the maximum salary of $2,400 for the season. That salary level did not last in the hard times that the club felt and Pepper soon found just $175 each month in his pay envelope, which added up to only $962.50 for the season. "I did some pitching for Greenville, played the outfield in pinches, but most of the time I was at second base.... I was socking the ball good, but I wasn't much shucks at fielding. I was always so anxious to make a play that I'd snatch at a ball before it was 'ripe' and I'd bobble on the stop. Or if I wasn't doing that, I was throwing wild every so often" (Martin, Philadelphia *Inquirer*, Oct. 13, 1931). If he was not playing well, he knew it very well. He knew he was letting the team down and letting down the owner who was paying his salary. "I wasn't at any time sure that I was good enough to hang onto a job even in Greenville. Fact is there were times when I thought my loose throwing might get me fired ... and that made me try all the harder to get a lot of hits and steal a lot of bases so as to make up for bad fielding" (Martin, Philadelphia *Inquirer*, Oct. 14, 1931).

To "make up" in other ways, Martin said he became "the whole advertising department. Every morning I'd hitch up a horse to a big covered wagon and drive around the town. On the outside of the wagon, they had big signs advertising the game that afternoon. I was also the assistant groundskeeper. After riding around that town all morning, I'd hustle down to the ball park and help smooth out the diamond" (New York *World-Telegram*, May 21, 1931).

After ninety-eight games, Martin's batting average was .340; he also hit eighteen home runs and stole thirty-eight bases. As a pitcher, he gave up fifty-two hits in fifty-three innings. Fielding second base in eighty-six games, he made thirty-three errors. "... I was not satisfied with my play-

ing and I didn't think I was getting along so good. What happens one day is this: L. K. Wise, the owner of the club, calls me in and says: 'I just sold you to the St. Louis Cardinals.' Folks, that was the nearest I ever came to fainting."

> That the Cardinals ranked with the most profitable National League clubs at this time owed to the genius of General Manager Branch Rickey. One of baseball's greatest innovators, ... Rickey made a contender out of the impecunious Cardinals by reviving the farm system and using minor league farm clubs to develop and train young players. By purchasing minor league clubs and establishing working agreements with others, and by deploying scouts to sign young players at low costs, Rickey built and stocked a network of minor league farm clubs which supplied the Cardinals with a steady flow of star players [Thorn].

Rickey's chief scout was Charley Barrett, who wrote to Rickey about Pepper that "he has speed and power, he can hit, and he has a wonderful arm" (St. Louis *Post-Dispatch*, Oct. 7, 1931), a kind of litany that Barrett would repeat often to his boss. He later added, "He was without a doubt the worst ball player I ever saw — but how he could run and how he could slug that ball!" (Bill Bryson, Des Moines *Register*, July 6, 1955). Rickey himself powerfully believed that fielding could be taught and that running speed was paramount in a player.

Having his contract purchased by a Cardinals farm team at Fort Smith, Arkansas automatically improved Martin's mobility within baseball. Either he would move up the Cardinal chain or he would be sold. If nothing else, Rickey was active with his players.

"The fellows in Greenville put on a little celebration for me the afternoon I played my last game there and they gave me a watch and asked me to make a speech, but I got scared seeing so many people looking square at me and hurrahing and everything and I couldn't get any words out of my mouth so I started for the clubhouse on a run and just was able to yell back at them, 'Thanks, boys, thanks,' and that was my farewell to Greenville and its fine people, in 1925" (Martin, Philadelphia *Inquirer*, Oct. 14, 1931).

Moving from a "D" level team to a "C" level team meant a raise of $25 a month. Martin said, "I went to Fort Smith to start my major-league education. Blake Harper, who now has charge of all the pop bottles, hot dogs and thirst-producing popcorn in Sportsman's Park, was the owner of the Fort Smith team and, after seeing me hop around the bases and listening to my line of chatter, he named me 'Pepper'" (Brundidge, St. Louis *Star*, July 21, 1931).

Another version was that Martin, arriving in Fort Smith, saw the headline "Pepper Martin to Join Twins" went to the newspaper office to complain and found Harper there. The story has been told that Harper picked out the name "Pepper" because he thought the name John Martin too ordinary. At any rate the newspaper liked that name.

In fact, on July 30, 1925, the Fort Smith *Southwest American* wrote: "Infielder Pepper Martin is en route here and will arrive here in time to take part in the series opener [against the Okmulgee Drillers] according to a telegram received from him by Blake Harper."

Little Rock then was a city of 31,139, and its newspaper paid attention to the Southern Association team in Little Rock as well as the four teams in the West Arkansas League. The six team Western Association included clubs in Oklahoma, Missouri and Arkansas. The Fort Smith Twins, who played at the 3,500 seat Andrews Field, were currently fourth in the league in the second half race at 14–17. They trailed the Muskogee Mets, the Drillers and the Ardmore Boomers.

In Martin's first game, a 7–6 win, he led off and played second. "Pepper Martin, recently secured infielder ... made his initial bow to the Twins fans," the unsigned story began, "by crashing out a double over [center fielder] Najo's head to open the Twins' half of the first inning. He also garnered one other blow, a scratch single ... and lived up to advance notices as to his speed and peppery playing"(July 31, 1925). He also continued his erratic fielding by throwing a relay from the right fielder into the Okmulgee dugout, causing two runs to score. This win put the Twins seven-and-a-half-games behind the league leader. Pepper made an error in his second game as well, but made three hits and two runs, and he showed the team what he could do: to begin the seventh, he grounded the ball, but hustled down the line, and when the throw went wild he moved to second. To third he advanced on a sacrifice, eager to increase his team's one run lead. He scored on a double and that began a four run inning for the Twins.

By July's end, the team had won thirteen of their last sixteen games. However, the Fort Smith team stayed seven games back of Muskogee and five games out of second place, tied with the Springfield Midgets for third. "They stuck me at short.... The throws from there are longer and you've got to get them away from you pretty fast, and my trouble was that I tried to get 'em away too fast and I didn't do much aiming and it was pretty near always an even money bet that I would throw it into the bleachers. ... but every time the manager had made up his mind to shoot me dead because of bad fielding I would make a hit or steal a base and that is how I saved my life from one day to the next" (Martin, Philadelphia *Inquirer*, Oct. 14, 1931).

On September 4, playing shortstop, Martin "started to sew up the

Pepper in 1925, playing for Little Rock when he first was given the name Pepper. (Copyright, *The Sacramento Bee*, 1941.)

game in the seventh by lacing one down the right field line that rolled to the fence. He made a brilliant sprint around the field and beat the ball home...." On the seventh, he hit two home runs and on the last day of the season "the fast little shortstop took the mound to hurl the closing game and got by three innings without yielding a hit." But then he gave up twelve runs though "slow fielding and apparent indifference accounted for some of these hits" (Fort Smith *Southwest American*). Martin finished the game at first base for the ninth inning as the second baseman gave up the last six runs of an 18–3 loss. So the team ended the 1925 season tied with third place Springfield at 40–35 for the second half.

Martin played shortstop for forty-five games making twenty-one errors, but he made a lot of hits, 62, in a short time and stole many bases as well — seventeen. This performance, no doubt, built his confidence.

4

1926–1927: Climbing and Stumbling

Martin's remarkable performance for the Fort Smith Twins in 1925 yielded Martin not only a raise of $125 per month, the raise equaling his entire salary when he first began, but also a three-level promotion to the team in Syracuse, New York. Martin remembered reading the contract for a $325 monthly salary and said, "I was just plain daffy I was that glad." The great jump from "C" to "AA" ball did not seem memorable to Martin so much as the jump in salary did.

The new contract, though, led to the first of the riding of the rods stories:

> ... In the spring of 1926 I was ordered to report to the Syracuse club of the International League, a Cardinal farm, for spring training at [Greenwood, South Carolina]. I looked at that check for my expenses, decided that 1,300 miles wasn't such a great distance after all, cashed the check, shipped my good suit and a couple of shirts to Greenville [sic] via fast express, walked down to the Oklahoma freight yards. A friendly hobo pointed out a freight that headed east and I grabbed it. It was a swell trip, but my fun spoiled on the last hop. I was sleeping in a freight car rapidly nearing Greenville [sic], when a thieving hobo got his hand into my pockets and took my expense money. I got off that train at 1 AM, flat broke. Did I look like a tramp? Man, go down to Market street, pick out the worst-looking pan-handler on the main stem and I'm him, see? I talked myself into an advance of salary, got my clothes from the express company and went to bed and slept around the clock [Brundidge, St. Louis *Star*, July 21, 1931].

This was a true story, so it seemed, according to a report on March 16 in the Syracuse *Post-Standard*: "John Leonard Martin, said to be a whale of an infielder, reached the Hotel Oregon at 2 o'clock in the morning, slept past lunch or dinner time and took his workouts minus food. He comes to the club with the reputation of being very fast and ... if he is, Syracuse fans can give three rousing cheers for Charles Barrett...." Scout Barrett remained one of Martin's biggest supporters and certainly talked Pepper up to the new president of the team Warren Giles, who bought the team from Phil Bartelme. Burt Shotton, team manager, played his last five years of fourteen with the Cardinals, ending his career in the majors—as a player—in 1923.

After some training season games against Wofford College in Spartanburg, and against the Greenville Spinners of the South Atlantic League, the team began to play its way north. In a game at Norfolk on April 10, 1926, Pepper homered.

There is no mention up until now of the playfulness that was an integral part of Pepper's makeup. Perhaps too intent on his career at this point to behave outlandishly, all he could be is Pepper. That is to say, Martin could be single-minded about something, like saving money on train fares, and not worry too much about the consequences of his actions.

The Syracuse *Post-Standard*'s reporter got information from Giles and manager Burt Shotton, then wrote, "Pepper is aptly named. He'll be a great favorite in this city. He'd be a favorite anywhere because he's always fighting. He wants to win all the time. He's high strung, full of zip and pep and he's drawn a lot of favorable comments from fans and sports writers in all the towns we've visited. In the field he'll get balls other third basemen couldn't reach. As a result he is liable to appear erratic at first but the more one watches him, the higher one rates him. On the bases he is even more of a go-getter than Jimmy Cooney ... and knows how to use his speed. He lacks ... experience ... but he will shape up as well in the field as any other third baseman in the league, and at bat will rank as one of the hardest hitting infielders in the circuit" (April 11, 1926).

The team's season began in Newark's City Stadium against the Jersey City Skeeters, with Martin hitting seventh and playing third base. After a series at the Reading Keys, the team, now 2–7, boarded a train for the ten hour trip to Syracuse for opening day at Archbold Stadium, used for opening day only. The team's permanent ballyard was on West Genessee. Called Star Park, it was the smallest in the league, with just 4,200 seats which sold for either 75 cents or 50 cents. The city of Syracuse seemed to be able to support a bigger park, since the city's population was 182,003 and the team, in the International League, was in the highest rated minors at "AA." It's true that Syracuse's weather can be brutal in late April but the season ran until September 19. This team was the largest (twenty-five players) that Pepper had ever played on.

The newspaper has a baseball poem called "That Old Sweet Song" by Joseph H. Adams to mark the home opener:

> I heard sweet music yesterday
> Like the song of a nightingale
> As it came to me in a morn in May
> In the depths of a flowery vale;
> And there's just one song as sweet as that
> One that makes you glad you're alive
> That's the song of the crash of a hickory bat,
> The song of a whirling drive.

For the home opener, the players reported at 1:00 PM and dressed in pin-striped uniforms and caps with short bills; the blouse had an "S" inside a circle over the heart. While batting practice began at the ballpark on opening day, bands, leading groups of fans, formed downtown near the team's office on Salina Street. The day was very cold as the band marched up the hill to the stadium for the game with the Twinks, the local nickname for the Stars.

Before the game, four Iroquois, dressed in full regalia, honored two Native American players, Guy Froman and Chief Nason. Floral horseshoes were delivered to the park. King Kelly, the field announcer, told the crowd that it was Mayor Hanna who threw the first pitch from the pitcher's mound.

But no matter the ceremonies, the Stars were playing badly. For example, on April 25, the Stars lost 30–5 in a game that took but 2:02. Manager Shotton tried Martin at second base for a while and then decided to move Johnnie to third base and to the third spot in the lineup. Soon rival pitchers tested him as with this incident on April 29: After a single and a walk began Syracuse's batting, "Spaulding dusted Pepper Martin off with a head high fast one. Pepper hit the dust, bounded right back again, and when Spaulding shot the next one through the middle, Pepper lost it beyond the right field barrier. As he made the circuit, he received an order from Bob Soule of the Citizen's Baseball Committee that entitled him to the pick of the new spring suits up on Nick Peters' rack" (Syracuse *Post-Standard*, April 29, 1926).

By the end of May, with Pepper now at shortstop, his team was 14–28.

Early in June, Martin was 39–144, .271, and in late June he batted 47–168, .280, playing in 48 of 66 games. Why was Johnnie not playing full-time? A story Martin told many years later may help to explain. The team was playing in Toronto and Eddie Dyer was pitching a 1–1 tie in the ninth. With one out, Dyer gave up a triple; the next batter blooped one that Martin chased down over his shoulder. Meanwhile, the runner bluffed running home and Pepper ran in, faking a throw, daring the runner to go instead of just throwing the ball in. It was then that the runner took off for the plate; "I was so darn surprised I just stood there petrified, not thinking to throw the ball. By the time I did the run was in. Shotton kept me in the dressing room for two hours, bawling me out," Martin recalled (New York *World-Telegram*, March 23, 1950).

By the usual half-way point, July 4, the team had not even won thirty percent of their seventy-eight games, and dropped to seventh in the International League. Martin had been moved into the second spot in the batting order and again to second base with 174 at bats and a .281 average. By month's end the team had performed better, their winning percentage climbed thirty-nine percent. How much of this was due to Martin, who had raised his average by fifty points, is impossible to tell.

In August, the fans could tell the team was not going to get much better, stalled as it was with wins equaling fewer than one in three. Just when there seemed to be no hope, the team went on a twelve and one winning streak with Johnnie maintaining his .310 average. Thus, the team climbed to over forty-one percent wins, some of the players no doubt bragging at the New York State Fair on their day off.

The next day, September 1, with twenty-one games left with the Syracuse Stars 58–82, .414, Johnnie was given a chance to pitch: "Pepper Martin was the last of the home artillerists … who temporarily deserted second for the box…" (Syracuse *Post-Standard*, Sept. 1, 1926) and amassed an earned run average of 108.0 in one third of an inning (the visitor's eighth) this way: four runs on two walks, one hit batsman and one hit. The batter he hit, Joe Brown, was carried off the field unconscious, and taken to the hospital.

On the second day in September Pepper seemed to have a typical day for him in 1926 when he doubled in the ninth to tie the game, and then "became a dub in the eleventh when he dropped Bill Urbanski's fly with three on and two out" against Jersey City (Syracuse *Post-Standard*, Sept. 2, 1926).

Seventeen days later he ended the 70–91 season at third base, hitting second. His year was summed up with this report: "With Syracuse Martin played second base. He was erratic. He swung at balls a yard away from the plate, kicked grounders and threw plenty of balls a mile over the first baseman's head." On a weak team, he made the sixth highest average. Still, playing in 129 games he had 29 steals, which number would have made him second in the National League to Kiki Cuyler's 37 steals in 1926. And, with just 480 at bats, he managed to score 103 runs. But he made ten errors in twenty-three games at third and thirty-five errors in eighty-eight games at second.

The jump from Fort Smith "C" to Syracuse "AA" was an enormous leap and Johnnie did not show Rickey or Cardinals owner Sam Breadon that he was ready for it.

1927

Johnnie Martin knew that he did not earn a promotion for 1927, and that he needed "additional seasoning. I wasn't quite ripe." Martin added: "Burt Shotton, boss at Syracuse, decided I was too bad at fielding and he had me transferred ... but when I got to Houston's training camp in 1927 my whole career was changed. 'You're no infielder and no pitcher,' said Joe Mathes, manager at Houston. 'From now on you're an outfielder.'" (Martin, Philadelphia *Inquirer*, Oct. 13, 1931). Another version of the story said that Mathes, thirty-five, and a former infielder himself in the Federal League, needed an outfielder. Since Martin was clearly no infielder, and since Martin had that speed, he would be used in the outfield.

The Houston team had very close ties to the Cardinals. Branch Rickey was the vice-president of the team, and president Fred Ankenman had his home in St. Louis. Classified 1A baseball at the time, the Texas League was a demotion for Pepper. Compared to Syracuse, the team had fewer players, eighteen (with one spitball pitcher allowed), the city was smaller by 50,000 though its West End Park did seat 1,000 more fans, and the season was a few days longer. The uniform, however, was similar, with a buffalo in a circle over the heart and Pepper's uniform number 15 on both sleeves. Others wearing the same uniform included Ernie Orsatti in left field, outfielder George Watkins, and Tex Carleton, a pitcher.

At least Martin knew that Rickey had not given up on him. Twenty-three years old now, he had to be content to stay in the upper minor leagues, and work for his chance at the majors.

A few days after the season began, Johnnie sent a letter home, using "The Baker Hotels" stationery:

> The Menger, San Antonio. April 24, 27: Dear Father, Mother and all; Well my last letter was rather brief so I'll try and write a little more. I am feeling fine and I only wish my dear Dad and Mother felt the same. I'm going to send some money the first of the month we are in San Antonio now we beat them 7 & 2 yesterday it makes our 6th consecutive win. We are in second place and going good. If we can keep it up and win the Dixie series it sure will be keen, won't it? San Antonio is an old town the Alamo is here I've not went through but I'm going to tomorrow. The famous buck house saloon is about 10 blocks from the hotel and I want to see it tomorrow. They had a big parade last night celebrating the (Battle of the Flowers) I don't know what battle that was but the parade was good they had some keen floats and the militia paraded. My room overlooks the garden court of this hotel and it sure looks pretty the palm trees and flowers I wish you and Mother and Geo could be here this is a real town for sightseeing. Today is Sunday and I expect will have a real crowd out for the ballgame. I got a swell "Electro Shave" safety razor for

WITH BERT AT THE PARK

A proud Pepper is shown as the hero of the day. (Copyright 1927 *Houston Post*. Reprinted with permission. All rights reserved.)

LOOKING OVER THE BUFFS

Some of the new Houston Buffaloes are drawn in 1927, the year Martin was made into a full time outfielder. (Copyright 1927 *Houston Post*. Reprinted with permission. All rights reserved.)

my home run it sure is a swell electric razor cost $10. it is just like a safety only the blade vibrates from the electric current and it sure shaves? Well I'll close for this time lots of love Johnnie

The move to outfield play was clearly a career change for Martin and his memories of his days in Houston were filled with affection: "Mathes ... is a wonderful fellow. He encouraged me all the time. He showed me how the outfield should be played. He noticed that I still had the habit of running into the other fellow's territory to try for a ball and he didn't scold me about it but what he said was that I shouldn't try to field balls hit to their territories but I should be there to help out if the ball got away from these fellows" (Martin, Philadelphia *Inquirer*, Oct. 15, 1931). His manager also played Pepper in all of the outfield positions, and in 145 games in the outfield Pepper responded by making but nine errors. While his defense improved, Johnnie's thirty-six steals again would have placed him second in the National League.

Houston did not get into the Dixie series, the seven year old afterseason games between the champions of the Texas League and Southern Association that meant extra pay days for the players.

The year 1927 marked the death of his father, George Washington Martin, and the very serious illness of his sister Mary, surely great sorrows for Martin.

Pepper in the Oklahoma City restaurant where he courted his future wife, Ruby. (Copyright, *The Sacramento Bee*, 1941.)

But from out of the cold on an Oklahoma City street that winter, Martin found himself in a small, warm, family restaurant drinking coffee. Years before, a family named Pope had moved from Arkansas to Oklahoma City and opened a small restaurant, their young daughter helping out. As the family's business prospered, they opened a bigger restaurant in a better location, across from the state capital. Perhaps Martin, passing by the place, looked into the window and noticed the cashier. The sight was enough to make him go into the restaurant one day. The lovely cashier, whose name was Ruby, was soon listening to how Johnnie would one day be a major league ballplayer. Ruby told me, "Johnnie came to the restaurant to eat a lot and talk to me. I went out to where he was out in the woods hunting quail and deer with the bird dogs he loved." There Martin found out how good a shot his young sweetheart was.

It wasn't long after their meeting that Pepper and Ruby started to write to each other and then date throughout the winter of 1926–27. Ruby Pope agreed to marry Johnnie Martin, and so on November 9, 1927, just two days after Miss Pope's eighteenth birthday, they were wed.

With Ruby he could always be "Johnnie" and not "Pepper." Here's how Martin told it: "That winter I forgot to tell you that during my big year in 1927 I got up my courage and committed matrimony with the sweetest girl in the world, Miss Ruby Pope" (Brundidge, St. Louis *Star*, July 21, 1931: 1). Ruby remembered that when "we were married I was still in high school. We went to Houston right away. That was the happiest winter of my life.... I love to hunt and so does Johnnie. George Watkins was playing with Johnnie in Houston then and all winter the four of us, Mr. and Mrs. Watkins, Johnnie and I, would hunt.... Whenever Johnnie buys a new gun he buys me one just like it. All that winter we hunted together, driving out in our Chevrolet and hunting quail, rabbit, and duck all over that part of the state" (Walter W. Smith, St. Louis *Star*, no date). The fact that Ruby was a crack shot and a restraining influence on the way Martin spent his money only endeared her to him more then and for almost forty years afterwards.

To his very fine performance at Houston in 1927 was added his desire to take care of his small family. Martin, so full of confidence and determination to succeed, felt those traits even greater now before the 1928 season.

5

1928–1930: A Cardinal, a Buffalo, a Red Wing

Johnnie Martin was brought up from the minors to the major leagues in 1928: "A letter came one day and when I read it I almost became one of those skyrockets. It was from the Cardinals and I was told to report to their Avon Park, Florida camp … at $600 per month" (Martin, Philadelphia *Inquirer*, Oct. 15, 1931).

But this team that he was to join had a young yet established outfield. The center fielder Taylor Douthit, who hit .262 in 1927, was twenty-seven; Chick Hafey, in left field, was even younger, twenty-five, and he had hit .329. While it was true that George Harper, in right field, was thirty-six, three other outfielders were on the team already: Ray Blades, thirty, and two twenty-five year olds, Ernie Orsatti and Wally Roettger. There was talk of moving the last outfielder, Wattie Holm, twenty-five, who hit .286, to third base in 1928.

Martin might have thought that this chance at the major leagues was his best, and last, chance. He was twenty-four now. Of the 1927 St. Louis Cardinals only Frankie Frisch, with forty-eight, had more than thirteen steals; only Frisch scored over 100 runs. Stealing bases and scoring runs were always Johnnie's strong points. But could he find himself a playing spot as a regular? Chick Hafey, one of the finest outfielders in baseball, had sinus trouble so terrible that he could not play at times and, in addition, due to a series of beanings in 1926, his vision was impaired. In short, he seemed to be fragile. Taylor Douthit, in center, was another fine outfielder, but his average dropped over thirty points from 1926 to 1927. So, for Johnnie Martin, there was hope.

3 6 28-Jacaranda Hotel, Avon Park, Fla. Dear Mother & all; I guess you think I've forgotten the folks at home but far be it from that. I am now in spring training, have been for 1 wk. I reported last Tuesday, the soreness is all gone now and I feel fit as a fiddle. I didn't look so good at the start but they are beginning to take notice now. we have played three practice games between ourselves and our team has won two of them. I've did very good in each contest. I'm sending a clipping out of a St. Louis paper which is pretty good I think. How is everything and everybody well and good I hope so. Tomorrow we go to Bradenton Florida from here we play the Boston Red Sox. Sure hope we beat them. Well I'll write more next time oh yes Ruby is coming back to O.C. to finish school in about 2 wks. Well bye bye and lots of love. Johnnie

This seems to be an early photograph of Martin, perhaps 1928. (Brace Photography.)

After an intra-squad game, the St. Louis *Post-Dispatch* reported that "Martin, playing right field, singled twice, walked once, stole a base and scored three runs. In addition he turned in the outstanding fielding play of the day in the first inning when he went far into center to make a diving catch of a low liner off the bat of Frankie Frisch." In one exhibition game, pitcher Jess Haines left his seat in the dugout to stand on the top step with Martin on base. Observed rising by Roy Stockton, Jesse Haines told the writer, "I wanted to watch Pepper run. I'd gladly pay to watch him play ball."

Ten days later, the same paper headlined, "MARTIN SLUGS BALL. Martin is one of the Cardinal Colts and is in right field every day of the training season." Martin got the chance to play against his hero Babe Ruth on March 15. He was in center on March 23 and in a few games split right field playing time with Douthit. Yet Hafey and Blades and Roettger were all tried in each outfield spot.

Pepper was kept on the team because of Blades' knee (wrapped in elastic all training season) and Hafey's sinus condition. Martin himself would later say, "They let me stay with them all season so I could watch and learn how the big leaguers operated" (Martin, Philadelphia *Inquirer*,

Pepper sitting on the bench for the Cardinals in 1928. (Copyright, *The Sacramento Bee*, 1941.)

Oct. 14, 1931). Martin studied such Cardinals quality players as Pete Alexander, Rabbit Maranville, Jim Bottomley and Chick Hafey. As a major leaguer, he could also observe players on other teams.

No one on his team called him Pepper. "He didn't like Pepper," said Frisch (AP, March 1965). John or Johnnie was used. Frisch and Martin were both former football players and it was Frisch who taught Martin the head-first slide. Martin later claimed that it was his football experience that taught him to be not afraid of diving. Frisch had had enough: "I had to quit that stuff. The guys started catching me with their knees and I was getting punch-drunk. But that Pepper he never stopped diving in" (Frisch, 58).

About learning that slide, Martin said, "I spent most of my time on the bench, watching the ball games, although I did run the bases," and that inactive role was certainly because Manager Bill McKechnie did not agree with Rickey's assessment about Martin's development. Martin was a burden to McKechnie. But Martin stayed the season and it was outfielder Ernie Orsatti who was sent down, only to be recalled in August.

So while Taylor Douthit in Martin's center field position accumulated 648 at bats, Martin came to the plate thirteen times, all but one as a pinch hitter. For another twenty-two games he served as a pinch runner "for a couple of stiff-legged catchers" and spent a small part of four games playing the outfield. He scored eleven runs in his few times on the bases (Brundidge, St. Louis *Star*, July 21, 1931: 3).

By season's end, the Cardinals got by the New York Giants by two games to win the National League pennant. In the World Series, the Cardinals were outscored 27–10, as Ruth and Gehrig hit seven home runs in the four game series sweep. Martin only pinch ran in the Series and scored one run. The young Oklahoman collected a full share of the losing team's post-season money. This meant that his World Series check for $4,181.30 was $800 more than Pepper's entire yearly salary.

1929

"Well, to get back to baseball, after my months with the Cards it was agreed that I could run like nobody's business but that I needed an education in outfielding and hitting, so I was kicked out of the post-graduate class and sent back to Houston to take my Junior year work over," said Martin (Brundidge, St. Louis *Star*, July 21, 1931). In fact he would toil two more years in the minors. His ambition to be a big leaguer was now spurred on even more with the pregnancy of Ruby with their first child.

Yet the added responsibilities of the oncoming birth didn't affect his joyous ways. It's told that Pepper, wearing overalls with no shirt, arrived back in Houston early in April in a junker automobile, two of his bird dogs with him. The parking lot he pulled into in Houston was quite large, since the new Buffalo Stadium seated 14,000. A league one step down from the International League, the Texas League was an "A" League, whose season ran from April 17 till September 15 in 1929. (Ruby, who had stayed in Oklahoma for the birth of their first child, Mary Aleyne, joined him not long after the season began.)

The team did not play very well, and it needed to change managers from Frank Snyder to Eugene Bailey in the course of the season. The Buffaloes finished sixth of eight at 73–86 though future major leaguers Ray Blades, Tex Carleton and Flint Rhem were on the squad. Martin was quickly assured of his spot in center field for the whole season of 157 games; he came to bat almost 600 times and made 175 hits for a .298 average. His assists rose to twenty-seven and his errors were down to twelve. His strengths as a player remained: he still scored lots of runs, 114, and he hit forty triples and forty-nine doubles; his steals numbered 43, which would have been good enough to tie Kiki Cuyler for the National League lead in 1929. Martin summed up the season by saying, "I studied hard, passed my exams, and Branch Rickey promoted me to the senior class at Rochester" (Brundidge, St. Louis *Star*, July 21, 1931).

He was also given a new Chevrolet in Houston for being voted most popular Buff, an award he won by almost 10,000 votes.

The cartoon has him, somehow, stealing first base. (Copyright 1929 *Houston Post*. Reprinted with permission. All rights reserved.)

1930

Once again, Martin was ordered to report to the major league Cardinals for the training season. Once again he knew he was in competition not just for a spot on the team but for playing time as well. Pepper, of course, played hard during the training season and hoped to stay in the majors because he was getting to be a little too old to be thought of as a prospect for major league play at age twenty-six. But still there remained Hafey and Douthit in the outfield, so the other seven outfielders were really all trying for one outfield starting spot.

But other things were happening to affect his future in St. Louis. In Rochester, New York, now the top Cardinal farm team, an elbow injury to outfielder Red Worthington left that team with just three healthy outfielders, one of them playing manager Billy Southworth. Either president of the team Warren Giles or Southworth called Cardinal vice-president Branch Rickey, asking for George Watkins or George Fisher from the major league team when the team cut their roster to the major league limit. Martin was not asked for.

Starting off weakly, the Red Wings were in last place by May 2 when Branch Rickey visited the team on the road and watched them lose to the Jersey City Black Cats at the New Jersey park. Worthington played in the outfield though his elbow was not yet fully recovered. But the team climbed to sixth place two days later, being 7–8, as they left Reading via the Lehigh Valley System for their home opener. While traveling, it was decided that Red Worthington needed to rest the fractured bone in his elbow for about three more weeks.

Not only did they lose the home opener against the Baltimore Orioles on May 6, but manager Southworth jammed his fingers during a fielding drill, an injury that was estimated to keep him out of play for at least two weeks. Sam Breadon promised to deliver a left-handed hitting outfielder to the Red Wings "as soon as the trial between" three players could be completed. "With ... four men out of play [of a roster of eighteen], President Giles managed to pry John (Pepper) Martin from the Cardinals as a reserve outfielder" (Rochester *Democrat and Chronicle*, May 7, 1930). Giles had been the president of the Syracuse club when Pepper played there in 1926. But it was true that although Giles really didn't want Martin, he knew that Pep was all that Rickey was willing to give him. Pepper was, after all, another right-handed batter. Rickey, too, apparently promised Giles that as soon as the "trial" was finished, Martin would be sent down to Houston.

So, having played six games in the majors in 1930, and having been designated as a reserve outfielder on a minor league team, Martin left St. Louis for the eight hundred mile trip to Red Wing Stadium a month into the season. Johnnie had about three weeks to prove himself, to get into the lineup, to keep himself ready for promotion to the big club. While Martin was in Rochester, he was paid $750 per month for 5½ months, which was a raise for him of $150 a month. (The average working man's salary was $92.00 per month or $1,196 per year.) The uniform Martin was given to wear had a high buttoned half collar, and over the heart was a large baseball with red wings on it; the red cap had a raised red "R" on it.

There's always some luck in any successful career, and here in Rochester Martin found some for him. Simply, the Rochester club was a great team. Captained by Specs Torporcer, the team included first baseman Ripper Collins and pitchers Paul Derringer and Tex Carleton. The Red Wings' season of 1930 was one of the greatest in the history of minor league baseball.

Yet, early in the season, the team was still jinxed. In Martin's first game, a game in which Pepper went hitless while playing left, catcher Gordon Hinkle was injured, his hand requiring stitches. Collins, with five homers already this year, carried his team that day with four RBI.

By Pepper's fifth game, on May 18, 1930, the team extended its winning streak to nine games and above the byline of Joseph T. Adams, the Rochester *Democrat and Chronicle* headlined, "MARTIN HAS FIELD DAY IN VICTORY. Collects Four Hits, Shows Speed to Upset Jersey Team in Thriller." Martin, moved to left field, doubled, tripled, stole a base, and drove in a run. His play in this game was a kind of model for his play for years afterwards: in the outfield, "he partially kicked the ball around ... as two runners tallied." Offensively, he tripled in a run in the first and "streaked around the sacks on the blow." After teammates drove in some runs, "Martin came right back to steal his place in the sun in the third. He singled, dashed to second on a steal and went to third as Jorgens threw to center field.... The fans enjoyed his running. In the fifth, Martin hit to right and as [Twinkletoes] Selkirk held the ball momentarily 'Pepper' dashed for second and slid in safely." The manager of Jersey City, furious at the call, was thrown out of the game, allowing fans to see the maddening effect Martin sometimes had on rivals. "Martin did some more fast stepping ... in the ninth. Martin singled to left and when the visiting shortstop let the ball roll a few feet away, Martin went right on to second with a display of foot-shaking that again had the fans talking." We can see that Martin moved himself up four bases just on his speed and daring alone. After an 0–8 start in his first two games, Pepper hit 6–11 to bring his average to .316. His play impressed so much that an outfielder, Ray Pepper, was sent down to Danville of the Three-I League. With his team hitting .301 and with the pitching staff having only one pitcher below a .500 winning percentage, the team moved into first place in the International League.

He was hitting so well that rival teams complained that he was not standing in the batter's box. Pepper's direct solution was to arrive at home plate, take a tape measure out of his pocket, and offer to let the umpire measure.

When Red Worthington reported back for active duty at the end of May, Martin had now played in sixteen of the team's thirty-nine games, was 22–63, had raised his average to .349, and was tied for fifth in team RBI with manager Southworth. Worthington had played in nine games and was hitting .206.

Around this time, Cray Remington, Rochester newspaperman, was searching for a phrase to describe Pepper's baserunning, and, considering Martin's Oklahoma upbringing, came up with "The Wild Horse of the Osage." Martin read and liked the name: "I was kind of proud of that name and the fans got a kick out of it too" (Wilbur Adams, Sacramento *Bee*, Feb. 21, 1944: 15). Perhaps the other local writers, Joseph T. Adams and Jack Burgess, wish they had thought up the name.

> Return J. L. Martin, Rochester Ball Club, Rochester N.Y. July 7–30. Dearest Mother; I guess you think I'm never going to write but here is # 1. Did you get the Mothers Day present? I'm sending a check for $10 in this letter and Mr. Merrick or Mr. Spears will cash it for you. I'm going to try and be a little more considerate from now on. Ruby and the Baby are getting along fine the Baby has 8 teeth and she is cutting her eye teeth now She is 4 months old an she can walk just fine but can't talk much yet. I'm sending a couple of camera pictures of her. Mother how have you been getting along good I hope I guess you raised quite a garden didn't you? Mother I realize I should write often is but even though I don't I love you and I think of you lots. I am going good up here been hitting great my average is .401 I'm just 2 or 3 points behind the leader of the league I'm sending the batting averages of our club Well hello to all and all our love Johnnie Ruby and Baby OX OX OX.

The batting averages of the Rochester club by the end of the season in the International League showed that it was, and still is, the greatest team in Red Wings history: ten men hit over .300 that year, and four scored more than 100 runs while four drove in more than a hundred runs. Johnnie performed spectacularly, especially in light of missing a month of the season. He hit .363, with twenty home runs, and drove in 114 in addition to being the first player to hit a home run over the 450-foot center field wall of Silver Stadium. Pitcher Paul Derringer was 23–11 with a 2.89 ERA,

Ripper Collins, the first baseman, led the league in batting, and the team featured pitchers Tex Carleton, Paul Derringer and Fritz Oestermueller.

With a .629 winning percentage, their 105 wins in 167 games easily topped the International League and gave them entrance into the Junior (or Little) World Series, which began on September 24, against American Association League champion Louisville.

By October 2, Rochester had won the series 5–3, during which games Martin hit 10–35. Louisville manager Alan Sothoron, seeing that Martin had scored eight runs, stolen four bases, hit two triples, and two doubles, was heard to say, "How could we stop that guy Martin?" (AP in Philadelphia *Inquirer*, Oct. 10, 1931). It was written about Martin in Rochester that "it used to pull you to your feet to watch him stretch singles into doubles … and then end up in a cloud of dust after a swan dive" (Mandelaro, 42).

Martin was a league all-star for the first time and he was joined on that team by Collins (180 RBI), Torporcer, Worthington and Derringer.

6

1931:
An Old Rookie

In February 1931, Martin spent his twenty-seventh birthday in an unusual way: "I got my expense money for the trip to Bradenton.... I looked at that check and decided that on account of all the automobiles, fast freights and passenger trains that were moving along highways and railroad rights of way that it would be a waste of money to buy a railroad ticket. Besides, if you've heard the call of the road once, you'll hear it again, and it's kinda like malaria, and other forms of chills and fever, for, once it gets in your blood, it's hard to get out.... I hit the hectic trail again and pulled out of Oklahoma City on February 26. I knocked off those 1,500 miles in a trifle over five days" (Brundidge, St. Louis *Star*, July 21, 1931: 5).

Martin sometimes left out of the story the fact that he was not all that skilled at riding the rails. This trip, he seemed to have ended up in Georgia being jailed for vagrancy. It was with the help of a local minister that he finally got into Bradenton and to the Cardinal hotel (*The Sporting News* March 28, 1970: 16).

"I was a day late getting to Bradenton, and Clarence Lloyd didn't even want to recognize me, but I was in condition to play ball the day I arrived." The *Post-Dispatch* verified the story this way: "He arrived in Bradenton on a freight at 12:20 PM on March 2, 1931 and then strutted into the lobby of the Dixie Grande Hotel. His hair was full of cinders, he was badly in need of a shave and bath, his clothing was wrinkled and stained, but he had the body of a prize fighter, the glow of rugged health and a broad, infectious smile."

Martin, later, would admit, "I wasn't a pretty picture walking into the hotel. The bellboy didn't carry my bag because I didn't have any." Bob

Broeg continued the story. "He went to the desk, grinned and nodded to the clerk and asked for Clarence Lloyd, traveling secretary of the St. Louis Cardinals"(Broeg, *The Sporting News*, March 1965: 29). Harry T. Brundidge described the rest of the scene in the St. Louis *Star*, as the ever-suspicious Lloyd arrived and, sensing a touch, backed away from the tramp as he asked, "What can I do for you?"

"Gimme a room."

"I'll give you a kick in the pants if you bother me again," said Lloyd earnestly. The tramp grinned.

"Aw, Mr. Lloyd, have a heart. I'm your new hard-hitting outfielder and I was ordered to report here for spring training. I just got in from Oklahoma City."

"What's your name?"

"Folks call me 'Pepper,' but my dad christened me Johnnie Leonard Martin."

"This is another one for the book," laughed Lloyd. "Give this guy a room."

The clerk picked a number, handed the key to a boy and whispered "Count the towels before you leave him."(Brundidge, St. Louis *Star*, July 21, 1931: 2).

Branch Rickey was not averse to such stories and encouraged them as being good for attendance. Rickey's biographer Murray Polner mentioned "Charlie Barrett's apocryphal story of driving 60 MPH in Oklahoma and suddenly looking up to see a jackrabbit run by his car pursued by Martin...." Pepper Martin could always run, as this story by ex–Houston teammate Roy Moore verifies: "He used to scoot alongside a bunch of rabbits and every so often he'd reach for one and heft it for size. If it scaled a little thin, Martin'd put it back down again; if it felt nice and fat, he'd drop it in his bag" (Carmichael, 153).

It may be that magical speed that had the St. Louis *Post-Dispatch* on March 7 report that "Pepper Martin is being touted as a regular in the outfield" and to ask the next day, "Is Pepper Martin as good as the scouts say he is? Will he break into the outfield as a regular?"

The combination of Martin's presence in camp and Hafey's high salary led to rumors "that the proposed deal of Hafey and three players and cash for Chuck Klein of the Phillies has fallen through…. It likely means that left field will be taken over by Ernie Orsatti [28], the colorful Italian, when a right-hander was pitching and by Ray Blades [34] or Pepper Martin when a southpaw was hurling against the Cardinals." Johnnie, always ready to play, was labeled a "strong-armed gentleman who doesn't need much training," and the paper also noted that "Pepper Martin is determined to remain

Martin angry for his chance in 1931. (Copyright, *The Sacramento Bee*, 1941.)

in the big leagues this time. After his turn at bat on the diamond, he hikes to the batting cages in center field and pounds the ball until his turn arrives again" (St. Louis *Post-Dispatch*, March 25, 1931).

Since star Chick Hafey was still holding out by opening day, and since Rickey always hated to be shown up by a player, particularly when that player wanted more money, Martin saw his spot opening: "I don't think the Cardinals were gonna play me regular at all in '31 even though I'd hit .363 at Rochester, so finally one day I got a hold of Branch Rickey and I said, 'Look, Mr. Rickey, I'm a little tired chasin' up and down these minor leagues and if you can't use me here, why don't you trade me so I can play every day.... Play me or trade me. I wasn't born to sit on anybody's bench'" (Carmichael, 153).

Rickey liked Martin's desire, his aggressiveness, plus he noticed that outfielder Taylor Douthit was no longer getting around on a pitch and no longer pulling the ball. But the opening day lineup had Orsatti in left, Douthit in center and Watkins in right.

Early in the season, after losing a ball game, manager Gabby Street grabbed Martin and said, "Where were you today? I wanted to put you in."

> "How could you miss me?" Martin answered. "I almost sit in your lap every day to try to get your attention. I can play as well as anybody out there and I just plain tired of warming the bench and not getting an honest opportunity to show my ability." Street came to Martin's room that night and apologized [Wilbur Adams, Sacramento *Bee*, Feb. 23, 1944: 15].

If we try to imagine Martin's frustration, after 738 games in the

1931: An Old Rookie

JIM NASIUM'S SELECTIONS OF STANDOUTS OF 1930

An unusual drawing since the year is clearly 1931. In 1930, Martin was playing in Rochester, N.Y. (Rochester *Democrat and Chronicle.*)

minors, after seven years and six teams, after playing the bench for the entire 1928 season, after "years of concentrated effort and consuming ambition" (Drebinger, *New York Times*, Oct. 11, 1931), we can understand his impatience. Without Martin knowing it, negotiations were instigated by Dan Howley, Cincinnati Reds manager, who had an unproductive outfield, and he began to pester Rickey and Breadon for the contract of outfielder Taylor Douthit through Sidney Weil, president of the Reds. If the contract purchase could not be brought about, Howley wanted Hafey or Martin. *The Sporting News*, however, reported, "Howley preferred Douthit because Taylor was a younger and faster man than Chick, and Martin was untried.... At no time did the Card bosses show any inclination to part with Martin, a player for whom they were very strong" (April 10, 1930). Cardinal bosses, however, were inclined to part with Douthit's $14,000 salary and replace it with Martin's $4,000. As the season moved on, though, Johnnie was called on for only seven at bats as a pinch hitter and probably played in six games as a pinch runner or defensive replacement.

By June 15, after thirty-six games, Martin was established the Cardinal center fielder for the rest of the season. June 15 was the day Douthit was traded to the Reds. That 1931 St. Louis Cardinal team, in Pepper's real rookie season, was remembered by Frankie Frisch in his autobiography: "They were the happiest, merriest ball club I ever played with. We had a great fellow as manager, Gabby Street. The Old Sergeant, as he liked to be called, said early in the season that the ball club was a team of destiny. He insisted day by day that we were going to win the pennant and the World Series, probably because we started early pulling games out of the fire in the late innings" (45).

Pepper was one of the merry Cardinals bunch. Typically he "sat on a bench in the Cardinals clubhouse with the reporter, laughing and talking. He was garbed only in shoes and a sweat shirt. He wouldn't be the least concerned if socks, neckties, hats and coats were withdrawn from sale. As usual, he needed a shave and, as usual, he was grinning. His dark hair was ruffled and wet and his blue eyes were dancing as they ever have. 'You've probably heard a lot of tales about me and most of them are true,' he said."

"Andy [High] recalled a game earlier in the season in New York which illustrated Martin's running skills as well as his boyish enthusiasm: 'Pepper got on first base and didn't get the steal sign, but stole second base anyway. He slides hard into the second baseman, knocks him down, and the ball goes sailing out into center field. Pepper gets up, sees the ball in center field and heads for third. He slides safely into third, gets up and sees the ball dribble by the third baseman. So he heads full steam for home, where he bangs into the catcher, knocks the ball away and scores the run. He then comes back to the bench all covered with mud and dirt, laughing to beat the band, and saying, "Boy, isn't this fun? This is real fun'" (Murdock, 121).

Martin played 110 games in the outfield, and 123 games total. He led the team's outfielders in putouts and was playing so well by August that owner Sam Breadon gave Martin $500 to add to his $4,000 salary for his excellent play for that year.

Part Two

7

The 1931 World Series Nears

In October of 1931, a cartoon by Hanny showed "Panicky Citizen" holding the candle of "Timidity" which created a lurking shadow of "Disaster." The caption read, "THE VICTIM OF HIS OWN IMAGINATION" (Philadelphia *Inquirer*, October 12, 1931).

On September 30, 1931, the day before the 1931 World Series, John Drebinger wrote in the *New York Times* that "men and women, especially where baseball is concerned, are made of more emotional stuff, and on every hand there is the same manifestation of throbbing excitement that has preceded every world's series since the event became a national institution..." (Sept. 30, 1931).

In St. Louis, where the 1931 World Series began, the Cardinals had to offer a lottery for Sportsman's Park tickets, because of the 150,000 applications for 34,000 seats. In Philadelphia, George Calhoun took the honor of being first in line by getting to Shibe Park's ticket window at 10 PM on Wednesday night, knowing that the ticket sales did not begin in Philadelphia until Monday morning.

The Philadelphia manager was timeless Connie Mack, now just short of his seventieth birthday, who supervised the Athletics' win over the Cardinals a year ago in the 1930 World Series. Most baseball fans knew the Philadelphia sluggers very well: Al Simmons, Jimmie Foxx and Mickey Cochrane. In the outfield, in the infield, and behind the plate these American Leaguers were daunting. Their star pitcher was Lefty Grove.

No team had ever won three World Series consecutively, and the Athletics, having won over the Cardinals in six games in 1930 and over the Rogers Hornsby–led Cubs in five games in 1929, saw no reason why they should not triumph again. The Athletics were ready to win the championship again, and at a Rotary Club lunch at the Bellevue Stratford, before a crowd of 200, Eddie Collins promised that "all the boys would be bearing down all the time to place their manager of the high pedestal of fame" (Baumgartner, Philadelphia *Inquirer*, Sept. 23, 1931). Mack "now stands on the threshold of a third fall classic gonfalon and he wants that title badly," the *Inquirer* supposed. "In fact, his objective ever since the dark days of 1915 to 1928 has been to be the first manager to make three in a row" (Oct. 1, 1931).

The press was getting ready as well for the series. Columbia "arranged a hook-up involving eighty-two stations extending coast to coast to take the story of the baseball classic into countless homes throughout the nation" (*New York Times*, Sept. 30, 1931). Meanwhile, some writers were ready to simply award the championship to the Philadelphia Athletics, a team that wore an white elephant on their uniforms as their symbol. "There is a feeling of hopefulness here that Gabby Street and his band of red-breasted Cardinals will finally contrive to bring down Connie Mack's heavily armored and highly trained White Elephants" (Drebinger, *New York Times*, Sept. 30, 1931).

Less noticed overall were the Cardinal players, because none of them were sluggers. Still, the Cardinals would have six of their squad go into the Hall of Fame: three pitchers, Dazzy Vance, Jess Haines and Burleigh Grimes; a first baseman, Sunny Jim Bottomley; an outfielder, Chick Hafey; and a second baseman who knew how to win, Frankie Frisch. The St. Louis ball club hit about half of the home runs that the Philadelphia team did in 1931, 118 to 60. Yet the Cardinals found a way to score 5. 3 runs per game while the American League Athletics were scoring 5.6. The Cardinals made more hits, doubles, and triples and stole 89 more bases than the American League champions. The Cardinals led the league for 154 of the 164 days of the season, and were in first place to stay from Decoration Day, winning 107 games, the best in their history, and taking the National League pennant by thirteen games. The Athletics had not stolen a base in a World Series game in either 1929 or 1930. Four of the top five base stealers in the National League in 1931 were Cardinals.

More than forty years later, Bob Broeg had the seventy-year-old Mack telling his team before game one, during just their third clubhouse meeting of they year, "'Gentleman, I don't worry about their big hitters— Frisch, Bottomley and Hafey—but they've got a young man named Martin who bothers me. He's the kind of aggressive, unpredictable kid who could be the hero or the goat.' About the same time, J. Roy Stockton, baseball writer of the St. Louis *Post-Dispatch*, prognosticated by noting that Martin ... had the spirit of adventure and abandon. Stockton picked Pepper to be the salt in the Series stew" (Broeg, St. Louis *Post-Dispatch* Oct. 25, 1975).

THE VICTIM OF HIS OWN IMAGINATION

A cartoon that shows the tenor of the times drawn in September 1931. (Courtesy *The Philadelphia Inquirer*.)

    Gabby Street, Cardinals manager, was not a novice to the game either. His career went back to the 1890 Kitty League and he had two nicknames pinned on him: one was "Walter Johnson's catcher," Street having played for the Senators for four years; the other was "Old Sarge," from Street's combat duty in World War I. Gabby had won pennants in 1930 and 1931.
    Under Street's byline, his pre-games article of September 26 pointed

out three new team members who "were especially helpful." First Old Sarge outlined the contributions of twenty-four year old pitcher Paul Derringer (18–8) and young relief pitcher Allan Stout, who won six games without a loss. And then, "In Martin, we have a great center fielder. He has speed, a wonderful arm and he can hit the ball against any fence. He has a fine spirit, is aggressive, and the winning type of ball player. No chance is too difficult for him and he never considers danger. And he has the confidence that enables a man to rise to great heights when the occasion demands" (Isaminger, Philadelphia *Inquirer*, October 1, 1931).

Following a post-season exhibition (a Monday afternoon game against the Phillies) that generated $8,528.50 for the jobless in the area, the Athletics left the Philadelphia train station on September 29 at eight at night "amid volleys of cheers from thousands of thousands ... who were near sardined on the platform to bid them adieu" at the North Philadelphia station. They were "enjoying the best equipment at the command of the Pennsylvania Railroad as befits champions.... It is a special train with the right of way...." (Isaminger, Philadelphia *Inquirer*, Sept. 30, 1931). The team brought its two mascots. Scouting reports read by Mack on the train said that Jess Haines, a pitcher who beat the Athletics in 1930, couldn't play and neither could regular center fielder Pepper Martin.

Those two Cardinal players, as well as their teammates, were saluted in a St. Louis victory parade that same day. Though Martin did have a damaged knee, manager Gabby Street said that Johnnie would probably play anyway. The city certainly hoped the team was at full strength, for there were "Red Bird statues, flags, emblems, banners and whatnots ... in every window, plastered on auto windshields and ... every department store window." The fans in the city "... feel sure ... that within ten days the thing will be over and the Red Bird will be the 'eagle' of the baseball world. David, the mite, slew Goliath, the Giant ... [so] why cannot a Bird beat an Elephant?" (Grauley, Philadelphia *Inquirer*, Sept. 30, 1931).

The next day, the Athletics arrived almost an hour sooner than scheduled, due to the speed of their special train, while the Commissioner announced that "all stalemates must be played off in the city where the tie takes place" (Isaminger, Philadelphia *Inquirer*, Oct. 1, 1931). The powerful Athletics checked into the Forest Park Hotel on "fashionable King's Highway" on the afternoon of September 30.

As his rivals were getting settled in, Pepper Martin appeared in the lobby of his team's headquarters, the same Forest Park Hotel, with a shotgun in his hand. Stan Baumgartner, covering the team, asked Pepper if he was going to shoot pitcher Lefty Grove with the gun. "'I can hit him well enough with a bat,' snorted Pepper. Then Johnnie and Burleigh Grimes went out to do some trap shooting" (Isaminger, Philadelphia *Inquirer*, Oct. 2, 1931). Few fans knew Grimes was still suffering from appendicitis; few fans knew that the National League clubs were contributing the services of some of their pitchers to throw batting practice. The notion of a non-roster batting practice pitcher, for regular games, was unknown in this era, that job going almost always to players not in the lineup on game day. But for today's practice, for example, left-hander Bill Walker of the New York Giants simulated Grove's deliveries for the Cardinals.

There were, of course, always many players who were ignored by the press when the sluggers were around. Base stealers were one such group. The usual player-by-player comparison in the newspapers before every World Series prompted the *New York Times*' John Kiernan to write that one contrast in center field was that Mule Haas, 27, of the Athletics "always smiles whereas Pepper Martin looks angry in a ball game and always seems to be getting ready to bite somebody, preferably an umpire" (Sept. 30, 1931). Martin was about to bite a lot of people.

This Cardinal center fielder, Johnnie Martin, "Pepper," was a twenty-seven year old rookie who had produced moderate numbers for 1931. He didn't lead the league or even the team in any category; in the National League he tied for nineteenth in doubles, placed twenty-fourth in home runs, tied for sixteenth in RBI, tied for third in steals, and tied for eighteenth in triples.

As the Series approached, St. Louis writer J. Roy Stockton "suggested that Martin, the unknown rookie, just might be the series hero" (Broeg, St. Louis *Post-Dispatch*, Oct. 25, 1975), and Martin later said, "The *Post-Dispatch* ran a story about me having a good chance to be the big shot of the series and I cut that story out and I agreed with it.... I sure was nervous" (Carmichael, 152).

Another column, one with the byline of John J. McGraw, Giants manager, said, "In centerfield, the situation is ... a little uncertain as to whether [Mule] Haas or [Doc] Cramer will play that position for the Athletics and whether Martin, [Ernie] Orsatti or [Okkie] Roettger will play for the Cardinals" (McGraw, New York *Times*, Oct. 1, 1931).

Martin understood that he was at the top of his profession. Of the more than twenty-five minor leagues that sent players to the major leagues where eight hundred play, he had been one of the few in the national pastime and he wanted his family to see him perform. Martin hoped to play his usual position and hoped that his mother might travel from Oklahoma City to see him play.

But the five hundred miles on very primitive roads wouldn't be traveled this year by his mother. Mrs. Celia Martin said she was afraid of the crowds, and would follow the games from her home in Oklahoma City. Because Mrs. Martin was deaf, her son George would relay the events of the game to her. "Mrs. Celia Martin ... has spent so much of her life in a little three-room house on the wrong side of the railroad tracks that, at 67, the world beyond the next street seems queer and all the praise showered on her son seems more or less a fantasy.... It was discovered that the electrical current and gas had been shut off from the house because she was unable to pay the bills" (*The Sporting News*, Oct. 22, 1931: 5).

8

Thursday, October 1, 1931: Before Game One

Thursday, October 1, 1931, was the day that David was to face the Philadelphia Goliath in St. Louis' Sportsman's Park. Photographers put Martin, at 5'8" and 170 pounds, next to Jimmie Foxx, whose nickname was The Beast, who stood four inches taller and weighed twenty-five pounds more.

Lefty Grove and Moose Earnshaw, the strongest pitchers on the Athletics, had pitched 570 innings in 1931 and had given up about eight hits in each game they had worked. Because of the Sunday blue law in Pennsylvania, Athletics manager Connie Mack could rest both of these men, pitching both of them twice if he needed to.

And Martin was quoted as saying, "There ain't a pitcher I can't hit" (St. Louis *Post-Dispatch*, Oct. 4, 1931).

In St. Louis, the evening *Post-Dispatch* nominated a number of candidates as the prime movers on the team. No one on the team had driven in more than ninety-five runs; no one had exceeded sixteen home runs that year. The paper first chose "the stalwart figure of the Kentucky mountaineer" (Sept. 17, 1931), Paul Derringer, a rookie pitcher who won 18 and lost 8 that year. The *Post-Dispatch*'s next pick was first baseman "James Leroy Bottomley, the smiling son of Nokomis" (Sept. 17, 1931), who hit .348, and the last selected was Chick Hafey, who hit one point higher than Bottomley, just enough to win the National League batting championship.

Only Hafey and Adams on the Cardinals led the league in any offensive category, but there were four .300 hitters on the team: Jim Bottomley at first; Frankie Frisch, the team captain, at second base; Chick Hafey at .349 in left field. And Pepper Martin in center at .300.

Long before dawn of game one, the concession men and women, the vendors and the ushers, shoved at each other as they entered the grandstand gate on Spring Avenue to make sure they didn't lose their "coveted" jobs for the series. Later in the morning, a hundred or more youths gathered and "clamored so lustily" (Alexander, St. Louis *Post-Dispatch*, Oct. 1, 1931) asking for jobs in the park that police had to move them in a body to a nearby parking lot where they still shouted for work.

From their beds of flattened boxes and spread newspapers, the impatient ticket buyers arose at seven o'clock to noisily plead for the opening of the gates. The waiting lines extended from Sullivan Avenue south to St. Louis Avenue, three long blocks on both Grand Boulevard and Spring Avenue. Bleacher and pavilion gates opened at 7:45 AM; many people in line were eager to sell their places "at prices ranging from $1.50 down to 25 cents. As newcomers walked down the lines to their ends, they are greeted with a volley of shouts—'number 18 in this line. 75 cents, Mister. I waited all night to sell you this place for a dollar, boss' ... there were few takers" (Alexander, St. Louis *Post-Dispatch*, Oct. 1, 1931). At least a quarter of the late arrivals were women, many of them "gay in Cardinal red berets and red ribbons..." (Alexander, St. Louis *Post-Dispatch*, Oct. 1, 1931). Meanwhile groundskeepers were wetting down the infield and "the diamond was marked with whitewash" (Alexander, St. Louis *Post-Dispatch*, Oct. 1, 1931) and ready for play at 9 AM. A "half hour after that, all 5000 of the one dollar bleacher seats were taken and the gates were closed. This day the attendance was 38,529, including a few fans who had bought standing room only seats at the Arcade Building ticket office. At 10:45, a twenty-five piece band marches out onto the field playing 'Happy Days Are Here Again'" (St. Louis *Post-Dispatch*, Oct. 1, 1931).

Before the game, the newspaper cameramen held forth. Al Simmons was posed with his monster bat which was almost as thick at the handle as at the end; Martin's saffron colored bat was a puny thing by comparison. The white-haired Mack, so photogenic, was going for a new record of three World Series victories in a row. Photographed wishing the Cardinals good luck were National League managers John McGraw from the New York Giants, Burt Shotton from the Phillies (whom Martin knew well), Jewel Ens of the Pirates, and Bill McKechnie from the Boston Braves. Victor Miller, mayor of St. Louis, and Harry Mackay, mayor of Philadelphia, posed with the two managers while the two World Series rookies, Pepper Martin and Dib Williams, were shot together. Photographs were taken contrasting the National League ball, which would be used in St. Louis, and the American League ball, "just a bit livelier," to be used at Philadelphia.

Of course, flashes burst as President and Mrs. Hoover, the guests of the Philadelphia club at the first game, entered the ballpark. There was also a burst of booing from the crowd for the president who led the country

October 1, 1931: Before Game One

This gag photograph was taken before game one; it would turn out that Pepper had the big bat. (National Baseball Hall of Fame Library, Cooperstown, N.Y.)

into the years of the Great Depression and who continued to refuse to repeal the Prohibition law, which would have provided the country not only with beer, but with jobs as well. The Athletics, who had never lost a game in Hoover's presence, viewed the president as their mascot.

A few days after the Series, under Martin's byline, Americans could read that Pepper thought that "Grove and Earnshaw hadn't heard anything about me.... I had heard about how great a catcher Mickey Cochrane was, but I looked up his record and I noticed a couple of things. One was that he wasn't throwing out many runners and the second was that nobody was doing much stealing on him. Right away I says to myself nobody is trying to do much base-stealing in the American League and Cochrane's arm must be bad and his aim can't be much good.... Gabby Street gives us orders to 'run any time you get a chance'" (Martin, Philadelphia *Inquirer*, Oct. 16, 1931). Martin and his roommate George Watkins, a thirty-one-year-old Texan right fielder, had talked baseball by the hour, figuring out what to do under many circumstances. They watched the pitchers throw on the sidelines and tried to see their weaknesses. "The Big Moose (Earnshaw) reared 'way back when he threw,' Pepper recalled years later, 'and shucks that Grove just wasn't used to pitching with men on base'" (Broeg, St. Louis *Post-Dispatch*, Oct. 25, 1975).

The umpires, four of them being used for the World Series games only, entered the playing field, as the game was about to begin. In this World Series the umpires would enforce the rule put into place just that year; that is, that a fair ball bouncing into the stands would be counted as a double, not a home run.

9

Thursday, October 1, 1931: Game One

Manager Sarge Street, early in 1932, recalled that "a day or so before the series, Martin came to me in the clubhouse with a newspaper. 'All these writers are saying who's going to be the hero of the series,' he said, 'but they don't mention me. I'm going to be the hero'" (St. Louis *Post-Dispatch*). Years later, Martin told John P. Carmichael, "… My stealing … wasn't because I wanted to show off or anything. No, we decided to run whenever we could against catcher Mickey Cochrane because he wouldn't be looking for it and Gabby Street … told both George Watkins and I to limber up right from taw" (154).

"I don't know how much hittin' we'll get off Grove and Earnshaw," said Gabby, "so we better not waste time on the bases. Let's run everything out" (Daniel, New York *World Telegram*, 1932).

Back in Philadelphia, the *Inquirer* told of how money was collected from baseball fans by having "every play reproduced in moving pictures as fast as it is made upon the field. The next thing to television. At the Academy of Music admission 25¢, 50¢ & 75¢." There were a few shows like this advertised all over town, for instance at the Elks ballroom.

Before the game in Sportsman's Park, National League managers John McGraw and Bill McKechnie came into the Cardinal dugout to give pep talks. Peter Golenbock's book on St. Louis baseball claims, "After the series, the heroic Martin insisted that the impetus for his great Series was a speech made by Branch Rickey. 'The National League hadn't beaten the Americans in the last four tries. The National League officials' pride was hurt. Mr. Heydler, the league president, talked to us first; then Mr. John McGraw spoke; but then came Mr. Branch Rickey. His theme was: "The greatest attribute of a winning ballplayer is a desire to win that dominates." I have

After making five hits in the first two games (three off the great Lefty Grove) and scoring all the runs in game two, Pepper is being touted as the surprise hero of the Series and an irritant to Connie Mack. (Courtesy *The Philadelphia Inquirer*.)

never forgotten those words. He brought every single Cardinal off his seat with an address that beat anything I ever heard. He reminded us that we had dreamed of this moment from boyhood. We had schemed and scratched and fought and gone hungry to get here, and here we were, and what in heaven's name were we going to do about it? Well, we rushed out of there cheering, and I personally got down on my knees in front of our dugout and kissed the ground, and I actually prayed to God to help me have the desire to win that dominates. And I meant every word I prayed. I really did'" (Golenbock 149).

But the speechmaking, as usual in baseball, had little effect, and St.

Louis rookie pitcher Paul Derringer was beaten 6–2. The Athletics took the lead in the Series due to "Jimmy Foxx, the … beetle-browed farmer boy from the Eastern Shore of Maryland" (Stockton, St. Louis *Post-Dispatch*, Oct. 1, 1931).

For the Cardinals, Pepper went 3–4 in the game. In the first, with "Frisch … on second, bawling a wild indecipherable entreaty," as J. Roy Stockton described it, "Pepper Martin, the wild horse of the Osage, whose ambition is to be a star of the series, made a fine start in that direction. He quickly had two strikes, but that didn't bother him and he finally slammed a double against the right field screen scoring Frisch and moving Bottomley to third" (St. Louis *Post-Dispatch*, Oct. 1, 1931). The Philadelphia *Inquirer* the same day claimed the double "missed being a home run by a few feet."

In the fourth, Martin singled to left.

In the sixth, after outfielder Chick Hafey singled to center, Martin singled for his third successive hit. When Hafey stole third, Philadelphia third baseman Jimmie Dykes protested Umpire McGowen's decision on the play. Martin dashed for second, and made it.

"Pepper Martin made a fine World Series debut against Grove, pumping a double against the screen in right to drive in a run." Martin told the St. Louis *Post-Dispatch*, "Grove fed me nothing but fast balls the first day" (Oct. 4, 1931).

The Philadelphia *Inquirer* had to admit, "Pepper Martin glittered like [a] highly polished mirror … [and] made good his boast of yesterday that he wouldn't need any shotgun to hit Grove. He spanked the offerings of the southpaw as if it were batting practice." If Grove was clearly the best pitcher in baseball and a raw rookie could handle Grove, then any Cardinal batter could. And people in the country were beginning to adopt Martin as an exemplar, as a symbol of what confidence and energy could achieve. The Philadelphia *Inquirer* ended its portrait of Martin by saying, "If it were not for Pepper, in fact, the Mackmen would be inclined to consider the series in the bag now. That boy can cause a lot of trouble during the next few days" (Philadelphia *Inquirer*, Oct. 1, 1931).

10

Friday, October 2, 1931: Game Two

For game two of the 1931 World Series on October 2, once again, some hungry men lined up outside the stadium for the purpose of selling their places in the line to others. "One man with two children who had been out of work for nineteen months, sold his position for $1.50 yesterday and had no takers today.... Last night, policemen on duty at the park drove from the bleacher line those suspected of intent to sell their places this morning. Fifteen-year-old William Ecker of 2509 Madison Street, who took his place in the line at 6 o'clock last night, intending to sell his place this morning, managed to convince the policemen he had no such plan. He offered his place, number three in line, for as little as 25 cents this morning and when there were no takers, decided to buy a ticket and see the game himself" (Stockton, St. Louis *Post-Dispatch*, Oct. 2, 1931).

The crowd that day for game two was smaller and the eagerness was not as strong. When the gates opened at 7:50 AM the line was three, not eight, blocks long. Thus, within an hour, when the bleacher line had diminished, it was possible for fans to enter the park after a wait of only a few minutes. The bleacherites carried their own food into the park for the most part and no one made a move to stop them; the game would not be over for another five hours.

As the Sportsman's Park staff scrambled to try to get the loudspeaker working, the bleacher discussion seemed to be about the four run win by the Athletics, and if Bill Hallahan, called Wild Bill for his high number of walks, could stop the slugging Athletics. And if the Cardinals could master Moose Earnshaw, a right-hander. Near game time, field announcer Kelly had to use the megaphone to announce the lineup. "He made the loud speaker sound quiet by comparison," noted Herman Wecke of the

Record (Oct. 3, 1931). Down on the field, Nick Altrock, the baseball clown, posed for a photograph with Martin before the game.

That same October 2 evening, St. Louis *Post-Dispatch* headlines read "MARTIN HITS SAFELY TWICE, STEALS TWO BASES, SCORES BOTH RUNS; HALLAHAN IN FORM." The lead said, "Bill Hallahan ... cast a spell of impotence over the bats of the slugging Athletics.... He held the powerful Philadelphia machine to three hits, all singles.... Martin stood out in the triumph as the hero of the Cardinal attack."

After noting that the fans cheered hard for Martin as he came to bat, the Philadelphia *Inquirer* praised Johnnie in its account as Pepper's first hit reached the outfield: "Simmons slipped slightly on the wet turf fielding the ball, it hit his glove and dropped to the ground, a mere momentary lapse that would have been overlooked by most runners, but Martin was off for second like a deer. The surprised Simmons hurried his throw. It went a bit wild" (Baumgartner, Philadelphia *Inquirer*, Oct. 3, 1931). Martin remembered: "As I hit second in a cloud of dust, I turned my head around to look at Simmons and he was standin' there, lookin' at me as much as to say, 'Oh, a smart busher, huh?... Then I took a quick glance at our bench, and Street looked sort of happy" (Carmichael, 154).

New York Times writer John Drebinger commented, "Earnshaw may have allowed himself to become slightly careless for he should have known that to move on is an inherent trait of the exuberant Cardinal outfielder. Next, with Jimmy Wilson batting, Martin touched his prominent hawknose, a sign he would steal. ' Jimmy and I had a pet play and we pulled it,' Pepper explained. Seeing the smiling approval of his manager, Martin heads for third on the first pitch. Catcher Ace Wilson's beautifully faked bunt causes third baseman Dykes to rush in and then to try to come back to cover" (Oct. 3, 1931). "The backstop's throw was wild. Pepper, sliding head first in Frisch style, hit the cushions safe by two feet" (Baumgartner). Then, when Charley Wilson flied to Mule Haas in center, Pepper scored easily. "What an ovation the thousands gave him. Ample proof that the good old game still holds other thrills than the thud of base hits and the thunder of home runs.... The bleacher fans gave Martin a noisy cheer as he took his position in center field...." (Stockton, St. Louis *Post-Dispatch*, Oct. 2, 1931).

After Martin singled in the seventh inning, Earnshaw, Martin thought, took too much time for his delivery. "It was a race between the screaming ball and the flying man." Safe at second, Pepper advanced to third when Wilson grounded out. "Street decided to put the squeeze play on, figuring Earnshaw was pretty apt to get Charles [Gelbert], so he told Charley to lay one down" (Golenbock 147). "... The Cardinals pulled another glorious trick from the almost forgotten bat bag of thrills ... Gelbert bunted toward the first base side of the diamond and Earnshaw, expecting the strategy, got to the ball quickly. He tossed to [Mickey] Cochrane and Mickey had the plate well blocked. But Martin made a desperate and well executed slide and scraped the corner of the plate as he catapulted his body past the catcher.... Martin had to make a complicated slide to get to the plate but he made it...." (Baumgartner, Philadelphia *Inquirer*, Oct. 3, 1931). "The sight of the wildly dashing Card was too much for [Earnshaw] however, and his toss to Cochrane was wild. Pepper slid under Mickey safe by three feet.... Once more the fans almost tore down the stands. Babe Ruth with his spectacular home runs never received a greater ovation that did the daring Cardinal greyhound" (Stockton, St. Louis *Post-Dispatch*, Oct. 2, 1931).

The game was not over, however, and one of the more interesting innings in World Series play was about to take place. The headline read, "STUPID PLAY BY WILSON GIVES HOME FANS SCARE IN A THRILLING NINTH." After Philadelphia's first baseman Jimmie Foxx walked and third baseman Jimmy Dykes also walked, two outs were made, the runners advancing. Pinch hitter Jimmy Moore was sent up to bat in the pitcher's slot. With the score but 2–0 and two runners on base, most fans stayed to watch the end of the game even as they had begun to make their way out of the park. When Moore missed a third strike, Wilson, as he would after any strikeout, threw the ball easily to third baseman Jake Flowers. Third base coach Eddie Collins, meanwhile, ran toward home and shouted for Moore to run to first, since Collins knew that the pitch had hit the ground before it went into Wilson's glove; the result was that the bases were now full of Athletics, bases loaded and two out in the ninth.

Max Bishop, called Camera Eye, hit lead off because he walked so often. The left-handed batter hit a high pop foul into the recessed section of the right field boxes. First baseman Sunny Jim Bottomley ran hard, lunged for the ball, and held on to it, as he crashed against spectators and the railing too. After the catch, his teammates would have carried him off the field, but Bottomley wouldn't allow it, saying, "Old Jim ain't done nothing yet. Go get Hallahan. He's the fair-haired boy in this ball game. And when you get him, go get Pepper Martin. I ain't done nothing."

And Pepper Martin had done everything, according to the press.

The *Times*' John Kiernan stated, "Pepper Martin ... roused the home crowd again today. Fighting spirit and speed carried him around the circuit twice.... A slower man than Pepper would have loafed through the inning.... At the end of the seventh, the score was Athletics 0, Pepper Martin 2" (Oct. 3, 1931).

October 2, 1931: Game Two

The Associated Press contributed, "John (Pepper) Martin ... is a husky young athlete with a piano-mover's shoulders, a sprinter's speed and a fullback's fight. He owns an arm that can rifle a ball from deep center to the infield with deadly precision and has cut off many a runner at the plate. On the base paths, his churning legs carry his 180 pounds along with amazing swiftness to finish his dash with headlong dive, arms extended, to clutch the bag" (*New York Times*, Oct. 2, 1931).

Even rivals were impressed, as seen in Eddie Collins' column: "Nothing else in the world won for the Cardinals today but Pepper's speed and daring on the bases. More power to him. Incidentally, it is too bad from the spectator's viewpoint that there are not more of his type in the game right now. He is my idea of a ball player's ball player" (*New York Times*, Oct. 2, 1931).

Pepper merely said, "It's a good thing we did a little runnin' that day, because we weren't hitting" (Golenbock, 147).

The modesty was not fake or contrived and people knew it. Writers seized upon one of the great truths about baseball fans: "Yet it was that grimy look, as if he were a mechanic or a laborer — an ordinary working man — that endeared Martin to the fans and to the country. That it was possible for anyone to be a major league baseball star and he allowed them to think so."

On its October 3, 1931, front page, the Philadelphia *Inquirer* printed a "picture wired from St. Louis" showing "Martin (Pepper to his friends, who now number about ten million....)"

Gordon Mackay in the Philadelphia *Record* commented, "The mantle of glory kisses the broad and brawny shoulders of an Oklahoma hombre, alfalfa bred and riding high, wise and rough over the champions ... Martin of the meteor speed and the blistering bat...." (Oct. 3, 1931).

Newspapers searched for language to fit Martin's achievement thus far:

"... a flying meteor from Oklahoma.... Not since Ty Cobb ... has baseball produced a daredevil of the paths equal to the sturdy, chunky Oklahoman" (Baumgartner, Philadelphia *Inquirer*, Oct. 3, 1931). Baumgartner called him "the red devil on the paths; the flying flychaser; a streak of fire."

The front page of the *New York Times* under John Drebinger's byline for Oct. 3, 1931, read, "A dash of blazing speed so bewildered a White Elephant today.... Part of the speed emanated from the whip-like left arm of one William Hallahan.... The rest of the speed was supplied by Johnnie Martin, called 'Pepper'.... It was Martin, who ... stole third base right under the nose of Mickey Cochrane, generally acclaimed as baseball's greatest catcher…. It was a spirited tug and the Athletics lost because of Martin's alacrity and punch and Hallahan's (the left-handed necromancer) strength in the two times he was on the ropes and could have been beaten by a base blow."

Two hours after game two ended, the train carrying the Athletics left for Philadelphia. The Cardinals were due to leave at noon on October 3.

11

Saturday, October 3, 1931: Travel to Philadelphia

Before the Cardinals traveled, they spent the night of October 2 at home in familiar beds. Then, at 2 PM on Saturday, Oct. 3, they climbed aboard the special train. The group of eighty players, writers, and officials settled in for the nine hundred miles to Philadelphia that took them over the Pennsylvania Railroad lines.

Published nationally was a photo of Ruby and Pepper Martin boarding the train, he in a white three-piece suit, the caption reading: "Unabashed looking at the camera." No doubt he had time to relax though there were times on the journey to Philadelphia when fans did wave from trackside and whenever the train had to stop, the crowd at trackside begged players to come out and talk. Manager Street came out, at times, but the remainder of the team, aware that there was not to be a game until Monday, October 5, due to the travel and due to the Pennsylvania Blue Laws that prohibited baseball on Sunday, just wanted to take it easy while they could.

The Athletics, who left St. Louis right after game two, were beginning to doubt their own dominance. Connie Mack ("The Mahout of the White Elephants") in his column said, "I want to call attention to the fact that Cochrane slipped and was on his knees when Pepper stole third in the second inning. It would have been different, perhaps, if Mickey had not fallen but I do not want to detract one iota from the wonderful game that Martin played. He made it possible for the Missourians to win" (St. Louis *Post-Dispatch*, Oct. 3, 1931).

And while Mack was making excuses for Cochrane, though no one who knows baseball really believes a runner steals on the catcher, others were giving Martin his due, including the Philadelphia newspapers: "Martin was a heroic, dashing figure in the victory. The wild horse of the Osage who threatens to go through with his avowed ambition to 'steal the show' was a whole team in himself on the attack...." (Isaminger, Philadelphia *Inquirer*, Oct. 4, 1931).

"Enroute to Philadelphia" was Joe Williams, who filed his column for October 3, describing Martin: "Nobody would call him an intellectual. Indeed I suspect if you called him that to his face he would insist you smile when you say those words. He is finely trained, lean-faced and belligerent. I am told he eats T-bone steaks and custard pies for breakfast. His favorite movie actor is Two-Gun Hoot Gibson. The Pepper will not read the newspapers unless his name is on the top of the page in big, black face type. His opinion of newspapermen who write baseball is not high. 'They are just a bunch of dopes,' he insists and he may be right" (*New York World Telegram*).

The Babe Ruth/Ford Frick column stated, "Make no mistake about this kid 'Pepper' Martin. Everything he does seems to stamp him as the player who cannot miss being the hero of the series" (St. Louis *Post-Dispatch*, Oct. 7, 1931). Gabby Street, in a William E. Brandt column in the *New York Times*, was more to the point regarding game two: "I always have believed that ... the game can be won on the bases.... That steal of third by Martin practically won the game. If Martin had not made his bold decisions, the game might still be scoreless."

Brandt's colleague, John Kiernan, seemed not to have seen enough yet to make up his mind about the winner of the series: "The Cardinals ... have played dull ball so far in this series with one shining exception, and that is Pepper Martin, the fiery, fighting speed boy.... He's a first year boy who might be expected to be handicapped by nervousness in a world series. But Pepper has been the red-hot sensation.... Probably the Cardinal players realize their own shortcomings.... The Athletics ... are the favorites. They figure to win.... The hope of the Cardinals lies in putting up a fierce fight that will upset the dope and the Athletics at the same time. So far only a few of them have been fighting. There's still a glorious opportunity for the others to stir themselves to brisk and belligerent action in this series" (*New York Times*, Oct. 4, 1931).

These American League champions, the Athletics, for the third year in a row forced the Yankees' Lou Gehrig and Babe Ruth to barnstorm in early October. On this day they played on rival New Jersey teams, West New York and Fort Lee, at West New York Stadium as the Cardinals train was chugging into Philadelphia at 10 AM October 4.

The column called "Sports Salad" in the St. Louis *Post-Dispatch* has this verse:

> We, upon John "Pepper" Martin,
> our encomiums bestow:
> he stole a flock of bases
> and he also stole the show
> [Davis, Oct. 4, 1931].

For those in Philadelphia who couldn't get tickets to the game, the *Inquirer* ran an ad that read, "Due to the lack of seats for tomorrow's World Series game, ... we have made arrangements to guarantee the first 125 people ... installation of their Majestic Radios in time to hear the opening 'Play Ball'" (Oct. 5, 1931).

And Connie Mack was quoted as saying, "I want to give Pepper Martin every credit for being an inspiring ball player.... I had almost forgotten Pepper Martin who played against us on more than one spring training trip. It was always a puzzle to me that he was sent back to the minors" (*Inquirer*, Oct. 3, 1931).

12

Sunday, October 4, 1931: Practice Day

Dora Lurie interviewed Martin on Sunday for the Philadelphia *Inquirer*: "I'm in the game because I love it and I want the money because it is my livelihood. But if there wasn't any money in it I would be playing every chance I could get. Big money hasn't got me but every one has his own idea on the subject.... Ballplayers are superstitious I guess but cats bother me more than anything else. I sure hate to see one cross the road on the way to a game" (Oct. 5, 1931).

Gordon Mackay didn't forget Martin's nickname in an interview published that day, and his own touch was to give Pepper the label of "the prancing pinto of the Osage.... The fans love that prancing, dancing, dashing hombre from Will Rogers' home state. The cheers he evoked, the plaudits that rang in his ears as he dashed to centerfield.... Here was a Moses from Oklahoma to lead the folks back to the time when daredevils on the bases performed exploits that go ringing down the years as mighty achievements and personal deeds of moment and glory." Martin was also called "our Achilles of the Alfalfa," and was described as having "... a look of baby frankness in his keen blue eye[s].... A real guy, too is the hombre from the Southwest.... Yes, sir, one simply grand guy is Pepper, with modesty in his mien, a wide smile cracking up his intelligent face, and those dimples bending into his he-man countenance, a wholesome regular, fellow.... Pepper hasn't any languorous drawl.... Pepper laughs with you, not at you and he 'can't just understand what all this fuss is about.... My wife is up here with me this series but we had to leave our little girl back home. Like to play baseball? Man, I love it. You hear folks say all we care about is the money. Sure, it's a good way to make a living.... But if a lot of these fellows were in some other business where they could make more money,

I'll bet you they would be playing ball just the same for the fun of it'" (Philadelphia *Inquirer*, Oct. 3, 1931:12).

Johnnie may be having fun, but Connie Mack was very serious about the series. "Back in his own wigwam again ... Connie Mack tossed precedent into the waste basket and his henchmen into fever heat.... Never before in the 28 years that spanned these October battles has any manager ordered practice for his men on an open Sunday" (Mackay, Philadelphia *Inquirer*, Oct. 3 1931). The Sunday blue law practice was without spectators. Coach Earle Mack, 41, served as catcher for Lefty Grove, to be sure his injured fingernail was healed.

And while this morning practice took place, the Cardinal special pulled into the city. The team checked into the Benjamin Franklin Hotel and then, after a lunch, rode to the ballpark for their afternoon practice time.

Pepper was new to the park, since the National League Phillies played in the Baker Bowl. Shibe was smaller than Sportsman's Park in St. Louis but both had a center field (468 feet) flagpole that was in play. A twelve foot high wall in right field was the shortest distance from home plate at 331 feet and the houses beyond the wall, the houses on 20th Street, seem to be bending right over the park, they were that close; many players new to the park would stop to stare at the sight. Gabby Street knew the Athletics pitchers were going to be alert now to base-stealing and "a pitcher who has to watch those bags closely isn't going to be as effective as if he had nothing better to do but pitch the ball to the batter" (Baumgartner, Philadelphia *Inquirer*, Oct. 4, 1931).

The park was now quiet except for the sounds of wood on ball and ball on leather. During games, Shibe was famous for the presence of the Kessler Brothers, Bull and Eddie, of Philadelphia, who sat "on opposite sides of the grandstand and conduct what practically amounted to a private conversation across the diamond" (Thorn).

Even those loyal fans might have cheered Martin, who was now being looked upon as someone who would "inaugurate a third era in baseball. First there was the Ty Cobb decade of speed.... Then there was the Babe Ruth dynasty of slug-brute power, and nothing else, and now say the momentary worshippers at the shrine of the fleet-footed Cardinal — the Martin era — a return to speed, hair-raising base running and trickery on attack" (Baumgartner, Philadelphia *Inquirer*, Oct. 4, 1931). John Drebinger also saw Martin as "a curiosity. When Johnnie walks though the lobby of the Cards' headquarters everybody looks at his feet, and the first stranger you meet will tell you that those feet are capable of going over the ground faster than a bullet travels through the air" (*New York Times*, Oct. 5, 1931).

Martin remembered his early, tentative years as a player and said that now "I have confidence in myself. Who wouldn't after knocking about the country like I did. I have been in many tougher situations than facing Grove in a world's series" (Baumgartner, Philadelphia *Inquirer*, Oct. 4, 1931).

Martin, too, knew how to use to the press to his advantage. He loved to "wear a broad-brimmed, high-crowned cowboy hat and play the part of a cowpoke right off the range" (Broeg and Vickery, 234). Branch Rickey encouraged him to play the part.

Gordon Mackay asked Pep if the games in the World Series were different than the regular season games. "That's mighty hard to answer right quick.... I know you have to be in earnest in this World Series if you want to do your best work.... I'm just up there a-trying to get all the hits I can.... Shucks, all you can do is pick out a good one and hit it and then when you get on the bases run as fast as you can." After he was asked about hunting and fishing as his hobbies, Martin brought the conversation back to baseball: "You know when you're a kid and you sit back and think about being a big league ball player and getting into the World Series and you roam all around the country before you get up there, man, I'm telling you, it makes you want to sit right back and enjoy every minute of it." MacKay noted that "Pepper looked like some neighbor from the west who came up to see ... the series, instead of being the outstanding star of the battles, and a name to hail and huzza from coast to coast" (*Inquirer*, Oct. 3, 1931).

After the practice, Pepper, Bill Hallahan, and Jimmy Wilson walked to a soccer match at the grounds at G. Street and Huntington Park Avenue. Wilson was a soccer teammate of one of the players and went there to see the match. The game stopped for a while for handshakes, and then it continued.

High above the field in his Shibe Park tower office, Connie Mack was saying, "This man Martin has made all the difference in the world in the Cards. Martin is hitting and he is a hustling ball player.... As is often the case on a ball team when one player hits, the rest follow..." (Shriver, *Inquirer*, Oct. 3, 1931).

13

Monday, October 5, 1931: Game Three

As he was having his breakfast, Martin could read, "Stix, Baer and Fuller. Hear the Broadcasts of the World Series in Our Restaurants While You Have Lunch. Games Start at 12:30. A Special Improved Enunciator System Has Been Installed Which Brings in the Reports Clearly and Distinctly" (St. Louis *Post-Dispatch*, Oct. 7, 1931). He also read about the threat of rain for that day as he got ready to leave for the ballpark at 21st and Lehigh.

In addition, the AP wire had a story about Martin's mother: "Deafness prevents the St. Louis outfielder's 57-year-old mother from listening to the radio broadcasts of the World Series so she devours the play-by-play accounts in the newspaper. 'I didn't want him to be a baseball player,' she admits. 'I thought it would be better for him to be a doctor or a lawyer. But he was crazy about baseball and I guess maybe he knew best. He wanted me to come and watch him play in the series ... but I didn't want to go. I would have been embarrassed to go up there in that big crowd'" (Oct. 7, 1931).

By 12:25 the field tarpaulins were rolled up and the Athletics began to warm up, and Commissioner Judge Landis okayed the opening of the gates to the park. Not long after, Johnnie came out on the field for practice, and he was asked to pose with a Philadelphia policeman who held Martin's arm as if in the beginning stage of an arrest, presumably for the stolen bases in the first two games.

The president, Herbert Hoover, was due to watch the game that day; some Athletics players even considered him their good luck charm. When Mr. and Mrs. Hoover were seated at 1:10, just as the Cardinals were finishing fielding practice, Butch Yatkeman, Cardinals mascot, shook the president's hand in their box near the Athletics dugout. After the photographers did their work, Sam Breadon, too, walked over and shook the president's hand and Gabby Street asked Hoover to autograph a ball.

Papers took note that Hoover was booed when he arrived, as the crowd let known its displeasure with Prohibition, some fans chanting, "We Want Beer." And when Hoover threw out the ceremonial ball for game three, Tom Shriver of the *Record* wrote, "The ball went wild [and] struck a policeman on the leg," at which point a fan yelled, "Take 'im out" (*Inquirer*, Oct. 6, 1931). "I'm not a dignified man myself," Pepper told John P. Carmichael, "… but I always remember how the fans booed President Herbert Hoover in the first game at Philadelphia. They cheered me, a rookie from Oklahoma who could run a little, and booed the President of the United States. It just didn't seem right and I sure felt sorry for Mr. Hoover and I was kinda put out with the fans because, after all, being President of the United States is a pretty big job and should command respect…." (153).

Martin is given respect from all sides. When Johnnie came to the plate in the second inning for his first at bat, Mackay wrote, "A cheer welled and rolled to the throng on the roofs of the 20th St., unbounded and unfeigned and unadulterated admiration for this … young man who has shamed no booster and mocked no word-painter" (*Inquirer*, Oct. 6, 1931). Isaminger added: "On his first appearance , the Cards' outfield flash received an ovation which welcomed him to Philadelphia as to the bosom of friends" (*Inquirer*, Oct. 6, 1931).

On the first pitch to Martin, he singled on a hit and run with Bottomley for the first hit off Lefty Grove. "From that moment on, Martin was the hero of the game, the cynosure of all eyes" (Isaminger, *Inquirer*, Oct. 6, 1931).

Once Martin was on base, Grove "squinted constantly at Pepper," perhaps helping Jimmy Wilson to single as Pepper raced to third. "This astonishing young man presently tallied on Gelbert's fly to Miller in right field. By this time Mr. John Leonard Martin owned the town. He was given an ovation and a rising vote of thanks from the centerfield bleachers for showing them stuff that their daddies told 'em about but which they had never really seen. In this case, legend became reality" (Mackay, *Inquirer*, Oct. 6, 1931).

In the fourth inning, Hafey singled, "and then a mighty thunder of applause, mixed with a kind of dull rumble of apprehension, rose from the throats of the packed thousands. A powerful-shouldered young fellow, swinging a bat in his heavy bare arms, walked to the plate…. Martin the deer-footed, Martin the strong" (Isaminger, *Inquirer*, Oct. 6, 1931).

"When I came up in that third game," Pepper said, "Grove said to

October 5, 1931: Game Three 73

SHIBE PARK DOINGS - - - By Chas. Bell

Cartoon with various vignettes:
- "Something is wrong Lefty! I just can't hit!" — THE TEAM
- "Grove pitched his head off but the boys were helpless at the bat"
- "You just try something"
- "Mickey Cochrane had his eyes trained on 'Pepper' Martin"
- "Burleigh Grimes Cardinal Ace who served 'em up sizzling hot"
- "It must be the heat!"
- "Simmons succeeded in connecting with his stick in the last frame to score two runs but it didn't mean anything"
- "Connie wig wagging from the dug out took a worse licking than the team" — SCORE CARD
- "The President proved a failure as a mascot to the A's — he made his first wild pitch of the season and landed on the poor 'ump'"

With two more hits and two runs scored, Martin was not only "the reincarnation of winged Mercury," but also a symbol of old-time thrilling baseball revived. (Courtesy *The Philadelphia Inquirer.*)

me, 'You country _____, I'm gonna throw this right through your head.' I said, 'You country _____, you do that'" (Heinz, 69).

Martin doubled to the scoreboard in right center. After Wilson and Gelbert were put out, pitcher Grimes singled "... and Hafey had scarcely tagged the rubber before the flying hoofs of Martin thudded over the guttapercha, too. And now, Pepper Martin owned the state" (*Inquirer*, Oct. 6, 1931). Bill Dooly wrote: "This hit of Grimes was not a long one.... The throw would have a caught the runner of ordinary speed, but Martin wasn't the ordinary runner. He was the reincarnation of winged Mercury ... a whirring figure shod in steel" (*Inquirer*, Oct. 6, 1931).

After the third out, many of the Philadelphia fans, including those who were called the "sun fish" in the bleachers, gave Pepper Martin a great cheer when he returned to his position in center field.

Mackay then reached for the language of imperial Rome: "*Morituri te salutamus*, Martin" (*Inquirer*, Oct. 8, 1931). Some of this hyperbole, obvious even for sportswriters, came out of fear for the National Game. After attendance had reached an all-time high for the major leagues in 1930, the number then decreased from that 10.1 million figure to 8.4 million in 1931. It would sink to 6,089,031 in 1933. Martin seemed to be some kind of savior, a symbol of that kind of old time and thrilling baseball revived. And so "baseball owes him a vote of thanks. Just as Babe Ruth and his mighty bat assuaged the anger and the wrath of the fans 12 years ago" after the Black Sox scandal, "so has Martin stimulated renewed interest when the public mind was at its lowest ebb over the current series" (Mackay, *Inquirer*, Oct. 8, 1931).

Grimes' two-hitter was given some consideration in contributing to the 5–2 win, but the 32,205 who saw the game were fixed on Pepper, as were the writers.

After the game, as usual, Pepper and Ruby bought a quart of ice cream and Johnnie ate most of it.

14

Tuesday, October 6, 1931: Game Four

The 1931 World Series began under cloudy skies for the fourth game. For those fans without tickets to the ballpark that day, the Philadelphia *Inquirer* again set up broadcasts from four parts of the city, bringing in Graham McNamee's radio play-by-play at each location from six loudspeakers "which will utter every syllable" mounted above a scoreboard, manned by "an *Inquirer* attendant clocking the count right before your eyes." Other fans, "2500 cliff-dwellers hanging to the Twentieth Street porches" beyond right field, had to pay the houses' tenants for a look at the game (Wiegand, *Inquirer*, Oct. 7, 1931). Even so, the attendance inside Shibe Park reached 32,295.

The Cardinals saw George Earnshaw, nicknamed Moose, on the mound and "held the big fellow in awesome respect, for the man of Montclair makes an impressing and commanding figure on the mound. But it so happens that Johnnie (Pepper) Martin knows little if anything about psychological complexes or reflexes" (Drebinger, *New York Times*, Oct. 7, 1931).

Earnshaw was in control that day, giving up just one walk and two hits. McGraw's column claimed, "Young Martin refused to be impressed by any sort of pitching, however … in addition to that, Pepper had the whole Philadelphia team and also the crowd in a flurry when he got to first base the first time.… Martin is the big shot in keeping the Philadelphia team worried. He is a real fighting ball player of the old type" (McGraw, St. Louis *Post-Dispatch*, Oct. 6, 1931).

In the Philadelphia *Inquirer* Harold J. Wiegand called him "that jumping jack from the prairies" (Oct. 7, 1931).

What they meant was that the two hits that Earnshaw gave up were both by Martin. Pepper truly did not seem to be impressed by the Moose. Taking Earnshaw to three and two, Pepper singled to left in the fifth inning and then "thumbed his nose at Mickey Cochrane ... who must have felt like a Chicago policeman yesterday. Both Frisch and Martin stole second right under his nose" (McCullough, *Inquirer*, Oct. 7, 1931). In the eighth, Martin came up to bat, and Cochrane asked, "Don't you ever make an out?" After faking a bunt, Pep hit a double that bounced off the left field wall. The Cardinals were all Martin.

Joe Williams wrote, "Yesterday Earnshaw was practically 100 per cent of the ball game. An exception should be made for that little mug, Pepper Pot Martin.... This bird continues to be the outstanding hit of the show.... I can't remember a World Series where there has been a performer who played with more zest, enthusiasm, determination, and effect. Connie Mack said last night that he didn't know whether Martin was the greatest ball player he ever saw or just a rookie gone wild.... Even the partisan Philadelphia fans rise on their hind legs and cheer when he comes to bat or trots out to center field to take his place. In his highest moments of glory, Babe Ruth never knew such acclaim. Through it all, the Pepper Pot remains terribly earnest and unconcerned. This may be a World Series with a lot of dough hanging in the balance to such men as Frisch, Grimes and Hafey, but to the Pepper Pot it is just a day's work. After the game ... the Pepper Pot was all hot and bothered because the Cards haven't torn into Earnshaw's pitching. With a tremendous youthful conviction that comes close to being amusing, he said: 'All that guy's got is a fast ball, and I've seen a lot better fast balls than that'" (Williams, New York *World Telegram*, Oct. 7, 1931).

And John Drebinger added: "The pepper-box from the Osage country may dwindle in importance in the remaining games but to date he has held the spotlight of fan interest more pre-eminently than any other player" (*New York Times*, Oct. 7, 1931). Babe Ruth's batting average was .625 in 1928, in a four game series; Martin was currently hitting .643 for four games.

The verse from "Sport Salad":

> But Martin once again was there
> With jingle bells and braided hair
> To give the fans a thrill;
> Again he played hair-raising ball,
> But Pepper cannot win 'em all
> Despite his dash and skill.
> The 'Wild Horse' Earnshaw couldn't tame
> Although he pitched a two-hit game
> And 'Pepper' got them both.

October 6, 1931: Game Four

Pepper's hits now totaled nine, his two hits in game four the only hits by the Cardinals. (Courtesy *The Philadelphia Inquirer*.)

> And while the race is getting tight
> The Cards have just begun to fight
> On that we'll take an oath.
> [Davis, St. Louis *Post-Dispatch*, Oct. 7, 1931]

15

Wednesday, October 7, 1931: Game Five

Pepper Martin told John Carmichael, "I guess I'll have to take the fifth game as my biggest day" (155).

A Philadelphia advertiser, remembering game four, announced that "Al Simmons will be in Gimbel's Men's clothing section today at 10 o'clock to be fitted in a new hand-tailored Parkleigh suit ... for hitting the first home run in Philadelphia in the World Series game." Meanwhile, at ten, rain was falling and former pitcher Howard Ehmke, now 37, and now Connie Mack's groundskeeper, made sure the tarpaulin kept the field protected from the showers. The protection worked, and a good crowd of 32,295 inside the park, plus thousands who rented roof space outside, were ready to see who would take a three-games-to-two lead in the 1931 World Series.

Against Philadelphia's Waite Hoyt, Gabby Street decided to move his center fielder to the cleanup spot in the order, and Pepper made Street look like a genius.

On this bank holiday, Martin began in the very first inning, after Sparky Adams singled and was run for by Andy High. Then, when Frisch singled, Martin came to bat, and the local joke circulated: "No wonder they're closing the Philadelphia banks, with that bird hanging around" (Isaminger, Philadelphia *Inquirer*, Oct. 10, 1931). Pepper sent a long fly to Al Simmons, driving in High. That run was the only score, even after "Pepper Martin showed something fancy in the bunting line to open the fourth inning. Pepper bunted down the first base line and it seemed that he was an easy out, but when Foxx fielded the ball and reached to tag Pepper he found the runner already across the bag" (Stockton, St. Louis *Post-Dispatch*, Oct. 7, 1931).

"We had agreed on the bench to talk to Gabby," Andy High recalled. "Don't say anything to him, Gabby; the guy stole second base; give him some encouragement." We didn't want him to slow Pepper down, but to give him some leeway. So when Pepper came into the bench after scoring a run, Gabby didn't mention it at all. We gave him some encouragement, and he says, 'Gee, that's the way I like to play.' Well, Pepper ran on Mickey Cochrane, who's a great catcher, but Pepper ran Mickey crazy. He just ran and ran. Not only that he was hitting like crazy, too. That sure was Pepper's Series" [Murdock, 121].

The score was still 1–0, "until Pepper hauled his ashen flail to the plate" (Isaminger, Philadelphia *Inquirer*, Oct. 8. 1931), in inning six, after Frisch had doubled down the third base line. "And here comes Martin, trotting amiably to the plate ... no strut about the little man and the fans like that." And when Martin came to bat, Cochrane said to him,

> "Well, kid, you're sitting on top of the world now and you deserve it."
> "Why man, I'm as dizzy right now as you are and don't know yet what it's all about. I'm just up here swinging, hoping to connect" [McCullough, *Inquirer*, Oct. 8, 1931].

The *New York Times* wrote, "Hoyt now called upon all his cunning as he faced this total stranger to world series warfare and who was now threatening to tear the thing apart all by himself.... Hoyt's [second pitch was] a curve, a trifle low and threatening to cut the inside corner of the plate. Martin brought his bat around with tremendous force and the ball shot in a line for the upper tier of the left field pavilion. What followed is almost unbelievable, for the crowd, seemingly forgetting in whose cause Martin had hit that ball, gave him a thunderous ovation, for there is no denying that Johnnie has captivated the fancy of all who have seen him play in this series" (Drebinger, Oct. 8, 1931).

The *Post-Dispatch* described how the Cardinal "players rushed out of the dugout to greet their hero and shake his hand" (Oct. 7, 1931). "At home plate, Frisch shook his hand and said, 'That's the way to hit so old man Frisch can walk home'" (Carmichael, 156).

In Pepper's version: "I think Hoyt got a little careless with me ... or maybe he figured I'd try to get Frisch to third by laying one down ... because he put a pitch right down the middle.... It looked so good I couldn't help swinging, and the ball went into the left field stands for a homer, my first, in my first World Series" (Golenbock, 148).

One of the Mack coaching staff said after the game, "How Martin got a homer on that curve Hoyt threw him is a mystery to all of us" (Brandt, *New York Times*, Oct. 8, 1931).

In the seventh inning with Pepper in center, a spectator tossed a torn-up scorecard over the pavilion railing toward Pepper. Martin called time to pick up the pieces and handed them back to some fans in the stands.

The next time Johnnie came to bat with roommate George Watkins on base, it was the eighth inning with the Cardinals winning 3–1. When Johnnie singled to left to drive in Watkins, it marked a number of milestones: it was Martin's third straight hit; it was his fourth RBI in a World Series game to tie the record of thirteen others; it was his twelfth hit in five games, already tying him with Buck Herzog in 1912 who made his twelve in eight games, as did Joe Jackson in 1919. Sam Rice did it in seven.

When Pepper tried to steal, Mickey Cochrane's throw to "Boob" McNair arrived to put Johnnie out though "the crowd was pulling for Pepper and yelled its disapproval of Umpire [Dolly] Stark's decision" (Stockton, Oct. 7, 1931). As Martin trotted off the field, the writers were getting their copy ready.

John C. McCullough of the Philadelphia *Inquirer* wrote: "Take down your garlands of immortelle from those pictures of the diamond great upon the wall, and wind them about the brow of a leather-faced, grinning, steel-muscled, fast-as-light hero from the land of oil wells and Cherokees. ... this swash-buckling pirate in dirt-grimed pants..." (Oct. 8. 1931).

McCullough said: "... The short set bogey man of St. Louis once again waved his bat dramatically to pound the Athletics into submission and put the Cardinals out in front again in the struggle for the baseball diadem ... Martin, as humble and unimposing as a spanked kid, but bulking big as the Empire State Building in menace ... dynamite in his bat, dynamite in his shoulders, breathless speed in his knotted calves.... He strikes out with color, dies stealing with color. A rainbow follows his every move" (Philadelphia *Inquirer*, Oct. 8. 1931).

"Hallahan sauce, flavored with Pepper, burned the throat of the elephant again," Stan Baumgartner wrote (Philadelphia *Inquirer*, Oct. 8, 1931).

Pepper, as usual, objected to the hyperbole: "But gosh, I wasn't the whole show. What about Bill Hallahan, Jim Bottomley and the others." The others, all the others, looked like they would receive a World Series share of almost $4500 each, much of the amount having to do with Pepper. And in the middle of this storm, "a faraway look in his eyes and a general restlessness indicate that this big boy from out of the oil country of Oklahoma doesn't like to say much. Off the field, he's pretty much what ball players call a loner" (Shriver, Philadelphia *Record*, Oct. 8, 1931).

Even the stately *New York Times* could not restrain itself as John Kiernan wrote, "The barefoot boy from Oklahoma was the whole show again.... In five games, the Cardinals have scored fourteen runs and Pepper has had

TOO MUCH PEPPER - - - - - - *By Bell*

The diminutive Pepper was incapacitating the powerful Atheletics, their symbol the elephant. He had now made twelve hits in the 1931 Series. (Courtesy, *The Philadelphia Inquirer.*)

a hand in making nine of them.... It didn't seem possible that Pepper Martin had any more hits in his bat when he came up in the eighth but he singled just the same. The fellow is absolutely fantastic."

"Unless Mr. Martin gets run over by a truck, it might be just as well for the Mackmen to concede it" (Baumgartner, Philadelphia *Inquirer*, Oct. 8, 1931). The Mackmen were not ready to concede the Series but Mack himself was "getting to feel that right now this fellow's weakness is a base on balls. He'll get a lot of walks from now on" (Brandt, *New York Times*, Oct. 8, 1931).

Frisch's column reveled in the win: "You should have seen us in the clubhouse today. No two players were ever more slapped on the back and congratulated than Hallahan and Martin. Did Martin give them another show? As usual, he was our whole attack.... He's simply thrown the Mackmen into a panic. They have done everything to try to stop him, but no use. He has the bit in his teeth, and can't be stopped" (Philadelphia *Inquirer*, Oct. 8, 1931).

16

Wednesday, October 7, 1931: After Game Five

With a 5 PM train to St. Louis to catch, the Cardinal team, Martin included, had to get out of the Shibe park clubhouse quickly. He did have enough time to say to the press, "I am just trying to do my best out there and I am having luck doing it" (Baumgartner, Philadelphia *Inquirer*, Oct. 8, 1931).

Paul Gallico wanted credit to go elsewhere and he filed this syndicated story after game five, a piece he titled "Darling of the Gods":

> NOW by what queer decision did the baseball Gods arrive at by which they showered down all their lavish gifts on the person of Johnnie Leonard Martin, a rookie playing his first year of major league baseball? They must have held a meeting in baseball's Valhalla, the annual pre–series meeting at which they voted favors and curses and began to bicker over the distribution of favors. They are jealous Gods and prone to play favorites. Some wanted to give all the glory to the pitchers (the pitchers are doing very well, thank you); others began holding out for their pets, the hitting and fielding Gods got themselves into a vulgar squabble as to which was more important in the series, offense or defense. And I presume when the nominations and vote for hero came up there was the very devil of a row, threatening to break up the meeting, until the chairman, who looked very much the way Judge Landis will look as an angel, banged on the pearly table with his golden gavel and bawled for order.
>
> "Lissen, you muzzlers," he must have shouted, "We've got to pick someone. Stop your bickering and listen to me. This guy wants Simmons, that one Foxx, another Hafey, someone thinks we owe Bottomley something — you no-hit guys over there in the corner shut up a minute, and let me talk. You can have a couple of no-hit games, so keep quiet. As long as we can't agree which star to make the hero, let's give it to some guy nobody ever heard of ... here. Here's a kid named Martin. John Leonard Martin. Nobody's touting him. Pick him and no hard feelings. What do you say, boys?"
>
> They must have agreed for ever if a boy was sprinkled with stardust,

it is this John Leonard Martin, St. Louis National center fielder, nicknamed 'Pepper.' He peers like Cyrano de Bergerac from behind an enormous hook of a nose, that distinguishing sign of a favored mortal, and he has all the courage and swagger and grim truculence of that ancient swashbuckler. He belongs in doublet and hose, with rapier and poniard at his side and a plume in his hat, but he has been doing middling well in a gray monkey-suit trimmed with red and two red birds embroidered on the breast and a stout club of ash or willow in his hands.

Cyrano, Jimmy Durante, Frank Merriwell and Douglas Fairbanks, rolled into one, Pepper Martin has intruded himself violently into the baseball-conscious world, leaving the writers high and dry for expletives, adjectives, and superlatives. I consider him a darling of the gods, a seventh son of a seventh son and best left unanalyzed. A report of his deeds suffices me. He does what he does because the gods will it and he cannot do otherwise. I don't know. Perhaps the Connie Macks needed humbling and Pepper is the instrument. Perhaps the petulant Robert Moses Grove was paying too much homage to his own fireball and not enough to the baseball gods. So they summon up an imp from pitcher's hell and sicced him onto Robert Moses.

Certainly a sacred spell is upon him. Perhaps she is a special undercover agent from the department of the law of averages, sent around to see that Connie Mack doesn't win any three straight World Series, an idea that is most abhorrent to the D. of the L. of A. ... Pepper's joints must be nearly worn out from rising to the occasion. Every time I looked up from my typewriter in Philadelphia last Wednesday afternoon, there seemed to be an occasion and Pepper was rising to it.

Before the fifth game in Philadelphia they said that if Pepper Martin never did another thing in the World Series this year he was established as a hero. But the gods did a good job when they voted him hero. They voted him 100 per cent hero, the whole show, or perhaps he was endowed with extraordinary powers by the Department of the Law of Averages. I prefer to think the last, because by all the odds and figures and averages, Pepper Martin should have fanned violently three times in that last game in Philly, or popped out to the pitcher, or grounded weakly to the second baseman. The law was all against him, but he was in that park as the Department's special agent. It was more important to the Department that Connie shouldn't win three series than that Martin should defy the records for World Series hitting. Not since the days of Babe Ruth has a man so electrified a crowd by coming up to bat as Martin did. And when he crashed that homer ... assuredly, a Darling of the Gods [© New York *Daily News*, L.P. reprinted with permission].

As the train steamed back to St. Louis for the games that would end the 1931 World Series, Martin, sitting next to his wife Ruby, told J. Roy Stockton, "I'm sure getting a kick out of the series. So is my wife. You ought to see her. Women are funny, ain't they? That first day when I started off with a hit and everybody was happy in the stands at Sportsman's Park and cheer, why she began to cry."

October 7, 1931: After Game Five

(Ruby Martin told me that "I was just so happy that I broke down and cried and had to go up to the top of the grandstand so no one would see me.")

"Martin, who lives with his wife and child in a five room apartment in downtown St. Louis, has seen his wife overcome with emotion before. Mrs. Martin said Pepper had always been a hero to her.... 'When this series is over, we're going to get somebody to care for our baby and go deer hunting in New Mexico,' she declared" (St. Louis *Post-Dispatch*, Oct. 7, 1931).

Back in Philadelphia, the *Inquirer*'s editorial department wrote, "They speak of Pepper Martin, thereby not doing him full justice. He's a whole gallon of Tabasco. We might lick the rest of the Cardinals with ease, but who thought we'd have to reckon with this batting, base-running fool? It ain't right and there had oughta be a law.... The A's catcher declared they had tried everything on Pepper, but he hit 'em just the same" (October 9, 1931).

Pepper's own manager declared at the end of his signed column that he "can't conclude this discussion of the series without saying a few words about our Pepper Martin. I believe that Martin has done more for baseball than any man who has come into the game since Babe Ruth. They're talking about Martin all over the country and he has given the national game advertising of unquestioned value." Later, Street adds, "Watch that kid a couple of years from now: he'll be filling your stadiums the way Babe Ruth does. He's a natural, ball-playing marvel" (Street, St. Louis *Post-Dispatch*, Oct. 8, 1931).

17

Thursday, October 8, 1931: The Train Home

In an interview with J. Roy Stockton, Pepper said:

> Gosh, but I'm happy ... but I can't believe it's real. It don't seem possible that one man could do what I've done and, don't get me wrong, I don't mean to brag, but in my wildest dreams, and I've had some pretty good ones, I couldn't have planned the things that have come my way. I'd have been ashamed to suggest even to myself that I'd bat .667 and knock in so many runs as I've knocked.
>
> Sure, I wanted to be a hero of the series [but] I found myself all tightening up and breathing short and I'd say to myself, "Look here, John, you got to shake that feeling off. It won't do." And so I'd make myself think about deer hunting. That's my big sport in the winter and I love it so much it wasn't hard to get to thinking about it and I get to breathing easy again and I'd be all right.... I worked hard and watched my food and got plenty of rest and that first day of the series I felt like a million dollars.... Maybe you think I haven't been lucky. Every time I hit a foul it's been out of reach.... I believe if I could bunt I'd be a star ball player.... I love to play and I love to win [St. Louis *Post-Dispatch*, Oct. 7, 1931].

When the train arrived, the St. Louis *Post-Dispatch* described how on the "station timetable bulletin board the train was chalked up as 'Pepper Martin and Redbirds due at 12:15 PM'" (Oct. 8, 1931).

The Philadelphia *Inquirer*'s Baumgartner wrote:

> Not since Colonel Lindbergh set his foot on Mound City soil ... has the populace of St. Louis tendered an ovation to a conquering hero. As Pepper's foot touched the station platform, three thousand throats bellowed a mighty ovation, three thousand necks twisted, turned and stretched until they looked like ostriches.... How did Martin take all this hero worship? He acted like any sensible ball player would do. He grinned,

By October 8, Pepper's great performance was becoming expected. (Courtesy *The Philadelphia Inquirer*.)

bowed, acknowledged with a wave of his hand and then when he got into a taxi with Mrs. Martin and two other Cardinals, he remarked, "Ain't that all the bunk. If I strike out tomorrow with a couple of men on they will give me the razberry. But it is nice to hear it once in a while — makes you feel good [Baumgartner, Philadelphia *Inquirer*, October 9, 1931].

The AP simply anointed Pepper as "the greatest baseball hero since Babe Ruth was in his prime..." (*New York Times*, Oct. 9, 1931).

The Cardinals rode right to the St. Louis ballpark for a three o'clock practice of hitting and fielding. After dinner that night, manager Sarge Street, second baseman Frankie Frisch and Pepper "spoke over station KWK at 9:45 o'clock" (St. Louis *Post-Dispatch*, Oct. 8, 1931).

After the broadcast, Martin walked into the hotel with two large bundles under his arms. Jimmie Wilson, Jake Flowers, and Sparky Adams, who were seated in the lobby, called out to him.

"What have you got under your arm, Pep?"

"Two gallons of ice cream."

"What's the idea?"

"Oh, ever since I was a kid I dreamed of being a big-league star making lots of money and buying as much ice cream as I could eat — and now I have done it" (Baumgartner, Philadelphia *Inquirer*, Oct. 10, 1931).

Street's column this day concluded with praise for Pepper. "They're talking about Martin all over the country and he has given the national game advertising of unquestioned value. And with it Martin has kept both feet on the ground and he'll keep them there. We were talking about all the cheering and the great work he had done and warned him not to let it get the best of him. 'Don't worry, Sarge,' he replied. 'If I hit a thousand, I'll still be plain John Martin.' And he will be. Martin is going to be a great drawing card and a great ball player next year" (St. Louis *Post-Dispatch*, October 10, 1931).

Catcher Jimmy Wilson said, "You can't go too far on Martin. I'll vote for him if they want to elect him to any office. In fact, I'll do better. I will go out and stump for him" (St. Louis *Post-Dispatch*, Oct. 8, 1931).

The opposition Athletics, who had scored only fourteen runs in five games, ought to have spent some time figuring out Cardinal pitching, but first baseman Jimmie Foxx thought, "Our best chance to win is by kidnapping Martin." Other Philadelphia team members tried to ridicule Martin by calling him things like "the ideal bellhop" (Baumgartner, *Inquirer*, Oct. 8, 1931).

But the fans weren't mocking him and Commissioner Landis wasn't mocking him. Stockton wrote:

> Whenever the Cardinal special made a stop on the long journey back to St. Louis, crowds gathered near the team's coaches, scurrying from car to car in search of their new baseball idol. He has the showman's instinct: ... he is naively sincere, outspoken and unafraid to voice his thoughts.... On the special train back to St. Louis, Judge [Landis] had to shake the hand of the man of the hour.

"Young man, I envy you. I would love nothing better than to trade places with you."

"It's all right with me, Judge. I'll trade my $4500 for your $50,000 a year any day."

Pepper didn't know that the commissioner's salary was $65,000 (St. Louis *Post-Dispatch*, Oct. 7, 1931).

18

Friday, October 9, 1931: Game Six

Before game six of the 1931 World Series, the United Press International interviewed Professor V. W. Lammon, Washington University psychologist, who said of Pepper that "it's just this confidence like Martin's that business needs. His confidence of being able to steal bases off Mickey Cochrane, his belief he could hit Grove and Earnshaw—all expressed in action—could be carried out in the business world. Let business place orders.... That's an expression of confidence, the sort the public needs" (*New York Times*, Oct. 9, 1931). Martin had clearly become a symbol and, like all symbols, open to a range of interpretations.

One reading was that he was useful to bring customers into theaters, and before game six Johnnie signed for a vaudeville tour, to open in St. Louis that night for two appearances and then more appearances each day after the Series ended.

Another interpretation was Martin's: "I'm like a kid with a little red wagon. I am playing the best baseball of my life. I am trying hard because it is a World Series and I want the Cardinals to win it" (Broeg and Vickery, 233).

Before the gates of Sportsman's Park opened at 7:45 AM on October 9, about 1,000 people were waiting. Eight hundred of them had waited in line the whole afternoon and night. The first woman joined the line at 7 PM and three more women showed up at 8 PM. In their red beach pajamas and white jackets, they were favorites of the photographers.

The *Post-Dispatch* found it to be an ideal day, with the "sun shining, air crisp.... There were splashes of red everywhere—hats, neckties, sweaters and hair ribbons" (Oct. 9, 1931). At 10:40, the Cardinal band took its place in center field and played, beginning with "the National Emblem

March," which the crowd cheered mightily. Then Robert McGilliway, the well-known singing usher, sang "Many Happy Returns of the Day." Many women in the crowd made cone-shaped hats out of newspaper as the day warmed "and found themselves the target of amateur hurlers of all ages, who tried to knock off the hats with bundles of paper, discarded frankfurters and miscellaneous rubbish" (St. Louis *Post-Dispatch*, Oct. 10, 1931). Pitcher Eddie Rommel, 33, in the Athletics bullpen, joked with fans who tried to razz him. Rommel reminded them that while they were working for the next four months he would be loafing around Baltimore.

When Martin arrived at the ballpark, there was waiting for him a watermelon brought up from Texas. Martin could not miss its size, forty-three pounds, and he saw that it had a label reading "To Pepper Martin and Gabby Street. " Martin said to the farmers from Fort Worth, "I sure am mighty grateful to you. This is sure a very nice present." People waited just to slap him on the back and wring his hand, but to their requests he gave a "deprecatory smile" and told them he was late. They saw his pockets stuffed with telegrams and he wore, as usual, his "two-gallon Western hat" (St. Louis *Post-Dispatch* Oct. 10, 1931).

Martin told a reporter, "A few months ago no once cared whether I could write my own name. Now I have signed it on everything from a paper towel to a postage stamp" (Baumgartner, Philadelphia *Inquirer*, October 10, 1931). Pepper came on the field at 12:15 and the band played "Hail, Hail, the Gang's All Here" as Martin began to hit at the end of the Cardinals' time for hitting practice. The *Times*' Brandt noticed "Babe Ruth [who] stepped down to the field to give Pepper some advice on not straining his hands autographing balls and score-cards. As soon as he was through hitting," photographers surrounded him, just in time for the Athletics to come out for their batting practice (*New York Times*, Oct. 10, 1931).

At 1 PM, the Cardinals came back out on the playing surface for fielding practice. Pepper was so busy signing things handed to him by fans before the game that he had little time for practice. There were fans who had come from Pepper's home in Oklahoma to see him play. "Thunderous was the applause that the crowd showered upon Martin" (Drebinger, *New York Times*, Oct. 10, 1931) during fielding practice even though he was "late getting to his place in the field and the crowd saved its cheers for him. No one else drew any attention" (St. Louis *Post-Dispatch* Oct. 10, 1931). Some of the crowd's attention was the presentation to Martin of two gift-wrapped rifles by two fans who came into center field. George Watkins, Johnnie's roommate, interested in the gift, came over from right field to Martin's position and examined the firearms. When practice was done,

Martin imitated a soldier by shouldering the rifles and marching to the dugout with them.

Then, "before the contest, movietones were made of Martin and Manager Street. Martin and Al Simmons, the Athletics' slugger, were photographed together. Martin had a gourd, which was bigger than himself, while Simmons had a small bat..." (Stockton, St. Louis *Post-Dispatch,* Oct. 9, 1931).

For the sixth game, Martin's bat seems to have failed him even though, when he came to bat in the second inning, "Martin's march to home plate was a parade, with the crowd cheering him at every step" (Drebinger, *New York Times,* Oct. 10, 1931). Johnnie popped out to Foxx on the third pitch.

In the sixth, "Martin was eager," said Isaminger, "and jumped into Grove's first pitch, but raised a puerile fly to Bishop" (Philadelphia *Inquirer,* Oct. 10, 1931).

He walked in the ninth with Roettger on first and one out, but the Cardinals did not score.

And while Grove pitched a five-hit, complete game win, Duke Derringer gave up four runs in the fifth inning. "GROVE STOPS PEPPER MARTIN" read the headline in the Cardinals' 8–1 loss. John Drebinger wrote, "He was simply a ball player having a quiet day [one putout] which in itself is considerably more than can be said for some of his less fortunate colleagues" (Drebinger, *New York Times,* Oct. 10, 1931).

Pepper saw all six games of the Series as a whole and said, "I've had my share of the breaks in this series. I'm not kicking" (Philadelphia *Inquirer,* October 10, 1931).

But the Philadelphia *Inquirer* wanted to know why Martin had failed. "Now what happened to Pepper Martin? The crowd ruined him — tired him out — before he ever started the ball game. Only a Sandow could have had the strength to hold up under the pressure the fans put on him" (Baumgartner, Philadelphia *Inquirer,* Oct. 10, 1931). The Associated Press agreed: "He was overanxious, trying too hard to live up to what they had said about him. Instead of just playing his normal game, he was trying to live up to his reputation as a hero on every pitch. He was weighted down with responsibility."

After game six, ticket sales for game seven began at 3:40 PM at the twelve ticket windows on Dodier Street, and within forty-five minutes, without a waiting line, a fan could buy any number of tickets. Windows closed at 11 PM.

The night following game six, Martin made his first appearance in a weeklong engagement at the Ambassador theater in St. Louis. These appearances brought him $3500 a week, one paper reported, 77 percent of the salary paid to him from opening day to closing day, for 165 days. (At other times and in other places, papers reported that show business paid him $1500 a week and $2500 a week.) For now, he was on stage only at 6:30 and 9 PM, along with "Al Trahan with 4 great acts" and the moving picture *Five-Star Final*, starring Edward G. Robinson. At the RKO St. Louis, Louis Armstrong played on stage.

> Catcher Jimmy Wilson revealed last week that Pepper Martin ... slept in his hotel only ten nights all season and that he was out all night the evening before the last World's Series game. Wilson said he accused Pepper of being out the night before the game and Martin admitted it. "You look it," Wilson told Martin. "Your face is all broken out as if it's been hit by a cyclone." "That's right," answered Martin, "those are mosquito bites. It was so hot I took my wife, my baby, two mattresses and the car and slept along the river" [*The Sporting News,* Oct. 22, 1931, p. 5].

19

Saturday, October 10, 1931: Game Seven

The gate might have been be smaller for game seven, 20,805, but those twenty thousand brought the gate receipts for the series to over one million dollars.

For this game against Moose Earnshaw, a right-hander, Ernie Orsatti, "the little Italian" left-handed outfielder, replaced Chick Hafey who, with four hits in the first six games, was hitting .167, so that Cardinal manager Gabby Street could now send five left-handed batters to the plate against Earnshaw.

It was a beautiful day in Philadelphia, clear and bright, when the bleacher gates first opened at 7:40 AM but there was no rush for seats before the game. Thirty minutes before the start of game seven the grandstand had only about 2000 fans and the $3.00 seats were less than half-filled, but the bleachers were packed.

Once again, the band paraded on the field at 10:30 to entertain the early crowd. They wondered if Burleigh Grimes, now thirty-eight years old, could pitch the Cardinals to the championship. Part of the uncertainty was due to the fact that Grimes had been having his side packed with ice, to keep the inflammation of appendicitis in check. As usual, the spitballer did not shave before a game, leading to his nickname Old Stubblebeard.

As the teams prepared for the game, they could see that some fan had climbed the flagpole on top of the YMCA building behind center field.

Andy High, who hit a Texas League single, preceded Pepper to bat in the first inning. After roommate George Watkins singled, Frisch's sacrifice moved High to third and Pepper came to the plate. Martin, still with twelve

Went to the Well Once Too Often - By Chas. Bell

Mack's dream of three straight championships is shattered by Pepper and his teammates. (Courtesy *The Philadelphia Inquirer*.)

hits, was looking for the record-breaker, hit number thirteen. Pepper's luck seemed to be running out; twice he ducked and twice the ball hit his bat. But then, with the count at 2–2, Earnshaw wild pitched High home and Watkins reached third. Martin walked on the next pitch and then stole second, "sliding hands first ahead of Cochrane's good throw," leaving first base open (Philadelphia *Inquirer*, Oct. 11, 1931). The steal meant that when the next batter, Ernie Orsatti, struck out and when Cochrane lost the strikeout pitch in the dirt for a moment, Orsatti could run to first, forcing Cochrane's throw to that base. While that play was competed, Watkins scored and Martin went to third base. So even though he did not hit, Pepper was making things happen.

By the ninth inning, Pepper was still hitless as High and Watkins had scored two runs each and made all of the team's five hits. But with the score 4–0, Burleigh Grimes began to tire. Hallahan, relieving, finally got the last batter, Max Bishop, to hit the ball in the air to center and Pepper later said "the ball looked like $1500 dropping in his hands."

In a column with his byline, Pepper remarked, "I never knew a happier minute in all my life.... I sure would have liked to have kept that ball as a souvenir but I had no right to it. Only one fellow had the right and I gave it to him. That fellow was Burleigh Grimes.... I didn't get a hit today but, shucks, what of that" (Philadelphia *Inquirer*, Oct. 11, 1931).

"Pepper Martin, the last man to reach the dugout, had to literally climb the shoulders of fans to reach his showers.... Cardinal players were actually too happy to talk. Even before they were off the field they hugged each other like kids. It wasn't surprising then that they strutted their stuff a little — stuck out their chests and told the world that they were good" (Baumgartner Philadelphia *Inquirer*, Oct. 11, 1931).

The Cardinals had beaten one of the best teams of all time, though "Street claimed nothing more for his players than that they were an organization of spirited men, men of speed and sticktoitiveness...." (*Spalding's Official Baseball Guide*, 1932: 17).

While Grimes and Hallahan won two games each in the seven game series, Martin was second in RBI (5), first in hits (12), and his five steals were five more than the Athletics team. He hit .500, made two walks, and made no errors.

From "Sport Salad," by L. C. Davis, this poem titled "The Leap Year Kid":

> Blessings on thee, little boy
> From my heart I give thee joy.
> With the sunshine on thy face
> Sliding into second base,
> Stealing Mickey Cochrane's shirt,
> As you deftly hit the dirt.
> Swiping everything in sight,
> Hitting pitchers, left or right.
> Pulling most amazing stunts
> Many times, not only once.
> Batting in a needed run,

October 10, 1931: Game Seven

Doing things that can't be done.
Scampering around the lot,
Putting pitchers on the spot.
You can have a birthday cake
Every four years—what a break!
Hero of the Redbird clan.
Six years old but what a man!
When you reach maturity
What a player you will be!
[St. Louis *Post-Dispatch*, Oct. 10, 1931].

20

Saturday, October 10, 1931: After Game Seven

When Pepper caught the last out in the last game of the 1931 World Series at Sportsman's Park in St. Louis, the city erupted in celebration; the noise was tremendous. Loud bursts were heard first from the motorcycle exhausts of the newspaper boys delivering the first evening editions. Then the clang was heard from drivers dragging tire rims and old cans behind their cars. Cars and trucks backfired as they drove through a storm of paper tossed out of office windows.

Drebinger wrote: "By his speed and daring on the bases and his vigorous manipulation of a bat, he had catapulted the Cardinals into their first three victories and even in two defeats he dominated the field as no man had ever done in world's series play.... [Though] apparently worn down by the attentions of an adulating public, the crowd acclaimed him to the end and tonight the big heroes of this astounding St. Louis triumph were Martin, the magnificent, Grimes, the indomitable, Hallahan, the courageous, and the grizzled Gabby Street" (*New York Times*, October 11, 1931).

But Pepper was about to cash in and others were about to cash in on him cashing in, though he tried to be realistic and truthful and generous, as he always tried to be, when he said, "When some of the other boys weren't hitting in the early games, I was lucky enough to be cracking them out and when Grove and Earnshaw finally got me tamed, why, High and Watkins soaked out a couple of hits apiece and won the game" (Martin, Philadelphia *Inquirer*, Oct. 16, 1931). And Martin told Frisch after the game, "It didn't make any difference that I didn't get another hit. We won the series and that's what we were after, no matter what anybody did" (Frisch, *New York Times*, Oct. 11, 1931).

October 10, 1931: After Game Seven

But winning the series *did* matter. If the team had not won the series, then chances were that many things would be different for Pepper. Change number one was the Martin "autobiography," serialized in papers all over the country so that "... people that want to can read something about a ball player that was just shucks before the World's Series," as chapter one said in the Philadelphia *Inquirer* of October 12, 1931.

Peter Golenbock interviewed Gene Karst, who remembered that "Pepper was the great national hero. He had all the headlines.... The fan mail poured in by the bucketful. Some were mash notes and simply admiring fans, and as head of the Cards' public relations department, I'd go through them." Pepper decided to "put all of the offers in Mr. Breadon's hands and told him he is my business manager and I will do as he says" (Golenbock, 150).

Influencing these decisions was the public belief, according to the St. Louis *Star's* Walter W. Smith, that the Cardinals had "become merely the ensemble background for the greatest one-man show the baseball world has ever known" (*Literary Digest*, Oct. 24, 1931).

The "one-man show" became literal truth after the Series. "Pepper was an outdoors guy, rough and ready. He didn't pay much attention to the adulation. After the World Series, he was signed up for an appearance onstage, though he certainly was not an actor. He'd go on the stage and imitate Will Rogers, twirl a rope and tell a few stories. He said he was getting $1,500 a week, which was a lot of money" (Golenbock, 201). In fact, it was a third of his year's salary with St. Louis.

So after the last game, Martin again taxied to the Ambassador theater in St. Louis to do two shows at six and nine-thirty. For the remainder of the week, since the games were over, Pepper performed six times a day. Breadon sent his secretary, Clarence Lewis, to mind Pepper, so that Martin was properly looked after on his vaudeville tour, at least for the first two weeks.

The plans Johnnie and Ruby had made for a hunting trip had to be canceled because "now I am doing an act and I'll be so busy in the big towns that the shooting party we had all fixed up is no go at all" (Martin, Philadelphia *Inquirer*, Oct. 12, 1931).

By the end of his week at the Ambassador, newspapermen were still interviewing him. The Associated Press writer recorded Pepper saying, "I know there was a lot of luck in what I did and I want everybody to know that Pepper Martin will always be as common as Oklahoma dirt. Nobody need think I'll get the swell head just because I was lucky to get hits off Grove and Earnshaw and steal a few bases.... I'm not promising to be a star or anything like that, but I'm going to bear down and do my best"

(AP, Oct. 15, 1931). Years later he told Carmichael: "They horse collared me in the last two games. It's just as well things didn't go on because my sombrero mightn't-a fit me after all the luck I had" (155).

While Johnnie was on stage in Chicago October 16–22, a *Sporting News* story had Martin say, "Money ain't everything. I'd rather live in a shack in the wide open spaces of Oklahoma with my wife and baby than earn $2,500 a week on the stage." But he couldn't turn down the money. He knew it was too lucrative an opportunity to pass up and it might never come again. Anyone who had taken from 1924 to 1931 to make it to the majors knew how short one's time in the big leagues could be. And to be someone who, as John Drebinger wrote, "has bounded from almost total obscurity into the position of a national idol" (*New York Times*, Oct. 11, 1931) was to be someone who knew very well how quickly obscurity returns.

"Anyway, this mail pours in," Karst continued, "and I go through it, and there's a lot. Anything involving financial offers, endorsements, money, was to be turned over to the club treasurer, Bill DeWitt, Sr. Bill would talk to Pepper."

One approved endorsement appeared in the October 18 issue of *The Sporting News*: "Pepper' Martin, World Series Hero, swings Powerized and Bone Rubbed Louisville Slugger Bat. Hats off to you, Mr. John Leonard Martin, World Series Hero Extraordinary. You and your Louisville Slugger Bat teamed well together. Three cheers and a tiger! Banzai! And what not!"

How much money Pepper made that fall is hard to tell. His year's salary might have been mostly gone by now, with the club paying only from opening day to closing day. The World Series check of $4484 could be added to his vaudeville money, and the story was told of Pepper holding onto $10,000 in cash which he showed to Branch Rickey on his way home.

Before he left, Pepper talked to Karst, who "had the rest of this mountain of fan mail, and we filled out a form letter or postcard to acknowledge the fans. I had a great big box full, probably two by four by four, and after Martin ended the stage deal, he said, 'I'm no actor. I want to get back to Oklahoma and go hunting and fishing.' We loaded up this pile of mail on a small trailer on the back of his car and he drove on to Oklahoma.

"The following spring training, I said, 'Pepper, did you read all that fan mail?' He said, 'You know, Gene, I never got around to reading any of it.' He never opened the package" (Golenbock, 150).

He did pay off the mortgage and repay the debt on his mother's home in Oklahoma City. He did pay off the mortgage on the farm back in Temple. He did play pro football with the Oklahoma City Chiefs as well as with the Hominy Indians featuring players from Carlyle and Haskill institutes.

When *The Sporting News*' Herman Wecke picked his all-star team of rookie major leaguers for 1931, there were three Cardinals on it: Ripper Collins, Paul Derringer and Pepper Martin.

But he was not just a rookie all-star according to the *Literary Digest*: "… Pepper Martin made himself a hero not only in St. Louis but in the entire country and turned himself, as regards popularity, into the Babe Ruth of the Nationals" (Oct. 24, 1931:34).

21

The Last of 1931

The *Spaulding Guide* of 1932 tried to sum up Pepper's play in the 1931 World Series: "... What actually happened was ... the grand entry into the big ring of base ball by a young St. Louis player, Martin, who mastered all others at the bat, in base running and fielded it without a blunder.... The success of Martin was extraordinary and so little expected that he established himself as a World Series hero.... He stole third base in the second game and with that he ... upset the equanimity of the Philadelphia players ... in the games that followed" (*Spalding's Official Baseball Guide,* 1932: 16).

When Johnnie was asked, "'Mr. Martin, where did you learn to run the way you do?' Well, sir," Martin replied, 'I grew up in Oklahoma and once you start runnin' out there, there ain't nothin' to stop you'" (Heinz, 70).

The Major League all-star team was announced on December 29, 1931, and only Frankie Frisch and Pie Traynor from the National League were on it. Earl Averill was the major league all-star center fielder. The Associated Press's choice for athlete of the year was Pepper Martin, who was given sixty-eight votes to tennis champion Francis Ouimet's 11.

In the voting for athlete of the year by American sports writers and editors, Martin received seventy votes and second place tennis champion Ellsworth Vines was awarded sixteen.

Bill Slocum, for the baseball writers' dinner, wrote words to the tune of "Goodnight, Sweetheart":

> Goodbye Mickey, this is Pepper Martin;
> I'm on first base, but soon I'll be startin'
> Off for second. I'll flit like a bird
> Then on my word I'll take third.
> So long, Mickey. Keep your glove and mask on;
> If your shinguard's loose, tie another clasp on.
> The way I feel, there's nothing I won't steal;
> So goodbye Mickey, goodbye
> [Broeg, St. Louis *Post-Dispatch,* March 16, 1975].

Part Three

22

1932–1934: The Gas House Gang

A story in the Daily *Oklahoman* late in 1931 guessed that "John Leonard 'Pepper' Martin probably will get a better contract or become a holdout. No young man has had better publicity since Lindy flew to Paris, and few have deserved it more. He has made a great show of a World Series people viewed with some apathy at the start, and he has given those who always insist the American League is the stronger much food for meditation."

It was Branch Rickey who negotiated the contracts with players and Pepper admitted, "He fascinated me.... He talked for ten minutes. When he paused for breath, I said 'Gimme the contract and I'll sign it, Mr. Rickey. I haven't the slightest idea what you're talking about.'" The contract was signed at noon.

Rickey was called Mr. Rickey by almost every one of his employees; it was a custom of the time and it was a sign of respect for your elders as Rickey was fifty in 1932. Rickey's biographer noted that "Martin was so taken by the educated Rickey and so pleased at the attention he had given him he had started patterning his speech after Rickey's." As for Rickey, he said, "Pepper Martin is the most genuine person I've ever met in my life. There was never an ounce of pretense in the man" (Broeg and Vickery, 234). Considering Rickey's high level of "pretense," Pepper must have been a constant reminder of the boss's affectation.

J. Roy Stockton saw Pepper after the contract signing on January 23, 1932, and the *Post-Dispatch* reporter knew, although the team had just won a pennant and beaten an almost legendary team, that "Martin is one of the few Cardinals who was expected to receive an increase in salary despite the major leagues' announced intention of reducing their payrolls" (AP,

St. Louis *Post-Dispatch*, Jan. 23, 1932). The times were hard in 1932 and Martin was pleased by his new pay. "Everything's fine and the Cardinals have sure done right by me. I'll be mighty glad when the season starts. This has been a great winter, even if the theater business did interfere with my hunting plans, but there ain't nothing like baseball" (AP, St. Louis *Post-Dispatch*, Jan. 23, 1932).

The money allowed Pepper to become a gentleman farmer. Hungry for a space of land of his own, Martin took a portion of his World Series money and bought eighty acres of bottom land, twelve miles west of Oklahoma City at Lake Overholster. "He liked to be out in the country," Ruby told me. Lake Overholster remains a fine fishing spot as well. Pep also told Stockton, "I bought myself a duplex flat out with some of the dough I got out of baseball and the theaters and I was pretty busy all winter getting things fixed up" (St. Louis *Post-Dispatch*, Jan. 23, 1932). The house at 2600 block NW 12th St. would be home to the family for thirteen years. Being a duplex meant it produced income and in addition there was a working oil well in the backyard. There was also room for Pepper's ten bird dogs, kept in a large pen in the backyard.

Martin was clearly aware of his fortunate position: he had always known of his limited baseball skills, particularly on defense, and he certainly knew the hard times that faced all the people back in Oklahoma, people who were about to become known as Okies.

Over the winter Pepper has been able to do some small game hunting, mostly quail, and it was this hunting that Martin loved so much that probably cost him in the 1932 season. While sleeping in tall grass on a hunting trip, he suffered a nasty insect bite which became a chronic skin infection. So it may be that when Martin went to St. Louis for his January 23 contract negotiation, his awareness of that skin problem may have led him to sign in just ten minutes.

When he was asked about his fantastic showing in the 1931 Series, he said, "I figure anybody who lets a little good luck go to their heads is just blamed foolish. Why, the President of the United States shouldn't ought to ever even get swell-headed about it, because look, ain't he liable to run into one of these depressions. No, sir, there won't be any swelling about my head if I can help it" (Stockton, St. Louis *Post-Dispatch*, Jan. 23, 1932).

Dizzy Dean and his wife Pat were in St. Louis at the same time as Pepper for his contract signing. The three went to a hockey game that night where Pepper "spoke a few well-chosen words to the radio and hockey audience through his 10-gallon cowboy hat," and the next night the trio attended an A. A. U. basketball game, where Dizzy volunteered to be a referee (St. Louis *Post-Dispatch*, Jan. 24, 1932).

Pepper much later claimed that he wrote letters for Dizzy to Pat: "I wrote all his love letters to his future wife and he won her. Pretty good, huh?" (*McAlester News-Capital & Democrat*).

Dean and Pepper had formed a friendship early, and the friendship would continue for some time. It was a friendship, Ruby told me, in which Pepper, six years older than the Arkansan Dean, acted as an older brother. "Johnnie liked to straighten him out," Ruby told me. "He got a kick out of that." The pranks Martin was famous for were planned pranks and the object was carefully selected. Dean caused trouble for people and did not amuse them and Pepper tried his best to advise Dean. Dizzy could be charming but he also irritated people. Pepper never made very many demands from his manager or owner or teammates and so was well-liked.

The year 1932 turned out to be horrible for Martin. Chick Hafey's trade to Cincinnati just before the season opened seemed to ensure Martin's job in the outfield but Martin was called on to play third base for fifteen games. But, in addition to his ongoing skin problem, Johnnie damaged his thumb and no one knew about the injury until, in Boston, he left a trail of bandage across the diamond on a throw to first.

The manager wanted to know how and why his third baseman was hurt. "Well, Gabby, you see right under my window some old dolls come out to walk their kiyoodles about ten o'clock every night so I thought I would have some fun. I got a pitcher of water and when a kiyoodle would come in range I let him have some. Gabby, you'd laugh fit to die to see 'em jump and holler. I ... had a bad accident. I hit the pitcher against the window sill. It broke the pitcher and I cut my thumb" (Heinz, 102).

This was just one of the physical problems that Pepper had that year, a year he spent unable to play for about 55 percent of the games. Teammate Frisch gave Martin suggestions:

> "If I had the shoulders, arms and body that you've got, I wouldn't have bothered about baseball. I'd have been the light-heavyweight champion of the world, knocking down twenty grand for each fight."
> "Oh, yeah?" said Martin.
> "Oh, yeah," said Frisch [Brundidge, St. Louis *Star*, July 21, 1931: 5].

Being idle, Martin now had more time for his pranks. His teammate from Rochester, first baseman Ripper Collins, had the gift of being able to suggest gags to Pepper that Martin went along with, while Collins stood in the background and watched. Sneezing powder spread in the crease of a newspaper and then held in front of a fan in a hotel lobby fan was one of Martin's favorites.

The worse he played, the harder, of course, he tried when he did play. And there were always, that year, the things written about him from the

World Series in 1931. Those pieces almost demanded to know why Martin was not playing at the level of his first five games in the 1931 World Series. But if he made twelve hits every five games, he would make about 360 hits for the year, a hundred more than anyone has ever made.

Yet another injury, this to his shoulder, happened after he dove into home plate, curtailing his ability to both hit and throw well. Then a leg injury sat him down for a while. Then he was hit by a pitch, causing a broken hand. Tried at third base, a bad hop ball knocked out two teeth.

Martin's reputation was not one of a graceful athlete. Broeg wrote that Johnnie was "an awkward athlete [who] batted right-handed, cradled his bat in the crook of his right arm and, strong and musclebound, he hit more to right field than to left" (*The Sporting News*, Nov. 26, 1977).

That year Martin saw the need to keep himself entertained and, inspired by trainer Harrison "Doc" Weaver's talent with a mandolin, "Pepper bought a guitar before starting on the recent Eastern tour. He couldn't play a note when he purchased the instrument. He still cannot play a note" (Sept. 29, 1932).

To change his luck, Martin tried rubbing his bat with a horseshoe and luck, or ability, did show up sometimes during that year. "And speaking of Pepper Martin, how is the gallant young man coming along these days? 'Well, he's just beginning to come again,' said the sergeant [manager Street]. 'It took him a long time to get over the fact that he was Martin, the world series hero. By that I don't mean he had a crush on himself. He was merely trying to pick up where he had left off last fall and he was overtrying and getting nowhere. Now he's Martin the ball player again and that's better for all of us because he is a ball player, all right'" (Joe Williams, New York *World-Telegram*, July 3, 1932).

On August 25, for instance, against the Giants, he doubled in his first at bat, stole third, "and so upset the New Yorkers," Charles E. Parker wrote, "that his teammate, George Puccinelli, sprinted from first to second before they recovered.... Thereafter, he kept Walker, the Giant hurler, on such tenterhooks, that the latter got himself into a hole and was forced to serve the plate-splitting drive that Dean turned into a home run.... [Martin's] second hit was nothing more than a legitimate single, but, upon noting that Lindstrom was fielding it as such, Pepper continued on to stretch it into a double. His third hit found the Giants prepared for another such move, so he was limited to one base. But he kept dashing back and forth in a way that threw [Sam] Gibson, Giant relief hurler, out of gear and thus sponsored the Cardinals' two-run tally in the eighth inning, to run their total of counters to an even half dozen" (Charles E. Parker, St. Louis *Post-Dispatch*, Aug. 25, 1932).

The season finally ended, and Martin, with only 323 at bats, produced nine steals and seventy-seven hits. The Cardinals' year, like Pepper's, was awful: a sixth place in earned run average for batting and slugging averages which led to a seventh place finish, ten games under .500.

1933

Perhaps worried about what his new salary might be (though the contract turned out to be $8,000 for the season), Pepper performed on radio early in 1933 in Oklahoma City, where he sang and played guitar. Martin also played football in the off season with the Hominy Indians and when Cardinals team management found out they quickly fined him $1000. Management knew very well how he would play football.

In Florida for the training season, the Cardinals tried to deal with the problem of one steady third baseman for the team, since seven men played that position in 1932. Then, too, since Ducky Medwick had locked up the left field spot, Pepper was asked to be the third baseman for the year. The bigger truth was that the Cardinal infield was in chaos. Ripper Collins was a strong player at first; Frisch at 34 and Rogers Hornsby at 37 probably could not be expected to fill the second base spot for the whole season; worst of all was the devastating injury to shortstop Charlie Gelbert who had shot himself in the leg before the season in a hunting accident. Sparky Adams, who was to be the shortstop, was playing hurt. Martin was needed in the infield.

Yet Martin knew he was not the best third baseman: "The fact is I aim to knock the ball down and scramble for it. All I want to do is get my hand on it and I'm quick enough to pick it up in time to make the throw. I'll bet I look funny to a seasoned third baseman, but I get away with the plays even if some of them are sloppy" (St Louis *Post-Dispatch*). Martin was untidy in other ways too, as Bob Broeg told Peter Golenbock: "Pepper was a mess, you know. He didn't wear underwear or a jock strap. He was wide-shouldered and very awkward. When he was playing third, he'd pick the ball up, and Rip Collins wasn't very tall [5'9"] at first, and he'd throw it down the right field bullpen. Oh, Pepper could throw. Rip would see it coming and retreat" (145).

But Johnnie did the job he was asked to do. Soon fans all over the league were used to seeing Martin with number 28 on his back at third base. In fact, there were only ten games in the 1933 season when he didn't play third base. As he seemed to become more comfortable at third, the

Cardinals traveled east in May. On May 5, Pepper hit a single, a double, a triple and a home run at Philadelphia. In contemporary baseball jargon, "hitting for the cycle," the feat was simply noted by the newspapers; Martin was the thirty-first player in modern times in the league to achieve this feat in the National League.

Not long after this accomplishment, Rickey contrived a trade. Paul Derringer, a starting pitcher, was traded to the Cincinnati Reds for the best defensive shortstop of his time, Leo Durocher. Durocher's abilities helped to bolster Martin's limited skills and Frisch's declining range at second base. Sparky Adams, an experienced third baseman, was traded with Derringer.

Martin often startled newcomer Durocher. Pepper, playing third, often had a sudden urge for a chew of tobacco. Even though a batsman was being pitched to, Martin didn't bother calling time. He simply removed his glove, tucked it under his arm, and reached into his hip pocket for his cut plug. If just then the batter drilled a sharp shot toward third, there was Pepper, glove in his armpit and a cut plug in his teeth. He would lean forward and let the speeding ball bounce off his chest. Then he leisurely picked up the ball and fired to first to get his man.

> May 31, 1933, The Branscome Hotel Rosedale 4000, 5370 Pershing Avenue, Saint Louis: Dearest Mother, Hope this finds you all well and happy. Ruby and the babies are just fine. I'm enclosing a check for $15. I guess will come in handy. The Texaco filling station across from the capitol will cash it Ask Monty or Sanders Merrick. I have been going good and our club is only one half game out of first place. I'm sure were going to win the pennant and you've got to come to the series if we do. I'm sorry I haven't wrote but I'm sure a poor hand to write. I love you Mother. Has Charlie straightened up any? I sure hope so. Well Ill write you soon and a longer letter all my love to you Mother Johnnie.

Charlie's problem seemed to be his drinking and there is a hint that eventually Charlie would be very badly hurt in an automobile wreck of his own making. Charlie's destructive behavior would make Martin very strongly anti-alcohol.

Martin was playing very well and the team was beginning to look like a winner again after their dive from first to seventh in 1932. "One of the pleasant developments of the season has been the return to greatness of Pepper Martin, now leading the National League in hitting.... The young man has contributed vitally to the Cardinals' upsweep.... By his work so far this season the Pepper Pot — called a flash in the pan when he bogged down last year — has definitely established himself as one of the great ball players of the day. He is playing with all the grit and fire and power that made him the most talked of figure in baseball when he overthrew the Athletics single handed" (Williams, New York *World-Telegram*, July 1, 1933).

On July 18, 1933, the very first All-Star Game was played. In an odd move, Manager John McGraw decided that Pepper would play third, though Pie Traynor was voted into that spot with Martin voted into the centerfield position. This exchange meant that in the first All-Star Game Martin was the very first batter. And Pepper in the sixth inning drove in the first National League run.

When Babe Ruth hit the first all-star home run, Pepper sent ushers out with a twenty dollar bill to find the ball and buy it from the fans who held it. Pepper got the Babe, then Crowder, Foxx, Grove, Hallahan, Lazzeri and Gehrig to sign the ball. At the same time he got National Leaguers — Klein, Hartnett, Wilson, Hubbell, Waner, Hafey and Berger — to sign another ball. (Martin kept that first home run ball — which he called "Babe Ruth's ball," and "my pride and joy"— all his life and it was not sold until 1995, when it brought $44,000 at auction.)

On Sunday, July 29, Martin's thrills continued with a game-winning three-run homer in the tenth inning. He was more at ease now with his play though often he drove manager Frisch crazy by seemingly disappearing before games. Soon Frisch learned that Johnnie liked to sit in the stands and talk things over with fans, so that Frisch learned to look for him in the crowd.

"The Cardinals fined me $1,000 last year (1933) for playing pro football and do you know they didn't give that one grand back to me until the season was durn near over..." (St. Louis *Post-Dispatch*, March 7, 1934).

At season's end, the New York Giants were in first place mostly because their pitching led the league in E.R.A. and shutouts; the pitching was strong enough to take the National League pennant. While the Cardinals led the league in runs, triples, doubles, and steals, their pitchers gave up too many earned runs. Only three pitchers made it into double digits in wins, and the team defense was last in double plays and assists. The team finished out of the first division in fifth place, still two places higher than 1932.

Martin, however, had a very good year. In the National League, he was first in runs with 122, first in steals with 26, fifth in batting at .316, tied for sixth in doubles, tied for fifth in hits with 189, fourth in OBP, tied for ninth in slugging average, third in triples, third in walks. So he had two firsts in the league and then he placed in the top five in five other categories.

Pepper had gone from his worst season to his best. It had been a season, as well, when Pepper clearly had baseball and not much else on his mind. His play was rewarded with a fifth place finish in National League

Pepper is in the front row, second from left, posing for the team picture of the first National League all-star team, in Chicago in 1933. (National Baseball Hall of Fame Library, Cooperstown, N.Y.)

voting for the Most Valuable Player behind the winner Carl Hubbell, then Chuck Klein, Wally Berger and Bill Terry.

It was around this time that Pepper went barnstorming with Dizzy Dean and others. Satchel Paige remembered pitching against Johnnie:

> All the boys'd been telling me what a tough out he was. That got me real curious, so every time a batter came up I asked, "You Mr. Martin?" Then this guy comes up and grins when I asked him that and I knew I'd found Mr. Martin.
>
> "They tell me you can hit," I said. He just grinned. "Then hit this." I threw my bee ball. I only fired the bee ball three times before Mr. Martin struck out and went back to the dugout [Paige, *Maybe I'll Pitch Forever*, 92].

In November, from a palm reader, a St. Louis *Post-Dispatch* reader found, "What Their Palms Reveal — Significant Lines in Pepper Martin's Hand ... from the studies of O. E. Largoe, 1416 Evergreen Avenue, St. Louis, MO.... The Mount of Jupiter reveals him to be incredibly ambitious. The first and second fingers are long and well developed and show the subject to possess accuracy, system, order and commanding power. The wide space between the first and second fingers indicates an unselfish, yet restless spirit that wants everything done quickly, on the impulse of the moment, without delay.... He is very sensitive and of a nervous temperament, although of a bright and happy disposition" (Nov. 30, 1933).

1934

Martin, back in Oklahoma, put in an active winter of 1933–34 hunting deer, coyotes, wild hogs and quail, some of the hunting being done in Mexico. Martin, being a true believer in baseball, "could have talked every night this winter if I wanted to. I don't go much for that stuff. But I do like them literaries. You know what they are? Everybody brings their harmonicas and git-tars and fiddles and they just up to old highjinks.... As I was telling Mr. Rickey, I'm a 12-month man. I play ball all summer and go preaching baseball all winter" (St. Louis *Post-Dispatch*, March 1, 1934).

Knowing how the team felt about his other off-season activities, Pepper said, "I didn't play no professional basketball. Course they pay you for playing amateur basketball out there but it's still amateur they tell me. Well, I only had seven men, but we were good enough to beat Carl Hubbell's team and Carl had about 30 players" (St. Louis *Post-Dispatch*, March 1, 1934). Martin always found a way to have fun.

On March 1, 1934, Martin drove to St. Louis in "his beloved motor truck" to negotiate his contract, bringing Rickey some Oklahoma venison he had shot. Pepper thought the gift game would make Rickey look more kindly on the talks. But Rickey, as was his wont, talked poverty, talked calamity, talked to confound and impress. Savings must be made, Rickey declared. The next savings must come from the salaries of players. Frisch's salary dropped by $9,500. Dizzy Dean signed at $7,500 for winning 20 games and giving the team 296 innings. The two chief rookies, Paul Dean, pitcher brother of Dizzy, and a catcher Bill Delancey, "Dee," signed for the usual rookie pay of $3,000. And Rickey sent out yet another warning. Pepper's roommate, George Watkins was traded to the Giants partly because his average had dropped in 1933 and partly because he was refusing to sign his contract. Branch Rickey, of course, assigned himself no pay decrease.

After Pepper signed, he drove south from Oklahoma City to New Orleans, to the home of Tex Carleton, twenty-seven, who had been Pepper's teammate in Houston, Rochester, and for the last two years with the Cardinals, and then he and Tex drove together to arrive on March 5 at the Hotel Dixie Grande in Florida (St. Louis *Post-Dispatch*, March 2, 1934). It would be the addition of three men — Delancey, an intelligent veteran player, Spud Davis, another catcher, and the superb pitching of Paul Dean — that would greatly help the team. Then too, Ripper Collins, a fine hitter, would be at his peak, Joe Medwick would be near to his, Tex Carleton would add sixteen wins and though Bill Hallahan would falter, Bill Walker would rally from his 1933 record, and Dizzy Dean would top all the pitchers with thirty wins.

Before the Cardinals broke camp, manager Frankie Frisch made a fire eating speech: "Don't let anybody push you around.... Your nights are your own, but your bodies belong to the Cardinals in the daylight.... Now if you'd rather go back to the mines and dig coal or ride around the country in Pullmans and live in the best hotels at the expense of the club, speak right up. We haven't any room for softies, no holds are barred. That's the way we're going to play ball" [Hood, 34].

Pepper still made his fun. Appointed honorary fire chief in Fort Myers, Florida, during spring training, Johnnie was photographed in his Cardinal uniform wearing a fire chief's hat sitting atop a fire engine. He and Dizzy knew how to get a crowd together for exhibition games. In late May, in Huntington, WV, they walked down both sides of Main Street, having a very loud conversation:

"You pitching today, Dizzy?"

"Sure am. You gonna play, Pepper?"

"You bet I am."

After another exhibition game, this one in Wichita, Kansas, a Wichita business man, S.A. Murphy, visited the Cardinal hotel with his son. Dizzy and Pepper Martin gave the boy an autographed ball and a Pepper Martin model baseball bat. They introduced both the father and son to other members of the team. Murphy was so pleased by the kindness of Martin and Dean that he gave them an interesting gift of an oil lease (UP, New York *World-Telegram*, June 24, 1938).

When the team took the field on opening day in 1934, Martin wore uniform number 1, and though it was his third different uniform number in three years, it was the one he wore for years afterward. Bob Broeg wrote that this team, "when they weren't supposed to win ... got down and dirty and played with all the effort of a man trying to hang onto a job just to feed his family for one more day. They came up smiling and boasting about how they knew all along they'd win." This was the team that would be known as the Gas House Gang.

In April, they could only find a way to win four games while losing eleven.

By the end of May, the team was in first place.

By the end of June, the pennant race in the National League was clearly between the New York Giants, now in front, and the Cardinals, in third. Only the Cardinals had established a winning record against the league leaders.

The All-Star break required the attendance of four of the Cardinals: Pepper Martin was named as a reserve and joined Frisch, the starting second baseman, Dean, and Joe Medwick, the starting left fielder, at the Polo Grounds for the second All-Star Game.

After watching Carl Hubbell strike out, in order, Babe Ruth, Lou Gehrig, Jimmie Foxx, Al Simmons, and Joe Cronin, Pepper was sent into the game to go 0–1 as a pinch hitter, but he also walked and scored.

By the end of July, 1934, Johnnie developed a swollen stiff elbow. The elbow was found to be full of bone chips. Restricted by the damage, Martin found time to have a foot race through the streets of Pittsburgh for a bet involving two gallons of ice cream. But then Johnnie tried to play too soon and so developed a painful pulled muscle in his side.

Martin kept active and useful to the team by throwing batting practice, and by using the skills as a pitcher used much earlier in his career. In the first of two games against the Boston Braves on August 19, Carleton, Haines and Mooney gave up seven runs in fewer than four innings. Pitchers were needed, of course, for game two. Frustrated by inaction, Pepper volunteered to pitch the rest of the fourth inning. At that half inning's end, he ran down to the bullpen to warm up some more for the fifth inning. In that fifth, no Braves could get on base, as Johnnie used his knuckler, fast ball and sidearm change of pace.

Later that day, Martin was asked to leave the team hotel by hotel management. The supervisor did not think it was good for the hotel's reputation and the peace of mind of the guests if Martin was permitted to continue shooting pigeons from his room's windows.

Luckily for the Cardinals, by the end of August, the team's performance improved as injuries healed. When Pepper came back to play, after missing forty-four days, Frisch moved back to second, freeing up the dependable Burgess Whitehead to be used both in defensive spots and as a pinch hitter. Soon *The Sporting News* saw Martin, at third base, now 30, "still daring and aggressive on the bases, still all spirit and sweat. [He was] the most popular player, a fun-loving toughie, who played so hard in every game that the paper suggested he get off the last week of each month" (quoted in Gregory, 140).

As the press had predicted, the pennant came down to the Giants and the Cardinals. The September 16 Polo Grounds doubleheader seated the largest crowd in the history of the National League. The New York City fire department ordered the doors of the park locked while fifteen thousand watched from the 8th Avenue Elevated tracks or from Coogan's Bluff. When the St. Louis team swept the two games, they were just three and a half games behind with fourteen to play.

In Brooklyn, Dizzy threw a three hitter and Paul Dean pitched a no-hitter. Now the Cardinals were two and a half behind.

On the twenty-fourth in Wrigley Field, much thanks for the Cardinals win went to two players: manager Frisch with his diving catch of Stan

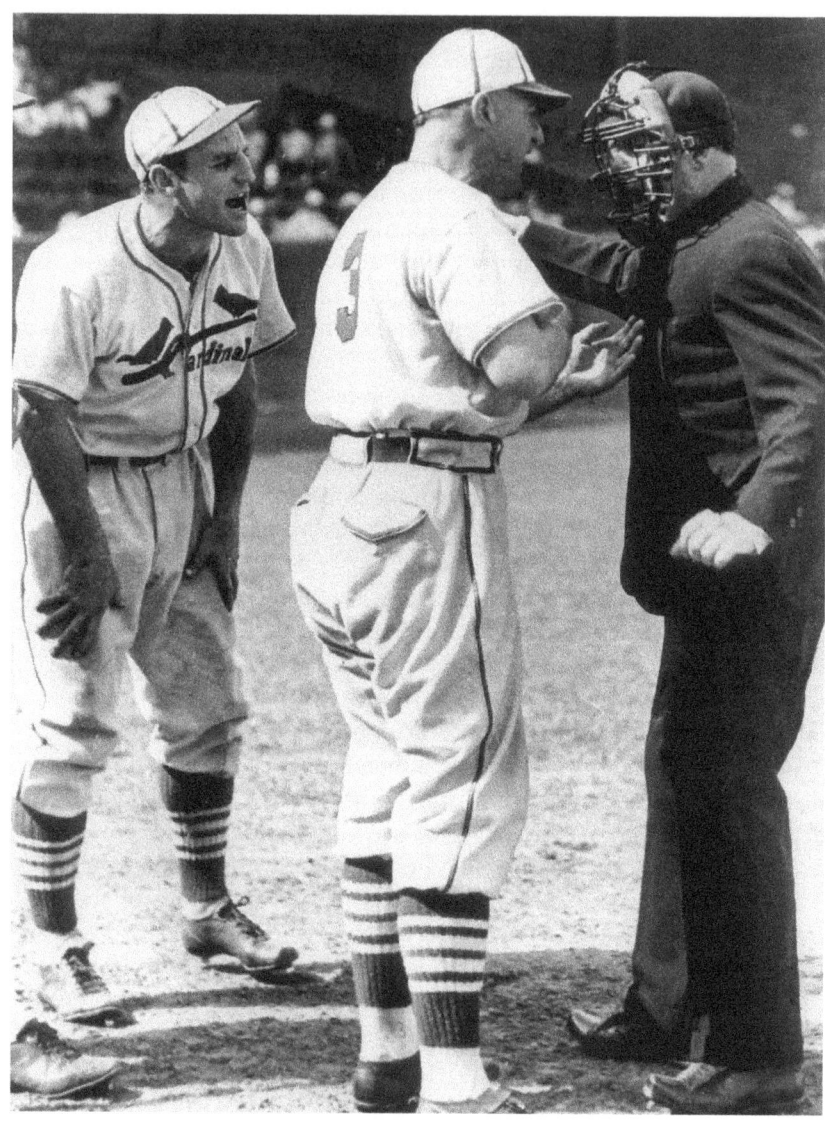

Frankie Frisch and Pepper explain the true nature of a play to an umpire who just doesn't seem to understand. (National Baseball Hall of Fame Library, Cooperstown, N.Y.)

Hack's line drive, followed by his throw which doubled the man off first; and John Martin for his catch of a line drive off the grass and another hard catch which he turned into a putout. The Giants did not play that day and their lead was down to two games.

When Dizzy won, the Giants' lead was one game with two to play.

On Saturday, the next to last day of the season, rainy though it was, many Dodger fans traveled to the Polo Grounds to see their Van Mungo go against the Giants' Roy Parmelee with the pennant on the line. The Giants lost again 5–1. They were about to lose the first place spot they had held since June 8 for good. On that rainy Saturday in St. Louis, Sportsman's Park's paid attendance was 11,500 plus 8870 women and 2671 girls. Pepper Martin in the first chased Koenig's foul, skidded in the mud and reached back to catch it. Paul Dean beat Paul Derringer six to one. The Cardinals were one game in front with one to play.

Sunday they won again and the Giants lost again. In the clubhouse, first baseman Ripper Collins, who made his two-hundredth hit of the 1934 season that day, sang "We're in the Money." In another part of the clubhouse, harmonizing on "I Want a Girl..." were first base coach Buzzy Wares, left fielder Joe Medwick, and National League stolen base champion Pepper Martin (Gregory, 206).

Martin had a fine year, hitting .289 in addition to his twenty-three steals.

The 1934 World Series began in Detroit's Navin Field. The newspapers that came out just prior to Tuesday's workout noticed that the Cardinals had five hitters at .300 or above and the starting lineup was hitting .301. Outfielder Ernie Orsatti, still limping, was to be used to hit against right-handers and Chuck Fullis would take Orsatti's spot in center against left-handers. Pepper still had bone chips in his elbow and it swelled up after games, a very painful swelling, but he insisted on playing.

This series was marked by the excellence of the pitching of the Dean brothers. After the two teams split the first two games at Navin Field, Pepper, playing full speed for his pal Paul Dean in St. Louis for game three, not only had two extra base hits but also crashed into Billy Rogell at second base on Jack Rothrock's probable double play grounder "like one of Knute Rockne's great tackles."

After the win, "[Dizzy] Dean was charging around the room with a white pith helmet.... Dean had a rubber tiger and was whacking Bill Delancey over the head with it and throwing it into the showers at Pepper Martin" (St. Louis *Post-Dispatch*, Oct. 5, 1934).

After the shower, Martin took his mother, Mrs. Celia Martin, now sixty, out for a fine St. Louis meal. She had not come to the 1931 series.

Martin being repaired after the 1934 championship season. (Copyright, *The Sacramento Bee*, 1941.)

Game four was a little different experience for Martin: "St. Louis never really has forgotten Pepper Martin after the series of 1931. The first excuse to put him back into the hall of baseball fame was his triple to start the game yesterday.... From then on he was the Mickey Cochrane of St. Louis. And just as we are writing this, he goes and makes his third error of the game. So the Wild Horse of the Osage was turned into a goat" (St. Louis *Post-Dispatch*, Oct. 6, 1934).

That 10–4 loss was followed the next day by another loss, this one 3–1, the loss given to Dizzy.

So it was back to Detroit, Pepper's Cardinals down three games to two.

In game six, Paul Dean again won to keep the Cardinals in the series.

The notorious game seven, remembered best for the seventeen-minute garbage barrage directed at Medwick after his slide into Detroit third baseman Marv Owen, ended with St. Louis winning the game 11–0 and winning the Series four games to three.

The team gathered for a meal guarded by policemen. Glossed over in the aftershocks of the near-riot in left field was the fact that Johnnie hit .355 for the seven games and, like his teammates Medwick and Collins, made eleven hits in the Series. Martin either led the team or tied a teammate in the Series for runs, doubles, triples, walks and steals. He also led all players in most errors with four. Soon Martin could say he had collected three World Series checks in seven years, this year's for $5389.57.

As the team members ate, the players discussed going home, even though Medwick, Orsatti, and Rothrock had invitations for two weeks' work in vaudeville as "The Flying Redbird Flychasers." Martin told the *Post-Dispatch*, "I plan to go down to old Mexico and slay deer, but first I'm goin' to Oklahoma to spend ten days with my mother and eat some of her cornbread" (Oct. 10, 1934). The elbow full of chipped bones had to be taken care of soon as well.

Durocher, in a signed column after the Series, made a clear statement of the ethos of all teams when he discussed Medwick's problems with Marv Owens: "If Joe wants to resent this it's his business. But if he gets in a jam it's ours. We're all together on this ball club. They've talked of cliques and so on this year but when you get right down to it, we're all in there making a living together and the only way to do that is to stay together" (Durocher, St. Louis *Post-Dispatch*, Oct. 10, 1934). It cannot be stressed too much that the two factors here — solidarity and cash — went together and still do. And it cannot be stressed too much that Martin was a true believer in that sentiment, so that one of the pleasures of the game of baseball, one of the powerful attractions of the game, was — and is — that ethos.

As a team member, he appeared in a Camels cigarette advertisement shortly after the Series in which he was quoted as saying, "You almost always find me with a Camel when I'm not playing or working out. Because I like 'em. And because when I light a Camel I can actually feel all tiredness slip away."

What would not slip away was the inflammation which caused his arm to be put into a cast by Dr. Robert F. Hyland. He was given instructions to return in three weeks.

A great baseball season was capped on October 27 with the birth of Pepper's second child, another daughter, christened Virginia Lee, but called Jennie Lee. After the birth, Johnnie then traveled to both Laredo, Texas, and Mexico to hunt.

In December, Pep "went to St. John's Hospital [in St. Louis] and Dr. Hyland removed two bits of chipped bone which were causing him trouble." Even there, Pepper wanted his fun and so "Martin's so-called brass band has disturbed the peace of nearly everybody in the hospital, so Pepper Martin was ordered to the sparsely populated north wing when he insisted that his cowboy band entertain him. The Cardinals star, demanding entertainment, hired the band from a radio station" (UP, New York *World-Telegram*, Dec, 21, 1934). Martin also took care of some business in the hospital by signing a one-year contract for 1935 with Sam Breadon on December 22, 1934, two months before his thirty-first birthday.

23

1935–1937: Maestro of the Mudcats

Martin brought his wife Ruby and two daughters with him to the Hotel Manatee River in Bradenton for spring training. Since he made about $11,000 in 1934, this travel was a burden to him. The cost of his family expenses had something to do with the fact that the average yearly salary in 1935 was $1,035.32, and there was no reason why the thirty-one year old Johnnie, making ten times that, ought not to be carefree, at least financially. Then, too, his arm had been repaired by the doctor who was called "The Surgeon-General of Baseball"; Pepper would be liable to feel very confident about his health. He had played in twenty-four percent fewer games last year, 1934, than the year before, 1933, and the fewer at bats, of course, lessened his output.

During the training season, *The Sporting News* wrote, " Joisey Joe and Pepper Martin are the only regulars who have batted with any degree of consistency," so at least in training Martin's optimism was justified.

To begin the regular championship season, Martin's roommate, Terry Moore, was not hitting, though fielding his center field position very well. Frisch decided that Pepper would replace his roommate in center and Frisch would now play third in Martin's place. Martin had not played in the outfield for two years and Daniel, in the New York *World-Telegram*, reported that "Pepper stood the ordeal for just four days. Then he walked in and told Frankie that he would resume his former job at third." Moore got back into center field playing 117 games in center in 1935, while hitting .287.

So being back at third satisfied Martin and he began some new amusement for himself. One very famous one was the pepper game. Using Jack Rothrock as the batter, Ernie Orsatti, "Showboat" Ripper Collins and Pep-

The Gas House Gang, of whom four are now in the Hall of Fame, with their newspaper nicknames (l to r): Dizzy Dean, pitcher; Lip Durocher, shortstop; Showboat Orsatti, centerfield; Dee Delancey, catcher; Ripper Collins, first base; Ducky Medwick, left field; Onkel Frank Frisch, second base; Jack Rothrock, right field; Pepper Martin, third base. (National Baseball Hall of Fame Library, Cooperstown, N.Y.)

per Martin were the three "fielders." What the three did resembled the famous Harlem Globetrotter routine performed to the music of "Sweet Georgia Brown." For their own as well as the fans' amusement, they threw the ball behind their backs to each other, they faked throws to one man while tossing it backwards to the other, they bounced the ball off their biceps, and so on. Martin was learning to juggle, and, "if the manager was in a good mood we were allowed to put on our act in front of the grandstand. The fans got a kick out of it and a laugh is a good thing. Any time you can do something a little unusual and amuse the fans I believe it is worth while as long as you don't make yourself look ridiculous. I'll admit our act looks a lot better in the movies that it actually is" (Wilbur Adams, Sacramento *Bee*, Feb. 25, 1944: 14). Martin also liked to bounce a baseball off the end of the bat while walking back and forth in front of the dugout.

By now, Pepper was also allowing two nine-year-old boys from Dago Hill in St. Louis named Berra and Garagiola into the clubhouse, by leaving a door open from them to duck through.

On May 14, 1935, in the New York *World-Telegram*, a column by Tom Meany referred to the Cardinals as the Gas House Gang, as did a companion cartoon by Willard Mullin, who had dressed a group of hoodlums in Cardinal uniforms. The thugs were carrying extra large bats and looked determined and belligerent, yet somehow free and easy. By late summer, as other newspapers picked it up, the nickname had taken hold, and it would stay in use as a synonym for the Cardinals through the 1930s and beyond. Frank Graham, in the New York *Sun*, described the team this way: "They fight among themselves and use quaint and picturesque oaths. They are not afraid of anybody. They don't make much money, and they work hard for it. They will risk arms, legs, and necks, their own or the other fellow's, to get it. But they also have a lot of fun playing baseball."

Pepper began a hitting streak in 1935 though most of May and into June. When Ed Heusser lost on June 3, the loss marked not only the end of the team's six-game winning streak but also the end of Pepper's twenty-three game batting streak.

That night, after dinner, Pat Warren of Chicago drove Martin's Redbird Special race car. Pepper had paid $1500 to have the midget racing car built as that midget kind of auto racing was just becoming popular in the East. The car, which ran to eight feet, was painted white and Cardinal red. Raced during the baseball season, the midget car would be brought to where Johnnie was playing for his nighttime fun, and for that of his friends, Pepper, Frisch, Dizzy and Don Gutteridge. At home, the men would travel to St. Louis' Walsh Stadium to see the car race. Sometimes the driver was Indianapolis winner Lou Schneider. If the racer stalled, the four teammates would hop the fence and helped to push the car. Pepper never drove the car on a race track, his family told me, but he didn't mind driving it around Oklahoma City or out on the farm. And it was at home that Pepper sold the car for $400 after Rickey ordered him to dispose of the racer.

On June 4, visiting St. Louis was at bat in the fifth inning at Forbes Field when Dizzy began cursing his fielders. By now Dizzy had a history of blaming his fielders.

A few feet away, Joe Medwick, who had wanted to punch Dizzy on many other occasions for his lackadaisical attitude, warned the pitcher not to say another thing.

"'Fuck you,' said Dizzy, and they started for each other and Dizzy's brother Paul moved to his brother's side. That is when Pepper and some others came between the two men" (Broeg). Years later, Bob Broeg, trying to describe the team, said that "Frisch had had a bunch of animals in that menagerie" and would tell them, "For Christ sake, take it out on the other goddamn club."

Meanwhile, Martin's family, who, during the St. Louis season lived briefly in an apartment each year, by now had moved into a rental house in the summer. Many houses in the Webster Grove area were put up for rental by people who would flee to the Ozarks to escape the heat and humidity of St. Louis. Often, to save money on the rental, the family would travel back five hundred miles to Oklahoma City when Pepper's ball club

Martin and his Cardinal Special midget race car from 1935. (Copyright, *The Sacramento Bee*, 1941.)

was on a long eastern swing, the seven city tour sometimes taking an entire month.

Both Medwick and Martin were hitting the ball well in early June of 1935. Pepper at .377 was hitting forty points higher than Medwick; the two were the only hitters above .274 on the team. By June 8, Frisch knew the teams needed a change, a boost. The manager put himself back at second base, moved Johnnie into center, Whitey Whitehead to third base and put Charlie Gelbert in for Durocher at short. It was Gelbert's first starting game since 1932.

June remained important for Martin. On the twentieth at the Baker Bowl in Philadelphia, there was an odd situation. Only Bill Klem was able to umpire the game that day. With Ducky Medwick on second, Pepper hit a pitch to short right field and right fielder Johnnie Moore threw in to catcher Al Todd while Klem, in front of the plate, turned to check on the sliding Medwick. Pepper, seeing how busy Klem was, ignored second base and cut across the diamond to third. Jimmie Wilson, now the Philadelphia manager, yelled to Klem and the umpire called Pepper out:

> "You didn't even see me. How could you call me out?" Pepper demanded.
> "No man in the world could have made it to third. You're out" [Blake, 62].

Pepper clearly had a conflict between his native honesty and his desire to help the team.

So long as he played third base, Martin did not like people bunting on him. He hated it so much it was one of the few things that would make him violent. There is a story from *Baseball Between the Lines* of a game in Boston:

Before the game, Pepper went up to manager Casey Stengel and said, "You'd better tell your guys not to bunt on me, because if they do I'm gonna hurt 'em." So naturally, they started bunting. After a while, Pepper got so mad that when he charged in and picked up the ball, he'd throw it at the runner going down the line instead of to first base. He was zinging the ball right over their heads.... Then Elbie Fletcher dropped one down the line that Pepper got a good jump on and when Elbie saw him winding up with it, Elbie cut away from the line and ran straight for the Cardinal dugout, ducking his head between his shoulders. I tell you that ball came like a bullet right over the button of his cap and smack into the dugout and damn near cleared out the bench. That ended the bunting [Honig, 158].

Elbie has memories too. "I used to hate to see that guy come to bat," Fletcher told Donald Honig. "He'd hit the ball and you could hear him leave home plate, stompin' and chuggin', going down the line like his life depended on him beating that ball. I used to try to get the ball and lift my foot off the base as quick as I could. I remember one time he cut the heel right out of my shoe. And that was a brand-new expensive pair of spikes. He wouldn't cut you on purpose; he was just an aggressive player" (Honig, *Grass*, 67).

It was time then for St. Louis to face the Cubs in Chicago for the 1935 Fourth of July doubleheader in front of a holiday crowd of 38,100. In these games, Orsatti made five hits and Medwick hit a low line drive through an exit gate below the center field bleachers. And in the Cardinal style of play—the Gas House style—there were two collisions on same play at the plate: Martin hit a soft grounder to second but beat it out; then, stealing, he kicked the ball out of Billy Jurges' hand. After Ernie Orsatti walked, Pepper went to third on an infield out. When he tried to score on the same play, Johnnie had to knock down rookie catcher Ken O'Dea and when he did O'Dea and the ball tumbled away from the plate. Ernie Orsatti, coming from first, saw a chance to score. Cubs' pitcher Lon Warneke was now forced to cover home plate, and in the second collision in less than a minute, Orsatti flipped Warneke over and scored. In this aggressive way, the Cardinals won two games and they gained second place at 42–29 trailing the Giants at 48–21.

The 1935 All-Star Game was played on July eighth in the three year old Cleveland Municipal Stadium. The National League team made four hits (Martin, Arky Vaughan, Bill Terry and Charlie Wilson) to eight for the American in a game that took 2:08 to play. Martin, playing the whole game at third and batting lead off, had the only error and the only steal, going 1–4. The game brought in $60,000 to make the three year total of support for needy ball players to $150,000.

Joe Williams chose this time to praise Martin:

> Pepper Martin. This fellow is at once the worst and the best third baseman in baseball. How can he be at once the worst and the best? My answer is enthusiasm. He loves to play baseball. He has none of the deftness that has been attributed to the great third baseman of the past, he is not in any sense an artist; he is in fact the worst infielder in baseball — but somehow or other the guy comes up with every ball that is hit to him.... Pepper Martins are unusual these days.... Why? Because he tries for everything. He tries to play the whole ball game.... I mean to say a guy who isn't interested in his own job is a mugg. There are so many muggs in baseball [Joe Williams, New York *World-Telegram*, 1935].

Martin still looked for his fun and found it in disastrous ways sometimes. That year, Martin wrestled with Dizzy Dean and Johnnie slipped on the clubhouse floor, falling against the locker, which cut his lip and forehead. Dean's stomach was bruised. Each had questioned the other's wrestling ability and wrestled for half an hour.

The next month, Johnnie Martin developed both a sore arm and stomach trouble. The intestinal illness passed quickly, but the arm problem was serious and would have to be treated at the end of the season, and so Martin, knowing that his pay could stop at any time, kept on playing. And playing hard.

On August 15, Pepper won the game for his team when he hit an inside-the-park home run to right center in the Polo Grounds over Mel Ott's head in the seventh, finishing with a great slide. On August 16th, Martin won the game in the ninth this way: he singled, stole second, moved to third on Frisch's single and scored on Medwick's high fly to George Davis in deep center. On August 17, after Dizzy relieved Strangler Heusser, Martin did it again:

> With two out, the Oklahoma wild man singled ... he stole second, picked himself up when Gus Mancuso's well-intentioned heave soared into the outfield and charged on for third. Even then the Giants could not stop him for Leiber's throw to third was a bit wide of its mark so Martin kept on going until he crossed the plate in a final cloud of dust that had the Giants fairly choking in rage [St. Louis *Post-Dispatch*, August 17, 1935].

The New York Times said: "Dizzy blanked the Giants in the final two innings with great gusto and then jogged off the field with the mud-bespattered Pepper Martin and the rest of the peppery Cardinals at his heels.... An entertaining, picturesque bunch, these Cards, who seem to have captivated New York as no visiting team has done in many years. All told 94,438 saw the four days of battling on the Harlem." The win cut the Giants' lead over the Cardinals to two games.

Five Cardinals (from left): Frankie Frisch, Pepper, Ripper Collins, Joe "Ducky" Medwick, and Dizzy Dean. (National Baseball Hall of Fame Library, Cooperstown, N.Y.)

A St. Louis writer said of the Gas House Gang, "Pepper may be the spark plug...."

The spark plug had decided to work in the corner of their bat boy, now a middleweight boxer with the ring name of K. O. Brown. In September, Cardinal teammates went to the fights at the Twentieth Century Club: Ripper Collins, Ducky Medwick, Moon Hallahan, Dizzy Dean and his silent brother whom the players called Harpo, Bob O'Farrell, the Lip Durocher and Frank Frisch. Though Pepper Martin gave K.O. a new ring outfit, Brown was beaten badly by Jimmie Webb and lost by a T.K.O. in the third.

The Cardinals also took a K. O. in the pennant race, unable to keep up with the one hundred wins by the Cubs.

Pepper finished the year in the top five in the National League in doubles, runs and steals for the year.

As the season ended, more rumors circulated concerning S.A. Murphy, the grateful Wichita business man, and the fabulous worth of his deeded five acres of oil land in Sumter County, Kansas. Wealth in the tens of thousands was going to be in the hands of Dizzy and Pepper very soon, the stories said.

And at season's end in 1935, Pepper Martin again checked into the hospital, this time for ten days for treatment on "a tear in the fascia or connective tissue" in his right elbow. Martin played hard, too hard, but Johnnie was well aware that his primary talent was playing hard. It was also his only chance for staying in the big leagues with the big league salaries. Not an equal mix of talent and dedication like his teammate Medwick, not able to get along mostly on his defensive abilities like roommate

Pepper is in front of the "boat," fishing, Ripper Collins rows in the rear, and Pepper's adopted man-child pal nicknamed Yo-Yo mans the middle of the craft, probably in 1936 during spring training. (National Baseball Hall of Fame Library, Cooperstown, N.Y.)

Terry Moore or Leo Durocher, Martin knew his limitations and counted himself lucky to have gotten to where he was for the five years of major league play.

One of the places he had gotten to was tenth place in the Most Valuable Player voting in the National League.

1936

Part of any player's salary negotiations with Branch Rickey in 1936 included the almost certain promise of money beyond the year's salary that a player would sign for. For some of the more popular players, Rickey would promise a bonus of $1000 if the club made enough money during the year (AP, New York *World-Telegram*, Feb. 21, 1938). Then, too, Rickey would promise the player that the World Series checks would arrive in October and the only person to blame if the checks were not big checks would be the player himself for not wanting the money badly enough.

Player moves were made by the club: outfielders Jack Rothrock, 31, and Ernie Orsatti, 34, were sent to Rochester while bought from Columbus were the contracts of Brusie Ogrodowski, a catcher, and infielder Stu Martin. The team said it was counting on Pepper to play third, but Pepper made thirty errors at third base in 114 games. The other Martin, Stu, was penciled in at second for the aging Frisch (38).

During the training season in 1936, the team stayed at the Hotel Manatee River in Bradenton and from there "Frisch posted an order that players must wear coats in the hotel dining room but had to take it down when he found out he'd have to buy about fifteen coats to enforce the rule. Pepper Martin was willing to go along a bit and rolled down his shirt sleeves" (Hood, 46).

In the clubhouse Pepper had adopted a man-child named Yo-Yo. Don Gutteridge explained to me that Yo-Yo was probably illiterate or retarded. Pepper Martin liked him, got him work in the clubhouse, and took him along on road trips. This seemed to be the mascot phenomenon that Pepper knew from his youth. *Total Baseball* explained one example: "Babe Ruth wasn't enough. Eddie Bennett became the Yankees' full-time batboy and official mascot in 1921, and, of course, the Yankees grabbed the flag.... During his years with the Bronx Bombers, with Ruth and Lou Gehrig and others rubbing his back for luck, the team won seven pennants and four world championships...."

The reporter Dan Daniel was in the clubhouse to tell this story:

> "Where's Yo-Yo," demanded Mr. Martin.... Yo-Yo is Mr. Martin's wrestling stooge. The night before [March 27] Yo-Yo and Mr. Martin had appeared in a professional wrestling card at the American Legion Stadium and in full view of a capacity crowd Mr. Martin had allowed himself to be thrown amid all the broad theatrics that characterize the modern wrestler. Yo-Yo is the town simpleton and is Mr. Martin's particular joy.... It was about time to take the field.... Mr. Frisch yelled for Yo-Yo. "Call the roll," he demanded. Yo-Yo pulled a book out of his pocket. "Frisch," he sang out. "Here," answered Frisch ... and so on until the full roster had reported "Here." Then at the finish, "Altogether, men: 'Fight, Fight, Fight for the Gashouse Gang!'" In a torrent of noise, Mr. Frisch and his bizarre hirelings roared: "Fight, Fight, Fight for the Gashouse Gang" [New York *World-Telegram*, March 26, 1936].

After the game, "with Martin gnawing away vigorously on a harmonica, Yo-Yo, a round-faced little man with a lisp went through the loose motions of the Harlem strut...." (Gregory, 287). Martin used a harmonica brace that fit around his neck so that he could strum his guitar and play the harmonica at the same time.

Pepper loved his rifles and carried many of them with him wherever he went. Those guns, combined with Pepper's optimism, seemed to be fueling his sense of delight. Frisch's autobiography told this story: "Down in Florida we were traveling along the Everglades Road in a bus and I heard shots.... [I] stopped the bus to investigate if we were being hijacked. It was Martin shooting buzzards from the back window with a sawed-off shotgun" (72).

Frank Graham told the story of seeing Pepper and Dizzy in a barbershop in Florida with Johnnie as the barber in a green smock being thorough with customer Dean. He gave Dizzy a hot towel to soften his beard, shaved him, dusted him with talcum powder and combed the pitcher's hair. Did Pepper, at thirty-two, think his time was almost up in the majors? Was he worried? Or was he too busy having fun?

On the way north, the Cardinals played three games in Georgia at Albany, Columbus and Atlanta. In the last game against the Crackers, Pepper Martin crashed into a tin wall and snagged his hand on a nail, cutting himself just under his thumb. The next day the team was in Birmingham, Virgil Davis' hometown, and the catcher was given a floral horseshoe before the game. After the game, "a Birmingham urchin snatched Pepper's hat.... Martin chased him five city blocks before bringing him down and recovering his cap" (Hood, 79).

Just before the season was about to begin, on the night of April 13, a dinner was given in St. Louis for the Browns and the Cardinals at the Hotel Jefferson. Hosted by the St. Louis Chamber of Commerce, the meal was attended by 750 fans who saw "silver life-time passes ... presented by President Frick to Jess Haines, Coach Mike Gonzalez and Manager Frankie Frisch ... earned by having served for 10 years or more in big league baseball" (Stockton, St. Louis *Post-Dispatch*). Dizzy spoke and so did Charlie Grimm, the Cubs' manager who was a St. Louis native, as did Ripper Collins and Pepper Martin. Some of the dinner conversation concerned the new rule for players, which prohibited them from talking to players on other teams and called for a $10 fine if the rule was broken.

Late the next morning, "... Hacks in which visiting ballplayers were conveyed from their hotel to the baseball park" were used to carry the Cardinal players, in uniform, to the park for opening day. "The parade used all horse-drawn vehicles partly to draw attention to the 60th anniversary of the National League...." (Stockton, *Post-Dispatch*, April 14, 1935). The Cardinals made their bow in their new white uniforms, the only noticeable change being a three colored trimming on the cap, running from the top button along the segment seams.

Since two longtime outfielders for the Cardinals, Orsatti and Rothrock, were gone to Rochester, Martin vacated third base and moved to right field, Terry Moore took over in center and Gelbert was to play third every day. But Charley Gelbert hurt his ankle to start the season and, though no one knew it yet, Gelbert would only play about half the innings that the regulars played. So by just the second game, Frisch had to make serious adjustments to his lineups with Gelbert hurt. Pep hoped to be a fixture in right field, his more natural position, but he had to move back to third base. It was just as well, according to Bob Broeg, as: "... he'd charge in, spread as if trying to fly, and, dropping to one knee, he'd catch the ball by cupping his glove hand on top so that the ball actually landed in his bare hand" (Broeg, *The Sporting News*, Nov. 26, 1977).

There was still time for fun. On May 17 or 18, Dizzy, Pepper and their new pal, another southwesterner, Texan infielder Heine Schuble, found a new source of amusement.

According to Robert Gregory:

> They were in Philadelphia on a rainy Tuesday and things were quiet at the Bellevue-Stratford Hotel. So Pepper Martin went shopping. "I needed a pair of unionalls to work around the machinery at home," he remembered, "and Diz and Heinie Schuble came along with me to the store. Well, they liked my pair so much they bought some of their own ['unionalls' were white overalls with thin black stripes], and before we knew it, we were buyin' us a railroad engineer's cap, too. We tried everything on when we got back to the hotel and danged if we didn't look just like plumbers. So Diz said we oughta have us some fun and we took off down to the barber shop to check on their plumbin'. We started gesturin' and talkin' about how we was gonna rip this pipe out and tear down that wall, and we nearly drove the guy who ran the joint crazy."
>
> Thus encouraged, they marched on the hotel ballroom, where about 200 people were attending a Rotary luncheon. The fried chicken had been eaten and the speeches just begun when Martin barged in with a ladder. Schuble was right behind with a hammer, a saw, and a can of paint. Foreman Dizzy brought up the rear, carrying only a pad and pencil, and when somebody asked what was going on, he said, "We got orders to fix this place up now."
>
> With their true identities unrecognized, they bumped into tables, scraped chairs along the floor, and even lifted several to move with men still in them. The speaker was having trouble being heard above the uproar when Martin climbed the ladder and hammered on the ceiling. Schuble climbed next to inspect a chandelier and declared it would have to come down, shouting, "Hand me some pliers." Simultaneously from a back corner, Diz yelled, "These walls are gonna look better red. Where's the paint?" Martin yodeled back, "All we got is green." And Dizzy yelled again, "That's close enough."
>
> The hotel manager arrived a few minutes later, unmasked the carpenters, and soon the Rotarians were laughing and cheering and escorting them to the head table. "They asked us to give talks," said Martin, "and that's what we did," so ending what one writer called baseball's piece de circus of 1936 [290–91].

This fix-up pretense happened more than once and soon Pepper and friends learned to mock fight while a banquet went on, including the Boys' Club banquet in Philadelphia.

In early June, still playing hard, Pepper scored in his thirteenth consecutive game. He began to tell teammates he was certain that his next child, due in about a month, would finally be a boy.

Don Gutteridge told me how Dizzy Dean and Johnnie Martin "liked to agitate Medwick all they could." They "agitated" so easily because Medwick was so serious about the game, far too serious for some.

Frisch claimed, "Everybody thought they were a wild, hard-living bunch. But they weren't at all. They were not a drinking outfit. Sometimes they had a few beers. They were just a fun bunch, happy-go-lucky mischievous, hilarious.... I didn't care what they did. They played ball for me and were strictly high class" (*Saturday Evening Post*, July 4, 1936: 34).

Trying hard against the surging Giants, Martin, playing all out as usual, hit his head on the concrete outfield wall and sat out a day. As the Giants were leaving, Tom Meany, covering the Giants in St. Louis, wrote, "The way things stack up now, the Cardinals have the best outfield in the league, a stronger unit than either the Cubs or the Giants.... The Cardinal fly chasing group is tops in the Frick wheel. Terry Moore looks like the best center fielder in the business, while Joe Medwick is having his best year and Pepper Martin — well, he's still the Wild Horse of the Osage.... And in the infield, Durocher is hitting .329, Collins at first is playing well and hitting for power, and Stu Martin has been a great surprise at second. Frisch is hitting .200 and Charlie Gelbert is at .177. The catching done by Virgil Davis and Brusie Ogrodowski has been competent. And the team was doing what it has to do, winning at a .654 percentage against first division clubs" (New York *World-Telegram*, June 6, 1936).

When the Boston Braves came in to Sportsman's Park on Tuesday, June ninth, Pepper Martin was playing one of the fifteen games he played that year at third and Johnny Mize was sent to right field for one of his eight games in the outfield, and given the sixth spot in the batting order. But there was still too much unsteadiness on the team, players being moved to fill in spots. When, on June 17, the Cardinals played at Boston during the doubleheader on Bunker Hill Day at the Bees, a number of typically Gas House Gang things happened. In the first game, Pepper Martin was replaced by Lynn King in right field because Martin, imitating professional wrestler Ali Baba, had injured his left hip wrestling with Paul Dean, the starting pitcher, in the clubhouse. Therefore Frisch had to play third base. But Frisch and the injured Durocher, who had been replaced by Charlie Gelbert at short, were both thrown out by the umpires in the second inning. This forced Pepper Martin, though hurt, to play third, but only after Spud Davis, a catcher, was sent in for his manager to play second base.

In the July 4, 1936, *Saturday Evening Post*, an article titled "The Gas

House Gang," by manager Frisch and J. Roy Stockton, tried to describe the team:

> Pepper Martin and Joe Medwick probably are responsible more than any other individual for the club's Gas-House reputation. Martin is one of the most spectacular players the game has ever known. Barrel-chested, broad shouldered, with a great competitive spirit, he is a picturesque figure as he charges down the base line like an express train, or takes off in a flying leap on one of his hands-first slides.... Nobody plays harder than Martin, but he has a highly developed sense of honor and fair play.... He has boundless energy.... Martin and Dean have a highly developed sense of humor and showmanship.... Pepper is the head man in a fancy juggling pepper game.... Pepper loves music as long as it is hillbilly music.... After batting practice ... the clubhouse ... was bristling with hillbilly musicians. Pepper had chanced upon a father and his five children wandering the streets with guitars, mandolins and fiddles and had piloted them ... to the clubhouse to entertain the athletes. Hillbillies were perched on uniform trunks and benches....
> If he offers you a cigarette, don't take it. If he tenders a match, beware. Either or both will explode. If you hear a wave of sneezing in the hotel lobby, Martin has probably been scattering powder [13].

On July 11, more fun. Dizzy decided to give his old pal Whitey Whitehead, now the Giants' second baseman, something good to hit when the second baseman came up for the Giants in the sixth. Too good: "Whitehead's drive bounded off of Dizzy's head into left field for a double and scored Davis as Dean falls unconscious...." Dizzy was carried off the field and remained unconscious for seven minutes. Ice packs were applied to waken him and Doc Hyland gave him a brandy. Pepper, who had followed his injured pal off the field, had to be brought back to the field by Frisch so the game could be played. The Cardinals, in first, were three games ahead in the win column over the Cubs.

On July 14, after losing a doubleheader to the last place Dodgers, and with Ripper Collins ill, Frisch put Gelbert on third base, moved Pepper back to right, and put Mize on first. The resulting 11–7 win came after Pop Haines zeroed the opposition for the last three innings. In this game, Johnnie had two home runs, one a grand slam.

Ruby gave birth to their third child in mid–July. Ripper Collins, interviewed for *True* by W. C. Heinz, said he always remembered July 19, 1936, "when Pepper's last daughter was born. You can't imagine what it meant to him. He prayed for a boy and talked about nothing else.... Well, it's the seventh inning of a tight ball game and an usher called me over near the dugout. 'Mrs. Martin just had another baby girl,' he said, 'Shall I tell Pepper?' I said 'Wait'll I talk to Frisch.' I told Frank and he said 'Jeepers! How're we gonna tell Pepper? We gotta win this game.'"

"I wanted a ballplayer," Pepper said years later. "I wanted a sidekick to go hunting with me and to help me mend fences and to grow up to be a cultured gentleman" (Heinz, 101).

Collins continued: "I got Pepper aside and told him, 'Everything's swell, fella. Ruby just had a fine girl and Ruby feels fine.' He said, 'Oh, no? No, the good Lord wouldn't do that to me.' Big tears started rolling down his face and just then it's his turn to bat. He pulled his cap down over his face to hide the tears and stepped up there. The park was full of people and nobody knew he was crying. He hit the first pitch for a double. The next guy singled and he slid home with the wining run; then he sat on the bench and bawled his heart out" over the birth of his daughter Alice Jane (New York *Herald-Tribune*, March 6, 1965).

"But that third one," Pepper said in 1959, "was the cutest one of them all" (Heinz, 101).

Only three days later, Pepper was tossing autographed baseballs to a horde of cheering children as the city celebrated "Pepper Martin Day." Dizzy won that day.

The Cardinals continued to play well, 23–18 in the last 41 games, but the Cubs were 31–10 in the same period. Pepper was hitting .309, fourth on the team behind Medwick, Stu Martin and John Mize. And he played aggressively as well, as Elbie Fletcher, the Braves' first baseman, remembered: "When we'd get him in a rundown, it was like being in a cage with a tiger. He'd never give up, and you knew that when it finally came to the tag, he'd be diving or kicking, doing anything he could to get that ball out of your hand" (Honig, *Grass*, 67).

Then, too, Martin always impressed writers and fans with his personal integrity. Red Smith wrote that "there was a passionate honesty in him, and an almost ministerial sincerity.... In one instance Pepper was at bat and Frisch bounded out of the dugout and screamed at the umpire that the pitch hit Johnnie. 'Did that pitch hit you?' the umpire asked Martin. 'I'm John Brown if I tell a lie, even to win a ball game'" (Frisch, *Saturday Evening Post*, July 4, 1936:14).

Pepper pitched on August 7 with his team behind 14–5, and gave up one hit in the last two innings. The team was glad to get home for five days with a two game lead.

After an August 12 contest, they traveled 611 miles to St. Paul to play an exhibition with the St. Paul Saints, managed by Gabby Street, Pepper's manager before Frankie Frisch. "The crowd of 10,000 was attracted to Lexington Park ... and Pepper Martin entertained with some witty asides as he broadcast the playing of the game over the loud speaker system." Then the team rode an additional 857 miles to Pittsburgh for games beginning on the fifteenth.

Pepper, asked to play third, right and center that year, played all three positions with something less than the grace of a Terry Moore, according to Bob Broeg:

> Everything with Pepper was awkward. He would try to hit the ball to left, and he'd hit a line drive to right. If he was playing in the outfield, I'd see him run in to get down on one knee and catch the ball cross-handed, and it looked like he would catch the ball with his bare hand. Pepper was a good ballplayer, just awkward. And, too, "he'd run to first base real hard, and he'd stop instead of running through the play and slowing down. I'd think, "Jeez, you're going to tear your knee ligaments" [Golenbock, 145].

Pepper did play hard, too hard, but it seemed to be the only way that he knew how to play. Like Pete Reiser, Martin injured himself over and over, unable to moderate his play. And as the 1936 season wound down, Pepper was hurt yet again. His replacement, Lynn King, wasn't hitting. To keep busy, Johnnie decided to neaten up his look. According to the papers, for a few days he sported pants that were neatly pressed and sharply creased. Before long, however, he apparently wearied of the effort, which didn't really mesh with his no-necktie, just-plain-folks style. Soon he was his old rumpled self, investing his energy not in the practice of neatness but in practical joking.

In *The Spirit of St. Louis*, Peter Golenbock interviewed Don Gutteridge, whose first full year was in 1936:

> I saw Pepper Martin drop a water balloon and just miss Frankie Frisch when he stepped out of the hotel. We were staying at the Kenmore Hotel [in Boston], which had a porch on top next to the sidewalk where you could sit down. So Pepper got a balloon and filled it with water, and he went to his room overlooking where Frankie was standing, about four or five stories up. He punched the button on the elevator, and when the elevator came he told the elevator boy to hold it right there. "Don't go away. I'll be right back."
>
> He dropped the balloon and just missed Frisch. If he had hit him, Pepper might have killed him. And Pepper ran and got in the elevator. "Take me down. Take me down."
>
> Frisch suspected who it was. He ran for the elevator. It opened, and Pepper walked out and said, "Hi, Frankie," and kept on walking. Frankie knew who did it, but he couldn't prove anything because Pepper had planned it so well. I don't think Pepper wanted to hurt anyone, but he sure wanted to deal him a lot of misery! He did it just to create fun [Golenbock, 234].

There are those who think that humor is hostility, that jokes are anger expressed as a prank. But anger is complicated. Was Pepper, for example, furious at his manager and teammate? Probably not. Could it be that in the midst of his merriment Pepper was angry? Of course that could be so. Was Frisch then a convenient target? Perhaps that anger explained some of his behavior. After all, Frisch was the Fordham-educated New Yorker, fond of the classical cello, and Pepper was the untutored Oklahoma farm boy.

He also, apparently, knew that teammates liked him for his pranks, as Max Lanier recalled: "Pepper'd tie up the manager's uniform in knots, nail your spikes to the floor. He was a great guy" (Golenbock, 231).

Martin knew that despite his injuries he could not stay out of the lineup. The team needed him and he needed to keep his job, even though he said, "With two jammed elbows, a lame shoulder and bruised knees [I am] not at full power. Until I hurt my elbow, I never had to worry about throwing, but now I got to do most of my throwing straight overhand, and the outfield makes it easy. At third sometimes you gotta side-arm 'em and it did not always work out" (Tom Meany, New York *World-Telegram*).

The team had been unhealthy all year and it showed in the final standings. The Cardinals finished the season tied for second with the Cubs while winning nine fewer games than in 1935. Dizzy, blunt as usual, said the team was "a bunch of bushers except for four guys: Pepper Martin, Medwick, Durocher and me" (St. Louis *Post-Dispatch*, Sept. 26, 1936). Pepper led the league in steals again and finished second in runs scored. Had Johnnie made one more hit, he would have batted .300 for the year.

Then "the South Ends St. Louis semi-pro team booked exhibition games with a 'major league all-star team,' featuring Pepper Martin ... and his musical Mudcats..." (*The Sporting News*, Oct. 8, 1936: 2). His performance and Dizzy's may have helped attendance as they took a train for the beginning of another barnstorming tour. Barnstorming was yet another way for Pepper to keep active and to produce income, although his family says that he often would leave the tour early, so eager was he to be home. At home or on the road Pepper seemed not be a reader or a moviegoer. Like many people in his era, Pepper seemed to simply believe that you had to make your own fun. And your own money, no matter what the method.

Though scheduled for the barnstorming tour's first stop in Wichita, Kansas, Martin "made several business stops along the way" to the next game 150 miles south in Oklahoma City, according to Diz. About halfway there, he stopped in Blackwell, Oklahoma, "where friends had installed him as president of an ice cream factory. 'I think we have something here,' he said, 'and if Diz behaves himself we'll make him vice-president of our chocolate department and pay him a thousand gallons a year'" (Gregory, 302). How wonderful it must have been for the child of parents so frugal with money for ice cream to now be in charge of an entire factory, surrounded by all the ice cream he could ever eat.

That business completed, Pepper went to another meeting, this one about a fifty percent investment in a Native American heavyweight boxer. As usual, as he traveled, Martin was on the lookout for shotguns and bird dogs.

The Kansas City Monarchs were the opposition against Johnnie and Dizzy that night in Oklahoma City, an 8–0 loss for the Negro Leagues team.

The next day, Pepper had to conduct even more business. And even though he had become the vice-president and general manager of a hockey team, the Oklahoma City Warriors, Johnnie was discouraged from playing on the team. The Cardinal management threatened to fine him $1000 if he played (Tom Meany, "Frothy Facts," New York *World-Telegram*, Jan. 13, 1936).

Virgil Cory wrote of Pepper's further plans in *The Sporting News*, noting that "Dizzy and Pepper were scheduled to play in four exhibition games on the Coast at Los Angeles, San Francisco, Oakland and San Diego. Pepper will then return to Oklahoma City to prepare for his annual hunting trip into New Mexico and Texas" (Oct. 8, 1936: 2).

That November, Pepper was told of the death of Yo-Yo, Pepper's pal in training camp, and it broke Martin's heart.

1937

Spring training for the Cardinals in 1937 had its headquarters at the Hotel Osceola in Daytona Beach from March 1 to April 9. Ripper Collins, who had been not only Pepper's teammate in both Rochester and St. Louis since 1930, but also the man who invented some of the schemes for Pepper to have fun with, was traded to the Cubs. Now Pepper was missing the man who encouraged the pranks he performed. Dizzy Dean had not yet signed. Something must fill that absence of friends, of fun.

First time Cardinals outfielder Frenchy Bordagaray and pitcher Lon Warneke were two components. The guitar presented to Johnnie by his wife Ruby for Christmas 1936 was another. A third was the mandolin playing of Cardinal team trainer Doc Weaver, whom Martin had admired for years.

The St. Louis *Post-Dispatch* had the first notice of a new musical group, but not in the Arts section of the paper. In the sports pages' "Extra Innings" column of March 23, 1937, J. Roy Stockton wrote:

Pepper and the Mississippi (not Oklahoma as the sign says) Mudcat Band in 1937. (Copyright, *The Sacramento Bee*, 1941.)

You never guess the name of the outstanding musician in Frankie Frisch's Gas House Gang. He can play the guitar, harmonica, violin, piano, trumpet or anything else anybody happens to have. Of all people it's Bill McGee.... Pepper Martin brought a new guitar to camp. He's been trying to master the thing ... but the only piece he can play is 'In Birmingham Jail.' McGee took it, strummed a few chords and now whenever the music department swings into action, the Wild Horse of the Osage hands the guitar to Bill. And Pepper turns to a harmonica, playing it lustily, while he glances enviously but grinning at Bill McGee....

"There's a club quartet now. Pepper Martin, Stanley Bordagaray, Mickey Owen and Bob Weiland...." The group changed as the training season closed and the baseball season moved along, but the band began to be known as the Marvelous Musical Mississippi Mudcats. Sometimes McGee would play the fiddle and Bob Weiland, another pitcher, would puff on the jug. Lon Warneke strummed the guitar and outfielder Bordagaray joined in on washboard as well. Of Martin as the band leader, Robert Gregory wrote, "Martin could be heard yelping at strategic moments, 'Pizzicato,' 'Obbligato,' or 'Sweet Po-tah-to,' as the boys tried to make it through the standards in their repertoire, 'Buff'lo Gal,' 'Birmingham Jail,' 'Cowboy Waltz,' and 'Possum Up a Gum Tree.' Said Martin, 'We play everything—we play anything—whether we know it or not,' as well as any instrument anyone gives them whether they can or not..." (315). It was said of the group that it was rare that they finished a tune at the same time.

The Mississippi label fit them well, too, because no one was from that state, or even close to it. John Carmichael wrote about the Mudcats that:

> It was no novelty of an evening to see and hear Martin on a street corner along with his "Mudcat Band" featuring Frenchy Bordagaray, Bill McGee, Lon Warneke and anybody else they could round up, standing around a big drum, the strains of guitar music, mingling with the toot of McGee's horn and the scraping stick against washboard. At intervals Martin would address the crowds that would stop to stare at the goings on, asking for alms for "the underprivileged of Patagonia." Sometimes they'd get as high as five bucks. They'd take the money and go to a recording store and make their own versions of "They Cut Down the Old Pine Tree" and "Birmingham Jail Blues." And take the platter back to the hotel, put it on the machine and drive all the quiet bridge players and soft-talking couples out onto the street in despair [Miami *Herald*, March 10, 1965].

The band had shirts and pants made that looked like a cross between western swing band attire and the St. Louis Cardinal uniform. The stage costume kept the birds perched on bats, like the Cardinals, but substituted the words "Mud" and "Cats" on each side of the shirt. Whenever the urge struck them, the band would start to play for players and fans in the dugout before games, on trains, in hotel lobbies and even at concerts.

It made no difference to anyone that the band really couldn't play. They were booked into Chamber of Commerce dinners and radio programs; once they were paid $700 to play on a New York City radio station.

When the 1937 season began, Martin, now thirty-three, was eight years older than the other outfielders, Medwick, Moore and Don Padgett. He would not play in one hundred games this year or ever again. He still played as wildly in the outfield as he had done back in Greenville, Texas. Often a fellow outfielder could be heard to say, "I hate to hear him coming."

Martin was still busy with his projects. One project was to be photographed sparring in trunks and boxing gloves, with his fighter, Junior Munsell of Oklahoma, who was about to box in St. Louis at the Auditorium.

On May 8 against the Giants, Pepper Martin made two bad throws from the outfield. On one play with the bases loaded, he deliberately dropped the ball to start a double play and threw home to Mickey Owen too late to get the lumbering Gus Mancuso. But then Owen threw the ball to Don Gutteridge on third base, making a force on Johnny McCarthy, and then Gutteridge threw it to Jimmy Brown on second base, who missed stepping on the base for a force. Saved from the third out, the Giants sent across five runs that inning.

Lon Warneke (left) plays his guitar. He would later become a major league umpire. Pepper plays his accordion and pitcher Bill McGee is on the other guitar. Teammates gather around the popular band to be part of the fun. (Brace Photography.)

Twelve days later, in the ninth inning, Dizzy threw at Jimmy Ripple, who got up and then, on the next pitch, bunted toward first. Mize fielded the bunt, but Dizzy ran right into Ripple and the Giant bench charged onto the field. Fights began. Gutteridge got a punch in the eye from Dolf Luque and Pepper pulled a Giant off of the pile and said, "I'll get to you later" (Blake, 68). Pepper lined up five Giants to fight. He was a team man.

Later, up in Boston, manager Casey Stengel, coaching at third, did a little dance to distract Martin, who was playing one of his rare games at third during 1937. It worked, keeping Martin looking and laughing at Stengel. Frisch came out of the dugout: "Don't look at that clown. Pay attention to the ball game." As soon as Frisch was back sitting down, Martin whispered to Stengel, "Do it again" (Daley, *New York Times*, March 8, 1965).

During these years, Ruby would only rarely go on road trips with her husband. But, if the trip was short, she might employ a hired girl to stay with the children. She told me that she "liked to go and learn the country and the people."

In the second game of the June 6 doubleheader at the Baker Bowl in Philadelphia, the Cardinals produced a big lead very early. The lead caused the Phillies' decision to begin to stall in the fourth inning, to prevent the game from going the official five innings before darkness canceled the game. When it was Pepper's turn to bat, he was slowly walked and then he stole second when catcher "Grace's throw was particularly leisurely." After a few moments' conference with colleague Bill Klem, with two out in the fifth (thus, not a "regulation game"), plate umpire Sears declared the game forfeit. When "a chorus of boos and a shower of cushions and other missiles ... greeted the forfeit announcement, ... Cardinals ... rushed from their dugout to protect the umpires.... One [pop bottle] narrowly missed Frisch and Klem who were walking together ..." (Stockton, St. Louis *Post-Dispatch*, June 7, 1937).

For such a passionate competitor, Martin's relationship with umpires was remarkably polite. "The best tribute I can pay Johnnie Martin is my wish that all players would comport themselves on the field as he does," Beans Reardon said. "Oh, yes, he has kicked on close plays and once in a while on a called strike but in such a way that no umpire would take offense. The main things is he never kicked as an alibi." Another umpire familiar with Pepper's play said, "There is no finer gentleman wearing a diamond uniform than Pepper Martin. There are not words enough to praise his attitude toward umpires" (Wilbur Adams, Sacramento *Bee*, Feb. 26, 1944: 15).

Martin was an interesting mix of honest man, cheat, fierce competitor, courtly gentleman, and prankster. No one seemed to know which one he was about to be next.

In the same month, Martin performed the public relations job that everyone on the team was assigned to throughout the season. "Pepper, aided by Bordagaray, Warneke and Ogrodowski, tossed two dozen autographed baseballs into the sections occupied by the [3587] Knothole Boys and the [1572] Cardinal Girls. The ensuing scrambles were terrific" (St. Louis *Post-Dispatch*, June 23, 1937).

Frisch had fun with Martin, too, playing a game they called "burn out." Sometimes after infield practice, Frisch and Johnnie remained on the field before a game and threw hard to each other, advancing a few steps after each throw. The two were, of course, major leaguers so they threw with such velocity that each pulled his hand out of the glove after each catch and shook the heat away. The game ended when Martin, as if in terror, ran for the stands and jumped in.

And sometimes, Frisch and Martin would share the same bill. Radio station KSD, for instance, hired J. Roy Stockton to conduct a pre-game show with the Mudcats and "Frankie Frisch, a pre-game frolic of fun and facts sponsored by Griesedieck Beer."

What did Frisch think of Martin? Frisch would say, "A streak on base, a great thrower. And what a fellow to have on a ball club, full of fun, never moody. And what a fighter!" (Broeg and Vickery, 233).

Don Gutteridge remembered that and many other things about Pepper:

> You know, when Pepper wasn't playing, you had to watch him, because in St. Louis our bench had two tiers. You could sit in the front row or the back row. And if you were sitting in the front row, Pepper'd sneak up behind you, crawl underneath there, and hotfoot you. The ball game would be going on, and you'd hear a guy go, "Aaahhhh!" And it could hurt you. Sometimes it would even burn a hole in their shoe. If you weren't careful and you were sitting in the front row, Pepper would get you sooner or later [Golenbock, 201].

Again, there are those who would take an act like that and accept it as good fun. Part of that acceptance would depend on how you feel about the funster. Martin's big grin and ingenuousness convinced almost everyone on the team that he did it for fun, to loosen up the team. And the team, the Gas House Gang, was an odd lot. "On one ballclub, we had Pepper, Dizzy, and Medwick. They were not ordinary people" (Golenbock, 201).

Medwick's uniqueness, for example, showed in this, his finest year, coming to the All-Star break with 105 hits, 83 RBI and a .404 batting average. And after the team went to the 1937 All-Star Game represented by four players, Pepper, Dean, Mize, and Medwick, they did not come out the same way after the game. Though manager Bill Terry appointed Jess Haines honorary coach "... as a tribute to the latter's long service in the game" (Drebinger, New York *Times*, July 2, 1937), though Frisch was selected as a coach and Medwick made four hits in the game, it was the line drive off the bat of Earl Averill that smashed into Dizzy Dean's foot that became the most shocking part of the game for most fans.

The catastrophic injury to Dean, the failure to hit at the catching, shortstop and center field positions, and Pepper's lame arm added up to too many positions manned by someone new every day. It wasn't, for instance, until July 12, 1937, that starting pitcher Si Johnson won his second game of that year. The team also lost catcher Brusie Ogrodowski to a foul tip and Arnold, now Mickey Owen, had to become the first string catcher. The team was second in most passed balls in the National League in 1937.

Pepper's lame throwing arm sidelined him and that led to some desire for fun, in this case fun that cost $200 when he broke curfew. Pepper Martin, resting his sore arm, bought a rubber stamp to use for autographs.

But the injury also allowed him to spend some time to hire the team's traveling secretary Clarence Lloyd as the business agent for the Mudcats band, now the Missouri Mudcats. Lloyd was able to sign Pepper's bunch for an appearance on a national radio chain. The band, in fact, appeared on such radio programs as *We, the People*. Max Lanier remembered, "Pepper took us on tour. We had a booking agent, went to Cincinnati. We just played country songs. We played on 'Ripley's Believe It or Not' program in New York. We played one song and got $750 for that — we had to split it up. We were staying at the Lincoln Hotel, and we had to slip out. We slipped away and went down the lower level and went out to Radio City to be on Ripley's program. I made as much money doing that as playing ball, about" (Honig, *Grass*, 211).

Martin signed on with the Wheaties cereal company and under the banner headline "WIVES LIKE WHEATIES TOO" fans saw Johnnie and Mrs. Mize pictured at breakfast with Pepper, the cereal box prominent on the table. "Johnny Mize, the ball-powdering first baseman, smiles at Pepper Martin and Mrs. Mize.... Says Johnny, 'Want to get off to a swell start tomorrow morning? Try my favorite — a "Breakfast of Champions!" ' Pepper Martin is another veteran Wheaties eater. He eats 'em about four times a week; his three daughters, too, eat Wheaties regularly."

Dean and Pepper were recuperating together through the rest of July and on into August. Johnnie got back into the lineup playing right field on August 7. That might have been too soon, but Don Padgett, who had been the right fielder while Martin was healing, had crashed into a wall and so Pepper felt the need to play. But not for long. On August 11, against the Reds at home, Pepper injured his knee, tearing a ligament sliding into third base in the fourth inning, "and play was suspended while he was given first aid. Gutteridge drove deep to George Davis and Pepper Martin limped home after the catch" (St. Louis *Post-Dispatch*, August 11, 1937). Mudcat Band member Bordagaray replaced Martin in right field. Fifth on the team in at bats at the time of his August injury, Johnnie had been hitting .314. Martin would have only fifty more at bats in 1937 for a total of 339. He could not know that this was the last season he would have more than 300 at bats in a year. He could still hit: he hit .304 in 1937 though playing irregularly.

Not so long before, Jack Miley of the New York *Daily News* wrote, "The toughest guy in baseball in this or any other season is John Leonard Martin.... He is so hard that when he catapults himself though the air in those death-defying slides of his, he doesn't cut or bruise; he chips. Pepper is not what you'd call an artistic athlete, but he is a violent one" (quoted by Bill Bryson, Des Moines *Register*, July 6, 1955).

This was Martin's reputation, what is now called his image, and reputation was a way of simplifying someone's behavior. There was truth in what Miley said, just as there was truth was describing Johnnie's limited skills and awkwardness. Yet some players learned how to play hard but still understand the length of the season and its demands. Every team loses at least a third of their games. Pepper always acted as if every game was the seventh of the World Series. It was his glory and his downfall.

A month and a half remained in the season. Bob Broeg describes an incident that took place about that time:

> The Cardinals traveling secretary, Leo Ward, taking over late in 1937, noticed only Martin and Joe Medwick carried a trunk on the road. Medwick's reason, an ample wardrobe, was evident. Martin, by contrast, started and finished a trip with only one suit and frequently one shirt. He solved the problem of changing underwear by not wearing any. Puzzled, Leo inquired one day about the trunk. Pepper opened it to disclose an electric motor and other parts for his farm equipment back home in Oklahoma. "Every town we hit," Ward said, "Pepper would make the rounds of the pawn shops, looking for spare parts or bargains. By the time we'd get back to St. Louis, the railroads hardly could carry the trunk" [Broeg, *The Sporting News*, March 1965: 29].

His son-in-law, Alan Cherry, called him a "toolaholic," remembering when Pepper was delighted to have found an anvil for only $60. So proud, in fact, that he paid additional freight to bring it home on an airplane, only to discover that he already had an anvil in his workshop on the ranch.

To pay for some of these items, Martin also signed on with the Laclede Gas Light Company. In the August 17 St. Louis *Post-Dispatch*'s sports pages, below his picture was a letter which said, "You can mark me down as a big booster of hot water showers.... It's a swell idea for anybody whether you are an athlete or a businessman, to take a hot shower after a tough day. It's just the thing to put a man back on his feet. As soon as every ballgame is over, I hit the showers. It keeps my muscles from aching and getting sore and seems to actually wash away my fatigue, and makes me feel like a million dollars."

By season's end the Mudcats were even more popular. Said Martin's manager Frank Frisch, "If the police ever hear this orchestra, you'll all get time."

Still, "They became so popular ... that a post-season, 13-week tour of the Orpheum circuit was organized and had them doing their stuff for $1,500 in cities like Chicago and Cincinnati," Gregory wrote. "At Dayton's Lyric Theatre, Martin came on the stage drunk and told the audience that the end of the world was coming. There wasn't much time, he said, and everybody should repent. Only loud hisses and boos could finally shut him up, whereupon he cued the opening theme. According to Bordagaray, it went something like this:

Mudcats, front row from left: pitcher Lon Warneke on guitar, Pepper on harmonica, Bill McGee in a vest, also on guitar; in the rear are Frenchy Bordagaray and Bob Weiland on jug. (National Baseball Hall of Fame Library, Cooperstown, N.Y.)

> We are the Mudcats,
> We're Pepper Martin's Mudcats,
> Our lungs are made of leather
> We are birds who play together —
> Don't you know? [315].

At the next scheduled stop the Mudcats called it quits. Martin missed his bird dogs and went home to hunt. *The Sporting News* of Oct. 21 carried this item under "Caught on the Fly":

> Pepper Martin returned to his home in Oklahoma with a carload of gadgets he had collected in a tour of second-hand machine shops near the end of the season. "I ain't sure just what I'll do with some more machinery," he confessed. "But I've got room for a couple of more pieces in my garage. Don't know as I'll make anything with 'em. I made a gunstock once, real, nice one too. And I'm working on my midget racing car again" [4].

For the 1937 season, the best Pepper could do was fourteenth in the league in steals with nine. The best his team could do was to finish fifteen games behind the league leader.

24

1938–1940:
A Captain of Cardinals

Over the winter of 1937–1938, Pepper rested his knee as much as he could and "built a fence, did some interior decorating in my home, attended midget automobile races, went hunting and managed my heavyweight fighter, Junior Munsell" (St. Louis *Post-Dispatch*, January 21, 1938). Always active, always a new project.

On January 26, Martin left Oklahoma City for St. Louis "at the request of the Cardinal management to talk over the salary situation" (UPI, New York *World-Telegram*, Jan. 26, 1938). Never a player to drive in more than seventy-six runs in a season, Johnnie's contributions, on paper, were as someone who stole bases and, much more importantly, someone who scored runs. But he would never again score even the sixty runs he contributed in 1937. Rickey worshipped speed and Pepper was a beat-up thirty-four.

But he was still a major leaguer. Maybe he would try not to spend so much of his $10,000 salary this year. Maybe he would try to hang onto his money a little more tightly for the sake of his wife and three girls. One of those economizing moves seemed to be driving to Florida by himself in March "in one of those tan, lacquered things called a station wagon. He had a mattress in the wagon. When he felt sleepy, he pulled over under the trees along the road and staked himself to a generous portion of shut eye" (Stockton, St. Louis *Post-Dispatch*, March 4, 1938). And not long after he arrived in training camp, he sought out the team owner.

"Mr. Breadon, I want to talk to you. I want it understood that not one of the Mudcats is to be sold or traded this season. You can't expect us to build up a fine musical organization and have you ruin it…. It isn't fair to art" (Stockton, St. Louis *Post-Dispatch*, March 4, 1938).

Breadon and Rickey had other ideas about the team that had nothing

Pepper at full speed crossing first base at Sportsman's Park in St. Louis. (National Baseball Hall of Fame Library, Cooperstown, N.Y.)

to do with music. Durocher, the shortstop, was traded to the Dodgers; Frisch would not last out the year; Paul Dean's arm could no longer be counted on. In Dean's first two years he had averaged over 250 innings per year. He had pitched 0.0 innings in 1937; in the next five years he would average 31 innings pitched per year.

Who was left of the Gas House Gang in 1938? Only Joe Medwick and Johnnie Martin remained from the 1934 championship team. Dizzy Dean was with the team, dead arm and all, but Dizzy Dean's contract was soon sold to Phil Wrigley, owner of the Cubs, just as the season started. Pep felt that with Dean went the chance for a "pennant and World Series money" (Gregory, 343).

Some Cubs thought they had just greatly increased their chances to win the pennant. Pepper Martin guessed that the $185,000 profit on the deal might be used to buy twenty-six year old strikeout pitcher Van Mungo from the Dodgers. Rickey did not buy pitchers; if anything, he traded for them.

So, on April 16, the 1938 lineup that started had Don Gutteridge in Durocher's shortstop place, Stu Martin at second base, rookie Enos Slaughter in right and then Don Padgett playing left and batting in Medwick's cleanup spot, since Ducky had a sore back. Mize was hitting fifth followed by Johnnie, age 34, at third and Terry Moore in center field with Mickey Owen catching. Fifteen game winner Lefty Weiland was the starting pitcher.

When the team went on to Chicago on the night of the twenty-first, Pepper left for Oklahoma City to be with one of his very sick children, Alice Jane, twenty-one months, who was recovering from diphtheria. When Pepper arrived, he found that his house had been quarantined, so Johnnie had to content himself with waving at his family through a window (UP, April 22, 1938).

Meanwhile the Cardinals made all sorts of adjustments. Terry Moore went to third base, Stan Bordagaray replaced Don Padgett in left and batted cleanup, and Tuck Stainback took Moore's center field spot. A few days later, on April 26th, Jimmy Brown played third, Stainback was in left, John Martin was playing center and Herb Bremer caught in place of Owen.

On May 8, showing he still had it, Pepper stole home on pitcher Red Evans in the sixth, a run that was the only one scored at Ebbets Field that day.

By the second week in May of 1938, with the Giants in town, a series of injuries added up to misery for the Cardinals. Pitcher Lon Warneke was still limping, Terry Moore had an inflamed eye, Mike Ryba a battered left eye, and both Stuart Martin and Pepper had charley horses. Even Onkel Frank Frisch was suffering with a severe bunion. Joe Stripp, who had held out until now, was the new third baseman. Stripp did not strike out much and he had played the outfield and all the infield positions. But, since 1928, he had only had 500 at bats in a season twice. (This year the frequent holdout, now thirty-five, will not have two hundred at bats.)

Later in May, Joe Medwick, while the team played in New York, invited Pepper to come to Cartaret, Medwick's New Jersey home town. Knowing of Joe's Mom's famous Hungarian cooking, Pepper gladly accepted.

After a team luncheon on Friday, June 3rd, at the St. Louis Optimist Club at which Rickey waffled, "We are aiming for the pennant," the Mudcat Band played three numbers.

On June 4, Saturday, the third place Boston Bees were scheduled in Sportsman's and a reminder of the Gas House Gang style of play came back in the first doubleheader of the season, when Pepper Martin made a pinch hit double to tie the score in the ninth and then came in to score on his belly later that inning.

While Pepper worked hard on the field, he also played his pranks. "Another thing he did, he did to me," Gutteridge told Peter Golenbock:

Pepper chewed tobacco. I wasn't playing, so my glove was laying down. He picked it up, and he spit into all the fingers with tobacco juice. Late in the game, Frisch called me to play, and I grabbed my glove and started out there, put my hand in the glove, and "Oh my God!" I turned that glove upside down and tobacco juice oozed out of it. I could have killed him. But he laughed. Pepper thought that was so funny. And Frisch would get mad. He'd say, "What happened?" Cause you'd look silly going out there, yelling, shaking your glove. Then I'd explain what happened, and Frankie didn't know what to say. He figured Pepper was the guy who was guilty of it. He'd say, "Why did you let that guy do that to you?" [Golenbock, 202].

That was always a good question. Clearly, Pepper saw part of his role on the team was as someone who kept things light, someone who didn't let anyone become too self-important. This role is a vital role in a group of very physical men playing under pressure in the heat and humidity of St. Louis. His teammates saw very little meanness in Pepper, and how could you answer Frisch's question? What Pepper had done was not awful. It might be annoying, or startling, but it was not mean.

Sometimes, team members are just fellow workers; they might not spend time with each other after a game. Some of that separateness was because there were different cliques on the team. Other players stayed apart because they valued their time alone. Medwick was one of those; so was Pepper. Pepper and Gutteridge were great friends and their families spent a great deal of time together.

Johnnie knew he was not going to be elected into the new Baseball Hall of Fame, as some of his teammates like Mize and Medwick might be. He knew he did not have in him the kind of greatness that those two men had. He was nearing the end of his full time play and he had not made 1000 hits. But he also knew that he had made himself a career out of his hard play. His love for baseball had not diminished over the years. Others might say nasty things about the owners, Rickey, and Sam Breadon, but Pepper never did. Except for things said in the fury of competition, Pepper was rarely cruel and the competition was but two hours each day.

On June 18, "more than 500 fans from Batchtown, IL, were on hand to help celebrate [Max]McGee Day and before the game the Card pitcher received an automobile. As soon as the car was rolled onto the field, the playful Cards climbed all over it, inspected the upholstery and motor, then, on behalf of the famous Mudcats Band, Pepper Martin presented a pen and pencil set to McGee."

Some writers wanted to present Martin with gifts too. On the night of June 15 in Philadelphia, the story goes, sportswriter Ray Gillespie of the St. Louis *Star-Times* bought a handful of different sized hairpins from a chambermaid at the Bellevue-Stratford Hotel. Superstitious ballplayers, and there were and are many, were willing to believe that finding a short hairpin would grant them a short hit; a longer pin meant a longer hit. Gillespie left them for Pepper Martin to find, but Joe Medwick scooped them all up. When told the pins were meant for Pepper, Joe said, "Let him find his own pins" (Gillespie, St. Louis *Star-Times*, June 16, 1938).

Again in 1938 the team was playing badly. With the Cardinals stuck in seventh place and not likely to rise much higher than the sixteen games they were behind in mid–July, the manager even gave up on Enos Slaughter, keeping the outfielder out of forty-two games.

Pepper still had his fun:

> Fans started gathering as early as 7 AM when Pepper Martin and his Musical Mudcats of the St. Louis Cardinals gave a concert at 10:30 AM, June 29, at the 132nd Infantry Armory, Chicago…. An assemblage of 7000 cheered Martin, Bob Weiland, Lon Warneke, Frenchy Bordagaray, Bill McGee and Max Lanier as they played and sang hill-billy songs winding up with a chicken dance by Weiland and Bordagaray. Martin was introduced by Rip Collins of the Cubs, a former Cardinal. Pepper tossed out a dozen autographed baseballs to the crowd.

When, afterward, newspapermen asked Martin about his bosses' attitude toward the band, Pepper said that "there has been some criticism of our band. They say it hurts our ball playing. We play as hard as we know how, but some folks just can't see us relax after a game. We never take our musical instruments into the clubhouse and I don't see why there should be any fuss about this thing" (*The Sporting News*, July 7, 1938).

Then July 16 was Pepper Martin Day at Sportsman's Park and friends from Oklahoma City had a ceremony at home plate for Martin. "Miss Virginia Estes of Pepper's home town gave him a baton, saying his friends hoped he'd have the genius of Stokowski, the rhythm of Lombardi and the swing of Goodman" (St. Louis *Post-Dispatch*, July 17, 1938).

On an eastern swing with the Cardinals, Martin and the team dragged up the center field steps and into the clubhouse of the Polo grounds after the loss of a doubleheader. Max Lanier recalled:

> The clubhouse is like a tomb. Buzzy Wares, our first base coach, goes to light up a cigar. Well, Pepper had switched matches on him. Buzzy strikes a match and it explodes. Buzzy explodes with it. "Damn you guys!" he yells. "Lose a doubleheader and you're still pulling pranks." He went and got another book of matches. But Pepper had loaded the cigar, too. Everybody's sitting there watching Buzzy light it. When twenty-five guys are sitting stone still watching you light your cigar, you ought to suspect something. But I guess Buzzy was too damn mad to notice…. Boy, he took a notice a second later. The damn thing blew up in his face, and he

had tobacco in his eyes, his ears, his nose. Twenty-five guys turned around and looked into their lockers, their shoulders shaking.... Pepper kept you loose all right [Honig, *Grass*, 212].

And the oil wells? The five acres of land in Sumter County, Kansas, given as a deed to a lease to Pepper and Dizzy by S.A. Murphy, the Wichita business man, turned out to be land on which oil was discovered. It was estimated (by the Chicago *Daily News*) that Pepper and Dizzy would reap cash profits of $50,000 apiece. A later report claimed the new well was supposed to produced 300 barrels per day. Part two of the oil story printed on June 24, 1938, claimed that Dizzy and Pepper's property was over a half mile from Murphy's gusher. Oil had not yet been struck on the two ballplayers' land. Another report said the well was producing 100 barrels a day, making it profitable enough so that the well could be sold for $2000 if they could find a buyer. Nothing ever came of it. Pepper's family, of course, still had the oil well in their back yard in Oklahoma City.

The 1938 season ended with the Cardinals seventeen and a half games back, Martin coming to bat fewer than three hundred times. With only minor injuries like charley horses during the season, it was age that was keeping him out of the lineup. Frisch would never be in the lineup again either; he was fired with a few games to go. There were two Gas Housers left.

After the regular season, Pepper went to Chicago to see a former Gas Houser pitch. Dizzy Dean, his arm dead but his skill very much alive, was called on by Gabby Hartnett to pitch the second game of the 1938 World Series against the Yankees. Before the game, "in center field," as Gregory wrote, "the Chicago Board of Trade Band was serenading early arrivals, and Pepper Martin, on hand to pull for Diz, was playing along on his guitar" (354).

The public was still eager to hear the Mudcats band, or to see the players, and so two weeks after the season ended, the Mudcats signed for an eight week vaudeville tour.

1939

With his salary cut $2,500 to $7,500, John Pepper Martin reported to the Suwannee Hotel in St. Petersburg ready for the 1939 season, Pepper's ninth as a regular. The team had a new ball park called Waterfront for its training season. And on the reporting date of March 1, not all of the team was ready to play, mainly because of unsigned contracts like Ducky Medwick's and Johnnie Mize's. In fact, the Cardinals had thirteen out of twenty-two players missing. Still, new manager Ray Blades appointed Pepper Martin team captain on opening day of the training season at Waterfront Park. Pepper, thrilled, said, "I will give all I have to make good, doggoned if I don't" (St. Louis *Post-Dispatch*).

Then Rickey decreed that there would be no more of the Mudcat Band in the clubhouse. Who knows why? Too frivolous for Rickey? Too many pitchers in the band from a staff that gave up too many hits and too many walks and had the sixth, of eight, best ERA in the league?

The Cardinals had dropped out of the first division for the first time since 1933. Joe Williams quoted Pepper saying, "'We might pull something like that again this season ... you never can tell what the governor might come up with.' To Captain Martin, Mr. Rickey is always the governor" (New York *World-Telegram*, March 23, 1939).

The governor thought that Joe Orengo, Herman Franks and Maurice Sturdy might be stars in the field and that pitchers like Bob Bowman, Mort Cooper, Tom Sunkel and Ken Raffensberger could carry the team upward.

Eventually, all of the returning regulars signed, and one day Johnnie Martin did some fishing with traveling secretary Leo Ward and Joe Medwick. Off Westbeach, Medwick caught a shark after a half-hour battle; Johnnie had nothing to show for his day, though sharks could be seen near their boat. Ward told this story to Milton Gross: Martin had a harpoon attached to a coil of rope. He threw the harpoon into a shark swimming by and the shark, hurt, began swimming away very fast. As the rope between Pepper's feet played out, he tried to grab the rope as it burned through his hands, angry because the shark got away (Gross, St. Petersburg *Independent*, March 8, 1965). But nothing else happened. The fact that Pepper had again done something without regard for the consequences is part of his appeal, after all.

New manager Blades was fond of meetings and discipline and lots of hard, physical work, causing Martin to say, "I got a jackass back in Oklahoma, and you can work him from sunup till sundown and he ain't never gonna win the Kentucky Derby" (Chieger, 54).

Martin also had another ward, another Yo-Yo. Sweet Pea was a bat boy and a kind of servant of Martin. "No kid ever wore a more worshipful look" (John Carmichael, Miami *Herald*, March 10, 1965). One day Pepper fed him a sandwich of ferns and flower petals which Sweet Pea gladly ate.

In St. Louis, at the annual baseball dinner in the Hotel Jefferson on April 17, Pepper Martin was one of the speakers to the 750 assembled fans along with coach Mike Gonzalez and manager Blades.

When the season began, Pepper, as captain, brought the lineup out

A more serious Pepper posed in 1939. (National Baseball Hall of Fame Library, Cooperstown, N.Y.).

to start each game but he actually played in fifty-one games in the outfield, twenty-two at third and in another fifteen games as a pinch hitter or pinch runner.

But he had his moments of excellence.

In Ebbets Field on May 8, against old teammate Leo Durocher, now the Dodger manager, Pepper Martin stole home for the only run in the first game of a doubleheader. The win helped the Cardinals to move into second place in the league at 9–6.

At Crosley Field, the remnants of the Gas House Gang ruled the day. In the first, after Stu Martin was forced by Pepper, Martin stole second base and when Joe Medwick hit a pop fly so high between home and third it was not caught, Pepper came all the way home. In the seventh, Stu Martin doubled, Pepper was struck by a Paul Derringer pitch and Medwick singled in Stu. On that single, third baseman Billy Werber cut off the throw from left and tried to get Medwick who was stretching his hit on the outfield throw. When the throw went wild, Pepper scored and Joe moved to third from where he scored on a force out.

In New York, three Cardinals drove to the New York World's Fair on June 3, and were shown to the National Youth Administration exhibits in the Consumer Building where they gave baseball instruction. First, mayor LaGuardia spoke to 3000 boy and girl scouts. Blades, Pepper and Ducky served as instructors in the Court of Sport at the World's Fair at 10:30 AM. Martin probably discarded his Beech-Nut tobacco before speaking.

Though by now Martin carried a little batch of hair from a mule's tail with him for good luck, later that same day Johnnie hurt his wrist in the eighth inning of the game.

He had his moments of fun. Once when the club stopped at the dignified Bellevue-Stratford in Philadelphia, Johnnie and some others were standing in front of a hotel after a game when a chauffeur and his passenger pulled up to the curb and passed by the players. Martin didn't like the disdainful look the chauffeur gave the men, and so the next day at the same time Martin paid the doorman at the hotel to call the chauffeur over for a chat. Martin quickly opened the limousine's hood, attached one of his favorite toys and waited for the passenger and chauffeur to exit the hotel. When the car was started, clouds of smoke came out from under the hood. The chauffeur couldn't miss the men watching and laughing. The passenger, an older man, called for the police. Martin, it seems, had insulted his dignity (King, New York *World-Telegram*, March 8, 1965).

The passenger was not a team member and therefore an outsider who could be attacked with justification. And more than that, he was attacked with justice. The man had treated Pepper badly and so Pepper treated him just as badly. Justice.

As the team was warming up to resume their season at home against Brooklyn, June 14 was the twenty-fifth annual Tuberculosis Day which featured "an elaborate program, including a 10,000 meter walk, drills by acrobats, bicycle riders, playground dancers, bands and drum corps"; the long entertainment meant that neither team had batting practice. But there was some exercise when Gutteridge, Bowman, Pepper and Slaughter grabbed a four-seater bicycle from its costumed riders and pedaled around the field. Pitchers Warneke and Cooper followed them on a more conventional two-seater tandem.

Four days later, June 18, fans and teammates celebrated Pepper Martin Day and around home plate gathered Pepper and Ford Frick, Jesse Haines, Carl Hubbell, and Charley Barrett, the Cardinal scout who signed Martin. Martin was given, by Carl Hubbell, a giant telegram from his friends in Oklahoma. John Drebinger described the ceremony: "In honoring Martin, the home folks forgot the customary luggage, fountain pens and wrist watches." Instead he was given two brood mares named, via a $25 contest, as "Osage" and "Cimarron," and a Holstein heifer, a pedigreed beagle, an electric churn, a sow with her litter given by pitcher and Mudcat Lon Warneke, rabbits, chickens, and, for tools, an electric grindstone, a hay rake, a cultivator and a large tractor. The large, metal plow he was given had his name engraved in large letters on it.

The *Post-Dispatch* described Martin's reaction to all the gifts, saying,

Bat Rifles: Don Padgett, Joe Medwick, Enos Slaughter, Johnny Mize, and Pepper Martin, on September 5, 1939. (National Baseball Hall of Fame Library, Cooperstown, N.Y.)

"Pepper was almost overcome. Hesitating for a few seconds before the loud speaker microphone, he said: 'If I just get straighter out here I'll say something.'" Listening to Martin's thanks were the mayor of St. Louis and the governor of Oklahoma. Drebinger ended by writing, "Martin, highly elated ... showed the fans how much he appreciated everything by driving the tractor out of the arena as if it were a Roman chariot" (St. Louis *Post-Dispatch*, June 19, 1939).

Stockton said about Pepper's career, "Martin is still going strong, although baseball age is closing in on him and he seems prone to injury. But as long as he can get into the game he will continue to be the team's greatest inspiration" (St. Louis *Post-Dispatch*, June 19, 1939).

Said Pepper, "I had to rent a box car for $400 and I had to build stalls in it for the animals to get them shipped back home. For a while, though, we had those animals out in the suburbs, where we rented a house in a dignified neighborhood [Webster Grove] and those city kids had never seen anything like it" (Heinz 102).

From the gifts Martin could see the affection in which he was held by his fans. Joe Williams, the sportswriter for the *World-Telegram*, was a fan of Pepper as well, calling him "about as pretentious as Bill Klem's old whisk broom" and stating that no one could measure "the ardor, will-to-win, self-sacrifice, and all the little intangibles that go to make up a team player" such as Martin. "He was as authentic as a 60-second minute. His whims, impulses and mad inspirations stemmed from an honest, prankish fun-loving soul ... [of] a grown-up man who still thought a boy's life was pretty swell and who wouldn't?... All he ever wanted was to be one of the gang. Captains don't have fun. They're supposed to set stuffy, painful examples, frown on normal human weaknesses and all that sort of thing. But

1938–1940: A Captain of Cardinals

All eyes are on Pepper as he horses around with, among others, Murry Dickson, Hal Epps, Ernie White, and coach Buzzy Wares, probably in spring training in 1939. (National Baseball Hall of Fame Library, Cooperstown, N.Y.)

captain he still was. Not Captain Fury, but 'way down in his heart, Captain Fury and a grand fellow" (Joe Williams, New York *World-Telegram*, Aug. 25, 1939).

We can tell who Martin thought a grand fellow was by whom he admired and in what words. Of Curt Davis, pitcher, Martin said, "What a man he's been for us. Starts games, goes in to relieve, and runs, mind

Two of Martin's three girls, Alice and Jennie Lee, celebrated their catch for the day with their father. Courtesy of the Martin family.

you, runs to the bullpen without being asked. Just a real fine worker." He points out the "potent bats" carried by left fielder Joe Medwick and first baseman Johnnie Mize (Joe Williams, New York *World-Telegram,* Aug. 25, 1939). Pepper admired team players and players who were outstanding contributors to the team. Did this mean that if he was no longer one of those contributors, he felt he did not belong on the team? That his time was up?

Still, he had an effect on the team. Max Lanier, then twenty-four, remembered Pepper clearly:

> Pepper Martin was still there. He was the most colorful ballplayer I ever saw. He did something funny every day, just about. Like he'd slide into second, and the fielder would have the ball, and he'd knock the ball out of his glove and would be called safe, and he'd laugh. I swear they couldn't tag him out. He'd stick his feet in the ground and go the other way quick as they run him, until they got so tired they had to drop over [Golenbock, 153].

But his teammates still had to be wary. On July 23, three Dodger runs scored when, after Medwick set himself under Ernie Koy's bases-loaded, two-out fly, Pepper crashed into him.

Being always a good team player, when the Cardinals played an exhibition game against the Washington, Penn., team of the Pennsylvania State Association, Pepper Martin pitched the last two innings, though very badly.

And after a game, "when you call on the Pepper Pot, you'll find him in a Cardinal cap, a pair of shorts which had once been white, but now are dyed a tea-rose yellow with honest perspiration...." (Williams, *New York World-Telegram,* Aug. 25, 1939).

He hit .306 in 1939 but only came to bat 281 times.

But it seems he came to bat again in California, barnstorming. There is evidence that Dizzy Dean barnstormed with his team but Pepper was not always with him. The Dizzy Dean All-Stars played in the southwest in 1939.

Even when Pepper didn't go with Dean, Dizzy would come to visit. His gambling and his drinking were not approved of in the Baptist home but he still had that charm. Childless himself, Dizzy was known to escort Pepper's daughter Jennie Lee to her room and tuck her into bed at night. Jennie, a kind of tomboy, was a frequent fishing partner of her father's and was becoming quite an athlete.

1940

Honest perspiration is fine but productivity is better. Pepper knew he was at the end of his productivity on the major league level and began to look around for other work in baseball early in 1940.

In the training season, there were new quarters for the team in the Hotel Bainbridge in St. Petersburg. Martin, who loved machinery and gadgets, tried a new contraption to cure his problem of throwing the bat after he had swung. So at the end of the bat he attached a leather loop that fitted around his wrist. When asked about his hitting, he replied, "Sure I got a theory on hitting. You'll notice the bat flies out of my hand only when I miss the ball or tip it. When I hit the ball solidly, the bat doesn't fly. I hold the bat loose until I'm at the top of my backswing; I figure that way I can hit relaxed. If you grip the bat too hard it may stiffen up your shoulder and tense your arms so you can't follow a curve. So I don't clinch until just before I meet the ball and sometimes I guess I forget to clinch" (UP, 1938).

When the team moved north, the Cardinals played an exhibition game in Oklahoma City, maybe as a favor to Pepper, since it was not unknown for a team to schedule a game in a player's town.

Less than a week later, Pepper was used in left field in place of Joe Medwick who again had muscle spasms in his back. Two weeks after that, Medwick returned and after he doubled, Blades put Pepper in to run for Joe. Pepper brought the winning run home in the tenth inning for Jack Russell, the thirty-five year old reliever.

Martin's wide-open swing, often leading to a thrown bat, is shown here. (National Baseball Hall of Fame Library, Cooperstown, N.Y.)

During this early season period, papers began loudly speculating about the end of Ray Blades as manager. Named as possible replacements were both coach Mike Gonzalez and captain Johnnie Martin. It is difficult to tell if the sportswriters were merely guessing that Pepper was a candidate because they had no real information. Choosing the team captain and a longtime Cardinal organization employee as manager simply made sense. Blades had been Rickey's choice and Rickey was known to favor Martin. Martin had been a very compliant employee, Rickey's favorite kind.

The fans were unhappy with their losing team, because for them it had been too long a time since the 1934 championship season and so anything was liable to set them off. On June 4, when Pepper Martin was thrown out of the game in the second inning and when umpire Bill Stewart twice reversed calls by umpire Magerkurth, "the fans in the left and center field stands rose and sent out the barrage of glassware. Within a few seconds, the entire left side of the field was littered with hundreds of bottles. Joe Medwick and Moore meanwhile scampered toward the infield to get out of range" (St. Louis *Post-Dispatch*, June 5, 1940). A photograph shows men in caps and fedoras hauling bushel baskets and buckets of pop bottles off the field. It took them seven minutes to pick up the trash.

On the kind of day when attendance was usually at its highest, a Sunday doubleheader, only 4,843 paid to see the games and the honoring of fan favorite Bill Delancey, back in the big leagues after four years recovering from his gunshot wound. At home plate Delancey was presented with an automobile and Pepper Martin, the team representative, gave Bill, from his teammates, a driving harness.

Soon the team left for an eastern swing trip without Joe Medwick, he and Curt Davis having been traded to the Dodgers. The trade meant that the Gas House Gang now had one member, Pepper. Johnnie, now 36, knew he also would be out of the picture soon. Knowing Rickey's regard for Martin, it seems certain that Pepper would be told his days in the majors were few.

Don Gutteridge remembered that Martin was still having his fun:

> Pepper and I were buddies. He played little tricks on me all the time. We were riding on a train, going from St. Louis to New York, and you'd sleep part of the time. I went to sleep in my chair and during a stop he got out and took some grease off the wheel, and he came back in and got a straw, and my hand was drooped down, and he put a little grease on my fingers. Then he tickled my nose like it was a fly, and I'd knock the fly off my nose, and I ended up with grease all over my face. He did that to several guys, of course. It was fun. We liked that.... And gum. Pepper'd shake hands with you and have gum on his fingers. Or he'd pat you on the back and put gum on the back of your hair. He was always doing that. Nobody ever got angry [Golenbock, 202].

How could anyone get angry at Pepper Martin? Did anyone think that these practical jokes were a way for Pepper to establish his status? If Pepper played the joke, then he was not the foolish victim of it. Though the humor was crude and the pranks harmless, at least they kept things light and relaxed, laughter being a great release. And Pepper almost always played these tricks where many could see them and, presumably, benefit from the laughter.

And Pepper himself sometimes had to pay for his antics. His injury when wrestling before a game, his slashed finger from the water glass prank, his being asked to leave by a Boston Hotel are all examples of both the payment extracted from a joke and his stoic acceptance of the payment.

Those who had jokes played on them by Pepper received two benefits. First, the victims had the opportunity to show that they were good sports and able to take a joke; second, they knew that a joke being played on them was a sign of acceptance on the team. Pepper was a veteran and a man everyone liked and if Pepper showed that he liked you through a prank, then the team was able to see that you belonged. So the jokes were a kind of initiation.

What happened next was no joke. In Brooklyn, Medwick was horribly beaned by Cardinal pitcher Bob Bowman. Dodger owner MacPhail rushed down to the field and, as Durocher wrote:

was standing in front of the St. Louis dugout challenging the whole ball club. Screaming at them. Out of control. The fiery Brooklyn boss shook off attempts of Dressen and Babe Phelps to restrain him, walked to the end of the St. Louis dugout, unloaded a tirade at the Cardinals team, inviting any of them to step under the stands. Johnnie Mize and Pepper Martin tried to cool him off. It was a miracle that there wasn't a riot [Eskenazi, 127].

Pepper had been hit by a pitch only thirteen times in his major league career but he, and many others, considered the beanball wars to be started by the Dodgers. Medwick's injury was then Durocher's fault, Pepper Martin suggested, since Leo considered beanballs an important tool for a team. In fact, in the space of two innings at Sportsman's Park on May 7 of that year, Dodger pitcher Hugh Casey had hit Padgett, Mize and Slaughter. Quite simply, using anything you can — insults, reminders of embarrassing moments, beanballs — to diminish a player's ability at bat was the common trade of baseball for some managers.

Less than a week later in Pittsburgh, an unusual event, for Pepper, happened: he was tossed out of a game for only the second time in seventeen years of professional baseball. For a man who played with so much intensity, this was a striking number. Pepper was back in the lineup since there was a left-hander pitcher, Dick Lanahan, throwing the next day in Forbes Field and, against Lanahan, Johnnie hit a grand slam home run in the ninth.

"Pepper was a very competitive ballplayer. He would do anything to win," Don Gutteridge claimed. "When he went out there, you had to beat him. He wasn't going to beat himself. You were going to have to be better than he was. He liked to win, and he never let up. He ran out everything. Some guys would run hard to first base. He ran hard all the time. When he went to steal, he did it headfirst" (Golenbock, 202).

As the 1940 All-Star Game approached, Daniel had something to say: "One of the biggest boners pulled on either side in the inter-league meeting is the snubbing of Pepper Martin, a bit old and a trifle brittle now, but still the Wild Horse of the Osage. Heroes come and heroes are sold or dry out in the St. Louis atmosphere, but Martin keeps charging. Particularly as the game is to be played in St. Louis, Martin should have been honored" (New York *World-Telegram*, July 3, 1940). Yet Pepper and his long time boss Branch Rickey were working on something that, if it did not do Martin honor, it certainly showed a regard for Pepper as a baseball man.

As a baseball man, Pepper was "asked by the magazine *Friday* about the quality of negro ballplayers.... Stars like Pepper Martin ... and Carl Hubbell praised negro players."

Pepper, still the same energetic and optimistic man after all these years, told Grantland Rice:

> There's only one way to feel and that's great. That's the way I feel. No alibis go in this game.... Play baseball from February to October and I hunt from October to February. I live outdoors. I live simply. I get a great kick out of life — especially baseball and hunting. I wouldn't know what a night club looks like. And I'm not going to find out [*The Sporting News*, 1940].

This may have been Pepper's last year in the big leagues, but it may not have been his last year in baseball. Pepper and baseball, after eighteen years as a player, were intertwined. And even when he was given his official release from a Cardinal contract on October 14, 1940, there was still plenty of Pepper in baseball and plenty of baseball in Pepper.

Part Four

25

1941–1946: War's Needs

Where Pepper would be in baseball in 1941 was formally decided within forty-eight hours of Pepper's official release, after some obvious long-range planning. Branch Rickey, head of the twenty-six team Cardinal minor league chain as well as vice-president of the Sacramento, California, Solons, had talked with Phil Bartelme, president of Sacramento, about signing Pepper to be the manager of that Pacific Coast League team. Bartelme, by the way, once owned the Syracuse Stars, where Martin played in 1926, and Martin had barnstormed in California before.

After a conference with Sam Breadon and Rickey, Martin signed but "before signing the contract he was assured the use of the Cardinal organization tractor on his Oklahoma farm" (UP, New York *World-Telegram*, Oct. 16, 1940). In fact, Pepper was given a tractor for leaving St. Louis and moving to Sacramento. He took the tractor to Oklahoma in a truck. That farm was his boyhood home in Temple which he had purchased with his 1931 World Series money.

Martin promised that he'll "teach his boys to hit the ball and run like hell" and "I'm going to teach Gas House Gang baseball to my team.… You can bet we'll wake up the coast league" (UP, New York *Daily Mirror*, Oct. 15, 1941).

This job was, in no small measure, an affirmation of Martin's baseball skill and maturity. The "AA" league, "founded in 1903, … was one of the oldest and most successful of the minor leagues.… The Pacific Coast League … offered sanctuary to fading major league stars who wanted to extend their careers two or three years. Some players actually preferred it to the majors; the money was often just as good, and for some its ballparks were closer to home" (Spalding, 36). The job may have been a reward to a faithful employee but it was, more importantly, a job for a knowledgeable baseball man.

Martin, interviewed "by long distance telephone" by radio station

KFBK, told Tony Koester that he intended his team to play "real Gashouse baseball" in 1941. "By Gashouse baseball I mean that every man gives a little more than 100 per cent and that they slide into the bases with no regard to their own personal welfare" (Adams, Sacramento *Bee*, Feb. 4, 1941:16).

As February 1941 began, Pepper had two send-offs from two St. Louis papers (though his home address was 2644 N. W. 11th St., Oklahoma City). The *Globe-Democrat* proclaimed:

> California, here he comes! ... He will show you how the game of baseball should be played.... To each game he gave every ounce of his energy ... and during the almost dozen years he cavorted at Sportsman's Park there was never a jeer or boo directed at him.... He will be greatly missed here next season but with him go the sincere hopes of his countless friends for a successful career.

The *Post-Dispatch* praised Johnnie's "will to win, competitive temperament, fighting spirit: ... all have been bestowed on him ... but there is more to the man's career. Was there ever a publicized difference with the front office? Elected forever into the fellowship of infinite zest, bleachers and grandstand unite in acknowledging, 'We shall not look upon his like again'" (quoted by Adams, Sacramento *Bee*, Feb. 28, 1941).

In Oklahoma City, Martin hooked up a trailer, packed up his wife, three daughters, and three dogs (two of which were a gift from Preacher Roe), and started the 1600 mile adventure for Sacramento around the middle of February.

In Sacramento, even as Pepper was unpacking the small trailer with the family's goods, he announced that he wanted "to get back to the major leagues in short order," John E. Spalding tells us.

When he arrived at the team office at Cardinal Field, on the corner of Riverside and Broadway on February 19, he was clearly excited about his new career. "I think I could have gone to one of the Cards' other AA clubs—either Rochester or Columbus. I chose Sacramento ..." (Steve George, *The Sporting News*, Feb. 27, 1941). The Solons played at an 11,000 seat facility in a city of 120,000. The 179 game schedule lasted from April 5 to September 21 and the team had a player limit of twenty-five, five of whom had to have less than two years organized baseball experience. Martin had signed to be a playing manager and he had been assigned some other players he knew well from the Cardinals.

As manager, Johnnie also had to get to know the traveling secretary, Joe Ziegler, as well as various civic groups in the city and the area. Within a week of his arrival, he spoke to Post 61 of the American Legion in Sacramento, the Sacramento Lions Club and the Lions Club of Brea. He was skilled at speaking to groups and any speaker who was enthusiastic was always popular with audiences. Pepper often appeared wearing a suit but with cowboy boots and a big cowboy hat.

Pep realized that the team needed a diathermy machine. He wired the Cardinals' trainer, Doc Weaver: "Alas, Doc, no diathermy machine out here and we sure need one. Club overhead terrific. Could you send one? I could give you an autographed ball, a right-handed pitcher or a couple of fat pigs. Hopefully, Johnnie Pepper Martin, manager, player, coach."

As W. C. Heinz reported: "'He sent me the machine,' Pepper said, 'and I got a couple of pigs, crated 'em up and sent 'em to him'" (Heinz, 106).

Leaving for Fullerton on February 26 for training camp,

Pepper and Jackie Coogan: Pepper became familiar with movie stars at work in the RKO studio during his time managing teams in California during the early 1940s. (Courtesy the Pepper Martin Family.)

Martin saw the team beginning to take shape. On the roster now were Red Munger, second baseman Gene Handley, twenty-six year old brother of major leaguer Jeep, and catcher Jim Grilik. Both Hadley and Grilik were eager for higher salaries and Bartelme made Hadley the team secretary during spring training in order to bring his salary up; Bartelme tried to convince Grilik to accept a $50 per month raise over the $300 per month he had been paid in 1940 in Asheville; the catcher wanted $100 more. Some of these men had played and would play in the majors. Others in the league, Debs Garms, Babe Herman, Marv Owen, Brusie Ogrodowski, had many years in the majors already. With the war seemingly unavoidable, many of these ex–major leaguers might be needed again to stock teams who might lose men to military service and to defense work.

Martin had a fine outfield that year, being able to use those two former teammates on the Cardinals, Lynn King and Sparky Adams. Another teammate and friend played second base in 1941, Don Gutteridge.

Though the west coast population worried about the Japanese and the threat of war, California was a lively place in the spring as major league clubs arrived for their training. Frisch's Pirates were in San Bernardino,

Martin visited the work of popular stars of the 1940s: Dennis Morgan, another RKO star, is in a white shirt (center rear). (Courtesy the Pepper Martin Family.)

Jimmie Dykes was in Pasadena with his White Sox, Connie Mack was with his A's in Anaheim and Jimmie Wilson, new manager of the Cubs, was in Santa Catalina.

As training camp progressed, Martin told the press that he planned on playing in right field all season. As is often done, he was asked to pick his own all-star team; from the Cardinals he selected Frankie Frisch and Dizzy Dean. Asked about the team's chances, Martin kept saying that they would play hard. The question was a loaded one in the sense that Sacramento had not won a pennant in thirty-nine years, and we can imagine the eagerness of the fans.

The team drew more than 6,000 for their first two home dates. They won their first three series in fact. On the road to the Pacific northwest, "Martin was miffed when the public address announcer introduced him as an Oklahoma 'hillbilly'" (Spalding, 104). Johnnie was still playing hillbilly music, though that was not the only music he liked. His daughter Aleyne told me that she remembered a bunch of musicians including her and her father sitting down to play "The Beer Barrel Polka." Aleyne, schooled in music unlike her father who was self-taught, "would call out the chords so my daddy could know what to play."

Martin knew how to bait an umpire when needed. Once Pepper and Gutteridge goose-stepped up to the umpire and remained silent for five minutes only to goose-step back to the dugout.

That 1941 season, Martin delivered. The team led by the league by fourteen games at midseason and "the hustling Solons were the talk of the league. The Sacramento *Bee's* Wilbur Adams likened Martin's Gashouse tactics to Hitler's panzer divisions.... They beat out bunts and stole bases with abandon, [San Francisco] Seals' catchers threw the ball away seven times trying to stop them on the bases," Adams noted (Spalding, 104).

When the team picked up catcher Clyde Kluttz from Decatur, they got even stronger. Martin tried to convince his old pal Paul Dean to come join the Solons, but Dean declined. Nevertheless, by June 15 the club's record was 50–19, a .724 winning percentage.

But then the first baseman was hurt and then the second baseman, Gutteridge, was hurt and then Kluttz was spiked and out for two weeks. The team's recent record for the time approaching mid-July was 13–14, yet the Solons still had a ten game lead. So on July 11, 1941, "an announced crowd of 14,300 — including 6,400 women who had paid a quarter to see the game saw ... Martin and his wife ... on the field ... for an event sponsored by the Sacramento Chamber of Commerce." The event was Pepper Martin Night, announced a month ago. "Martin broke down and could barely thank the appreciative fans for the gifts they had given. 'Darn it, I can't talk,' he sobbed, looking over the loot, a 1941 Chrysler New Yorker four-door sedan, a shotgun, a hunting dog, a rooster, several hens, electric welding gear and a set of dishes" (Spalding 105).

Martin had good reason to be overcome. In a photograph from *Sacramento Senators and Solons,* Ruby Martin looked stunned by it all and a little uncomfortable. Praise from newspapermen and attention from fans asking for autographs or to pose for pictures is one thing. But it is an entirely different matter when these thousands of dollars are being spent in appreciation of someone who has been in town for five months.

(There are, of course, few days for players in the major leagues now. How could today's fans even match what a star player is paid for a single game? One day's pay for a star now matches what all the gifts cost in 1941.)

Another honor for Pepper came later in the month when Martin and seven of his players were picked for the first Pacific Coast League all-star game, opposing the north all-stars and the south. Pepper's team lost. Then the Solons lost Lynn King, sold to Seattle.

Then something happened that Pepper blamed only himself for, as W.

C. Heinz recorded. On a Sunday night trip to Marysville, with Ruby driving and the children in the car, the family car came to a stop and was lightly tapped from behind.

> There wasn't any damage but the three guys in the car that was drivin' alongside of us, hollerin' vicious remarks. I finally shouted at them to pull over and I took the biggest one and gave him a punch on the jaw and knocked him down. Then I jumped on him and I was chokin' him but Ruby was screaming for me to stop and the girls were crying so I let up. I told the three of them, though, "That ought to teach you a little courtesy."
>
> I shouldn't have done that. I broke one of my knuckles and I couldn't play for ten days [106].

By September, the Senators were 91–61, with a four and a half game lead over the Seattle Rainiers and five games ahead of the San Diego Padres. Martin was credited with increasing the gate in many of the league's cities.

By September 4, the Solons' lead was down to two games over the second place Padres. Then Pepper severely injured his ankle sliding into Bill Rigney at second trying to halt a double play. When his team's lead withered to one game, Martin could be seen throwing his cap in the air and calling the umpires "hoss thieves," an insult of more power in Oklahoma than Sacramento. Martin couldn't help his team as a player, adding only three more at bats and one more hit for the rest of the season after his injury.

By September 16, it was the Solons who were two games back. When the regular season ended, Sacramento's record was 102–75, three-and-a-half games back, tied with San Diego for second place in the eight team league.

Spalding wrote:

> While the Solons unquestionably had a fantastic year, Martin's managerial style came under fire by the second guessers. They were behind him when the team was 50–19 in June, but the 52–56 record after that date was too much to bear. "It could be that Martin's tactics weren't solid in the first place and the law of averages merely caught up with him," theorized Tom Laird in the San Francisco News. "It would seem that Martin's record this season indicates that he needs considerable seasoning before he takes rank as a major league manager" [106].

Laird remembered Martin's dream announced back in February.

But the league had post-season play, called the President's Cup, and Martin brought his .322 batting average into it. The win of the first playoff game established the Solons as the second place team in the league. With Martin playing center field in two of the games, his Solons beat San Diego in four straight games 5–4, 3–0, 3–2, and 6–3 to qualify for the finals.

There they met Seattle who had beaten the Hollywood Stars in their playoff series. After seven games, Seattle took the championship.

Pepper, the player, hit well in his ninety-two games and with 245 at bats, totaled twenty-five percent of the at bats of teammate Don Gutteridge. All in all, Martin had a memorable first managerial year. No doubt he excited the fans in the city, he put extra money into the team's purse with eleven post-season games played, and he helped to put about $100 extra into each team member's pocket for the post-season games.

1942

Within two weeks of the end of the playoffs, before Pepper went back to Oklahoma, he signed again for the 1942 season with Sacramento.

At home in Oklahoma City, Martin received news that in the Hall of Fame election that picked Rogers Hornsby for election, he was given two votes; the total was the same as Wahoo Sam Crawford's.

When Johnnie called the Sacramento team office at 3-3929, he learned that the team limit had been cut by five down to twenty players.

Once war was declared the city itself began to change. Sacramento had grown by twenty-five percent and housing might have been a problem for Pepper and his family. The fact that Sacramento is the state capital and much wartime business would be contracted there added to the problem. "As an inland city, Sacramento had less to fear than coastal communities from the threat of attack by Japanese aircraft and submarine," Spalding wrote (107). Night baseball "was permitted only in the early stages of the season ... and clubs were forced to try morning and twilight games to entertain workers engaged in round-the-clock production" (Spalding, 107).

Personnel was a problem too: the team lost Clyde Kluttz, Nub Kleinke, Al Hollingsworth, and Buddy Blattner; Don Gutteridge, who was sold to the Browns, would not be back either. Certainly the remainder of the team from 1941 saw their chance to do well again in the league and must have been eager to report in late February, though only sixteen showed up originally. One of them was Debs Garms, who hit .358 for the Pirates in 1940. Buster Adams would anchor the outfield and Don Gutteridge's cousin, Ray Mueller, could be counted on the catch most of the season. Garms could also be counted on to play harmonica with Pepper.

Martin even ran a tryout camp in Fullerton on February 23 in preparation for the first training season game on March 2 and for the season opener on April 2.

Juggling rain-outs and injuries, even the death of Jim Grilik in an automobile accident, Martin kept his team close to the league leaders, the Los Angeles Angels. The Angels came in on September 15, 1942, for a seven game series, because extended series had to be scheduled in a time of military travel priorities. Down two games in the loss column, the Solons lost the next two games. Martin would not allow the team to give up. Down four games now, they took the next three games including wins in the ninth and the eleventh innings. The last day was a doubleheader with the Solons down one game. They made the race a tie with a 7–5 win in the first game and swept on to the pennant with 5–1 win in game two.

The season was a success for Sacramento, with Pepper, playing in the outfield and at first base, appearing in more games than in 1941 but with fewer at bats and a lower average. The Sacramento Solons won the city's first pennant in thirty-nine years. Attendance was low—1618 per date in an 11,000 seat park—mostly due to the odd game times, many of them scheduled at the usual dinner time.

Seattle prevailed again in the playoffs.

Pepper did not re-sign with Sacramento that October, partly because of the leadership vacuum brought about by the final break between Branch Rickey and president Sam Breadon of the Cardinals. Rickey had moved on to Brooklyn. No one seemed to know how the organization would settle out and with the confusion that existed, the farm system appeared to be on hold.

1943

No matter what else Pepper Martin was, he was a rancher and a farmer and that meant he worked much of the time with tools and machinery. Whether on the family farm in Temple or the land bought near Lake Overholster, Pepper had to do hard manual labor, but it was not necessarily work that brought in a lot of money. Though three natural gas wells on the ranch brought in some income, his future employment was still unsettled and with the rumors being published of a "Work or Fight" rule to come out of Washington, he enrolled in welding school at an Oklahoma City trades school late in 1942 (UP, New York *World Telegram*, Jan. 26, 1943). His skill as a welder may have been demanded by the government if it decided that all able bodied men should be doing defense work. Certainly the welding tools given to him in Sacramento could now be used with much more skill. Many of the things he did with welding tools on the ranch still stand: cow pens, a water trough.

This was a serious time in history and Martin, almost thirty-nine now, was tired of hearing the same old stories of water balloons dropped and sneezing powder put into fans. He began to think about how he would be remembered. People seemed to have forgotten that he led the league more than once and in more than one category, that he played in two World Series, that he was a part of some great Cardinal teams, even those that did not win. In Pepper's twelve seasons with the Cardinals, his team had finished first or second half the time and in the first division three quarters of his years there.

Meanwhile, it seemed as if the Sacramento club was doing Oliver French (president of Rochester in the International League) a favor. On January 8, 1943, Pepper signed with that upstate New York team which had finished last under Ray Hayworth in 1942. He was probably paid $10,000 to manage. Again Martin was signed by a team in the high minors. Not only that, Martin was given a job with a team that was in one of the ten remaining leagues in 1943. There were but fifty-two jobs in a league at B or above. There were no "C" leagues, two "D" leagues and one short-lived "E" league. Thirty-one minor leagues had disappeared just since Pepper had started managing in 1941.

Ruby told me that she was glad to be out of California as well. "California was smart-alecky." It was also family policy by now not to join Pepper until the school year was over.

Her husband received one less vote in the Hall of Fame balloting for 1943 than for 1942.

Martin told the Rochester press that he would try to play in sixty games that year, partly because many players might be doing defense work in the beginning of the day and playing in the minors in the evening. In addition, some of the players, listed as 4-F with their draft boards, might not be able to function full-time. Yankee pitcher Red Ruffing, for example, was drafted even though he was missing toes. Ford Frick, meanwhile, was suggesting that Pepper travel to entertain soldiers in the company of Dizzy Dean, Babe Ruth and others. The trips never materialized, probably because of defense travel priorities.

Because of the hard weather in upstate New York's spring, Martin started out for Rochester later than he did for California. He reported for work at 500 Norton Street in the northwestern New York city in mid March. Playing at Red Wing Stadium in 1930, no doubt Pepper had fine memories of the place where he had been given the nickname of the Wild Horse of the Osage.

A veteran manager by now, Pepper took the other twenty players assigned by the Cardinals, or at least those players who had not been drafted into service or were unlikely to be drafted, and tried to develop the players he had and finish at the top of the league. One of his players was a twenty-year old shortstop called Al Schoendienst, who at six feet and 155 pounds reported to the clubhouse in the middle of a team meeting. "Pepper Martin ... had been one of my favorites growing up and all I could think of on the train ride to Rochester was what an honor and thrill it was going to be to play for him.... Martin walked over and I could tell he was eyeballing me up and down," Schoendienst wrote in his book, *Red, A Baseball Life*. Martin said, "I've got enough bat boys," and turned back to the meeting. "I'm in last place and they're sending me bat boys, babies" (29).

Bob Broeg wrote: "A great believer in the mischief of idleness, Martin took his players bowling on off-days. He even bought red and green bowling shirts out of his own pocket so that they would be two pin squads on the ball club," as well as organizing two basketball teams and two units of pool players (*The Sporting News*, March 26, 1965: 29).

"Pepper was always playing games," Schoendienst remembered. "If it was raining and you couldn't take batting practice, he would form teams for a game of touch football.... He was always pulling practical jokes on people" (26). Though he was no longer a young man we can see that he was still giving hotfoots, setting newspapers on fire as one read them. Still capable of acting like a little boy, he was known to drop ice cubes out of hotel rooms to see the ice fracture on the pavement.

He also taught "his players practice slides on the outfield grass, wearing football pants to avoid thigh burns," his best-known player, Schoendienst recalled (Broeg, *The Sporting News,* March 1965: 29).

The team was not a strong one and Pepper took the losing hard. From *Silver Seasons*: "Although the team would win fifteen more games than it had the season before, the experience would be a bad one for Martin. Many fans turned on him, and at one point Martin became so fed up with the criticism that he quit. The players persuaded him to return, but Martin clearly had been hurt by the incessant booing and second-guessing" (Mandelaro, 234).

One of things Pepper liked, however, was his garden "behind the left field fence that he kept along with one of the groundskeepers. One day, Pepper got kicked out of the game. He went into the clubhouse, showered, changed into his street clothes and walked back onto the field. He called time, then strolled out toward left field, hopped the fence and into the garden.... He got the hose out and just stood there watering. There wasn't a darn thing the umpire could do about it" Schoendienst says, "except stand there smiling and trying not to laugh" (31).

This was typical behavior for Pepper. First, it created laughter. Second, it exhibited on Pepper's part a complete lack of acceptable behavior. Third, the act wasn't done to show anybody up, but because it seemed right to Pepper. Martin wanted to get to his garden and there was no law against it. If he was aware of the conventions of the situation he surely did not seem to know them. This kind of behavior made him charming to many people and they liked it that he broke tradition and custom and broke them out of the most innocent motives.

Pepper didn't help the team very much in his forty-six games at third base and in the outfield. His own pitching was something else that made him angry. In the game at the end of July against Baltimore, he entered with his team down 5–1. The third inning saw him walk five batters in a row before he got the side out; in the fourth Martin gave up three straight hits, took himself out, and sailed his glove into the dugout (AP, New York *World-Telegram*, July 30, 1943).

Martin was given a high minor team to manage as the total number of teams still in business shrank during World War II. He returned to the upstate New York town where he had starred in 1930. (National Baseball Hall of Fame Library, Cooperstown, N.Y.)

The Red Wings finished fifth in the league at 74–78. The team had been last the year before. The one bright spot was the offensive play (.337 average) of Schoendienst, who was named the League's most valuable player, even though Red made forty-eight errors.

1944

In the opinion of *Total Baseball*, "never before or since did the major leagues face a talent shortage of such proportions as occurred" in the World

War II years. In the off season, Johnnie was offered the job of radio announcer in St. Louis but the AP reported that he had declined the job, saying, "I had better stick with baseball" (*New York Times*, 1944).

On February 24, 1944, he agreed to terms with Sam Breadon by telephone from Oklahoma City to play with the Cardinals again. Martin said, "I feel—and I'm not throwing bouquets or glamorizing myself—that I can contribute more to baseball by playing with St. Louis" than by being a radio announcer in that city. Martin promised he will "be a player for the Cards and will hold down whatever position Billy Southworth thinks I can best fill" (AP, *New York Times*, Feb. 24, 1944). When Martin last played in St. Louis in 1940 it was for manager Southworth. Billy, still the manager in 1944, told reporters, "He told me he feels he can play about eighty games.... He was the best outfielder on the Rochester club last season and he could outrun any man on the team on the bases" (AP, Feb. 24, 1944).

Martin told newsmen he was engaged "in serious business right now." Pepper understood that his playing could help baseball survive. He knew he was still something of a gate attraction and that might help the game. "I don't want to give the impression of being a character.... I'm holding down the fort for the ballplayers who are soldiers so that when they come home the game will be alive and they can practically pick up where they left off."

Breadon told *The Sporting News*: "While we expect Pepper to be a live wire on the club and to add to the team's spirit, Martin wasn't signed as a coach or a pensioner but because we believe that in a year like 1944 he can help us. Of course, we believe the fans will be glad to see him back, for Martin still can run faster than most younger men" (March 2, 1944). The same issue of *The Sporting News* editorialized, "The fans knew that Martin, who never went to college, ranked summa cum laude in giving every chance the 'old college try.'... He will add new zest to the game by his penchant for the spectacular and the unexpected."

It was clear to see that many, many players who were in the majors in 1944 would not be there in 1945 and even fewer would be playing in 1946. Players, like many others in the rest of the country, could see the war coming to an end very soon, could see the major leaguers returning from service.

Teammate Danny Litwhiler said Martin was as good as his word about showing loyalty to baseball and to the Cardinals: "He was a fine man on the ball club. He didn't go through any antics. He filled in, did a lot of pinch hitting and pinch running" (Golenbock, 260).

Once Martin had made clear to all that he was not on the team to take

Southworth's job, he was listened to as a veteran and as someone who knew the game as both a player and as a manager. Danny Litwhiler said:

> In 1944, ... Billy Southworth ... might substitute Augie Bergarno or Pepper Martin. Pepper was fairly old, but he was still agile. Do you know the trunks they use for traveling? He could take two of them, lay them side by side, and jump over them without a run. And then he'd put one on top of the other, and he'd jump up on top of them without a run. Pepper just had tremendous legs. He still ran pretty good.
>
> I remember one day Pepper got a base hit, and it looked like a triple. He hit the ball between the outfielders, and as he rounded second base, one stocking came down, and by the time he got to shortstop, the other stocking was done, and the first one was over his shoe. And he's running. The sock is flopping, and he went headfirst into third.
>
> Pepper was a good man on a ballclub. He paid me one of the nicest compliments I ever had. He said, "Danny, you're the greatest two-strike hitter I've ever seen." And I got to thinking about it, and I thought, "Maybe I am," so he made me a tougher hitter with two strikes [Golenbock, 260].

He contributed to the club at the end as a batting practice pitcher, though in the regular season he hit .279 in forty games.

By season's end, the Cardinals had won the pennant. They played the Browns in the World Series called the Trolley Car Series. It would have been Martin's fourth. Martin's family told me that he was greatly disappointed by not being put on the roster for the 1944 series.

After Sam Breadon gave Pepper his unconditional release on October 17, Martin signed a one year contract with president Bill Starr, owner of the Pacific Coast League San Diego Padres.

So with the job contract signed and some World Series money in hand, Pepper bought what he always wanted, a ranch. Johnnie signed papers for a 960 acre ranch, at $12.50 per acre, on a rural route ten miles from Quinton, Oklahoma. The house on the property ranch had no electricity or indoor plumbing. And so the winter of 1944–45 was spent repairing the house and getting it ready for the family to move in.

Ruby and Pepper had to consider the ages of their children now. Aleyne, their oldest, was nearing the end of her high school years in Oklahoma City just as the second daughter, Jennie Lee, was about to enter high school.

1945

The San Diego Pepper Martin and some of his family traveled to in February of 1945 was a wartime boom city of 465,000. There were many defense plant workers and ship builders in the city and many servicemen to come to games (in the immediate area were Camp Matthews, the Naval Training Center and Camp Pendleton). Some team members would also be affected by the demands of war, even as it was in its last months.

As the Martin family traveled west from their new home, Johnnie could hear that three players received just one vote each in 1945 in the Hall of Fame election: Joe DiMaggio, Max Carey and he.

> In the outfield at Lane Field painted on the fence you read "Stay on your Job and Let's Finish the Japs." The local joke was that the park had been built so close to public transportation that the only rubber involved was in home plate and only gas used was by the fans insulting the umpire [Swank, 321].

By this time, it was not unusual to have team members who played in games while also working in military defense plants. "As the war wound down in the winter of 1944, a ruling made it possible for men to play ball and not be classed as job jumpers, but still you had to ask your draft board for permission to play," Lou Vezilich, shortstop, remembered, in the book *Echoes from Lane Field*. "The draft board had me go to work at Rohr Aircraft and then switched to the shipyards" (Swank, 335). Vezilich's schedule was often to report to the shipyard at 7 AM, work through the day and then play ball at night, a schedule that lasted from season's opener until May 8, V-E day. San Diego had the virtue of being a very active city, but for the team the wartime activity also meant instability. It seemed for awhile that Martin and his family might have to live in the clubhouse. Pepper put an advertisement in the local papers offering a season's pass to anyone finding him a five-room apartment.

There was a Hot Stove League banquet for 325 in San Diego on February 20 at which Martin and Connie Mack were honored. "A packed house of 325 turned out to welcome the Wild Horse at the swanky San Diego Club," *The Sporting News* reported. Pepper was quoted as saying, "Yep, it will be a long time before I forget this welcome."

> Starr didn't promise San Diego fans a pennant, but declared he would make every effort to give them a winner. And Martin would field a fighting, hustling team, whether or not it was a winner.
> Mack amazed those present with his remarkable memory as he told of the thrills and disappointments in the game. He gave Pepper all the credit for the Cardinals' World's Series triumph over his club in 1931 [Earl Keller, *The Sporting News*, February 16, 1945].

The next day Martin took charge of the Padres baseball school at Lane Field. With a player limit of twenty-five, Pepper knew that he and thirty-four year old president Bill Starr were probably going to have to work very hard to keep the roster up. Starr, from his Franklin 1371 telephone, was going to have to search hard for players this year.

Meanwhile, in El Centro, spring training had begun for rookies and veterans. Exhibitions started on March 14 against a Marine team and then later against the Hollywood Stars. By March 23 the team had settled into its Lane Field quarters and by then Johnnie had a new coach named Marvin Gudat, a former major leaguer from Goliad, Texas. Other managers in the league included Marv Owen, Dolf Camilli and Lefty O'Doul.

The year for Pepper would be an exciting one. There would be fifty-two players on the roster, including sixteen different pitchers full time, and seven more part time. At different times during the 1945 season, it was said more than once that the Padres lineup was virtually a new roster.

A younger man on the roster was first baseman Jack Harshmann. Pepper scouted him at the San Diego high school championship in order to see him hit. Others, the Dodgers and Cardinals, expressed interest in Harshmann, but Starr tried his best to convince Harshmann to wait before signing with a major league team and to sign with the unaffiliated Padres in the meantime. Harshmann, then 17, remembered Martin's part in the contract negotiations. The young player wanted $3,000 to sign and a bonus of $4,000 if he made it to the majors. Harshmann said, "Pepper was very honest and up front. He said, '... Give him the money'" (Swank, 340). If this was desperation on Pepper's part, or just his typically candid honesty, or a mix of both, it is hard to tell.

There were veteran major leaguers on this team too: Pitcher Jim Brillheart, 41; Tony Criscola who had played for the Reds in 1944; Butch Wensloff, who had made his debut with the Yankees in 1943. Some of these players were waiting to get back into the majors; some were satisfied to stay in the Pacific Coast league; some had local draft board obligations.

One man on the roster, pitcher Vallie Eves, was Pepper's roommate. Eaves, an alcoholic, was offered $1000 if he would stay sober the first week of spring training and $5000 if he stayed sober for the season. One of his teammates recalled Eaves "throwing bottles off the roof of a hotel in Sacramento and pissing into a potted palm" (Swank, 345).

There were many troublesome players on that team but there were also elements of Padres team life that seemed wonderful. Some players would go drive down to Tijuana for lobster and deer steak. Some would play golf after the game or go to Carl's Baseball Inn at 469 16th Street in San Diego. The team owner had a ranch, and on some Mondays the players and their families would go out there for a chicken dinner.

By April 24, the Pads moved into third place, four games in back of the league leader. In addition to having to manipulate the coming and going of so many players, Martin and his teammates had to contend with the San Diego fog and the strong wind off the ocean that would blow balls back into the park. The United Press, on May 3, stated that Pepper was "handed a bunch of misfits,... the experts, fans and opposing teams responded without the fire that Martin has instilled in his men. Martin has set up a small-pay bonus system: $2 for a slide that breaks up a double play; $2 for a pitcher who doesn't walk the first batter to face him in the first three innings of the game; $1 for a stolen base; $1 for going from first to third on a single, etc...." The system, by May 31, had the team in fourth place, six and a half games back.

But Johnnie still believed in fines. During a game in Oakland, Tony Criscola tried to sacrifice bunt but he hit the ball so hard that the runner was out at second; Tony stole second and then third at which point Pepper took off his belt and looped it around Criscola. The ump, seeing what Martin had done, called time and told Pepper to remove the belt, after which Tony scored on a base hit. After the game Pepper said to his wandering player, "You were fined $25 when you fouled up the bunt, but I took off the $25 when you stole second. Then I fined you $25 for stealing third, but I took it off when you were safe at home. If you ever do that again, you'll be fined $100 if you make it or not!" (Swank, 343).

Richard Goldstein's book *Spartan Seasons* tells of a team visit to San Francisco in May of 1945, during which time the organizing of the United Nations was being transacted. The Padres were without hotel rooms but a hotel came up with twenty-five cots and "the cots were transported to the Seals Stadium visitors' clubhouse.... Pepper Martin provided a touch of home with an electric coffee pot" (141).

Meanwhile, Pepper was working on rehabilitating pitcher Vallie Eaves. Pepper was very strongly anti-alcohol his whole life. Some suppose that it was the drinking and fighting of Johnnie's brother Charlie that affected this attitude. Eaves, who had been rumored to go to the railroad tracks and drink wine with his friends, was not just a social drinker. Some guessed that his missing front teeth were caused by his drinking. Pepper, with wife Ruby's influence, had begun feeling more religious and was convinced that he could help to save the pitcher. In Oakland on Sunday, July 23, Pep set a date to go to church with Eaves. After the pitcher failed to appear, Johnnie saw Eaves strolling into the lobby of the team hotel. Manager Martin approached the pitcher and threw a hard right to the chin of the 6'2" Cherokee. "He had it coming to him," Martin said. "He let me down during the game yesterday besides upsetting the discipline of the club and setting a bad example for the rest of the players" (AP, *New York World-Telegram*, July 23, 1945). Eaves would lead the league in strikeouts

1941–1946: War's Needs

Charles Coburn and others familiar to moviegoers of the 1940s pose with Pepper. (Courtesy the Pepper Martin Family.)

with 187 but his negative effect on the team was still something that had to be dealt with.

But if Eaves went off on his own to drink, most stayed together as a team. One player told the story of how "every Sunday after the ball game, we would all go out to Morrie's (Morrison) restaurant in La Jolla and he would not only gives us the upstairs room but being a great fan would serve us wonderful dinners where we would dance, play cards and party.... Monday was the day off and we would go to the beach: ... all the wives would bring potluck and take beer and soda water and stay at the beach until it was dark, playing with the children" (Swank, 72).

The team functioned well as a unit off the field, some of that Martin's doing, but still there was no cohesiveness on the field. By July 20 the Padres were in sixth, nine and a half behind Portland while Martin was trying anything to motivate his team. Around this time a pitcher recalled that "Pepper Martin came out and told me to throw under their chin or at their ankles" (Swank, 319). Pepper was not playing very much in 1945: he played second for eleven games and went 30–97; he had fifteen RBI; he pitched five innings pitched in one game for a win. Martin appeared in fifty three games.

By August 7, the Padres were twenty-one and a half games back. It

Pepper poses with RKO comedienne ZaSu Pitts (center), Dennis O'Keefe, and others. (Courtesy the Pepper Martin Family.)

was clear to the team that they weren't to win, or even finish in the first division that year. So they relaxed and had fun. Shortly after V-J day in a game against San Francisco, Dick Geyselman's son was in the dugout with his father and the boy was playing with his cap pistol there. Snuffy Ballinger borrowed the cap pistol and stuck it in his pocket before he walked up to home plate. While at home plate, the umpire called a strike on Snuffy that he didn't like. The player reached into his back pocket, took out the gun and "shot" the umpire. The umpire, furious, threw Ballinger out of the game. Ballinger walked back to the dugout, passing Tony Criscola who was coming to bat. When the umpire insisted on frisking Criscola, the fans began screaming (Swank, 342).

Although it is not known if Martin approved of that particular prank, it was the kind he still pulled, though always off the field.

Martin was using a lot of players in each game. He obviously was trying his best in a difficult situation. His work was rewarded with a renewed contract on August 31.

Ten days later the season ended with the team's 101st loss in a 183 game season, finishing sixth in the league.

But attendance was good, even while finishing thirty-one and a half games behind the leader. The Padres averaged 3802 fans per home game for a total of 346,057.

1946

The level of frustration of 1945 seemed to rise even higher for Pepper during the 1946 season. There was a sense of dissatisfaction all around the league because questions went unanswered or the answers were not pleasing. Would there be a new ballpark in San Diego? Should Lane Field be used by the West Coast Negro Baseball Association? Would the Pacific Coast League become another major league? Should it? Were the ballparks in the league up to major league standards?

The league president in 1946, Pants Rowland, handled some of these questions. Rowland managed the White Sox from 1915 to 1918 and had been an American League umpire as well.

To get ready for the March 29 to September 23 season and to try to recruit some players, Pepper held a rookie camp at Lane Field early in February. Later that month, the 27th, Martin was quoted as saying that: "We may not come up with any more new Sislers or Cobbs, but we're going to have players who will at least know what they should do when they try to beat out a bunt" (Swank, 358). Pepper clearly had low expectations. Pitching coach Jim Brillheart tried his best with players limited in number and ability.

Pepper was very angry when Training Camp officially began on March 1 and only eighteen of the sixty expected players showed up. But there were clearly problems with getting enough players to report. Some problems had to do with competition for players from the new Mexican League. Many team members were just now getting out of service, which was added to the very serious post-war transportation problems. The other managers in the league — Marv Owen, Jo-Jo White, Casey Stengel, and Lefty O'Doul — faced the same problems. Martin had Vallie Eaves back again. The troubled pitcher reported without his baggage, and he had no spikes.

After exhibition games against the Mexicali All Stars, the Los Angeles Angels and a doubleheader against the Chicago Cubs, it was almost time for the season opener. Meantime, groundsmen decided to install, as baselines, "2 × 3 inch boards set in the ground and painted! This, the crew felt, eliminated the old-style laborious and dangerous use of lime baselines" (Swank, 356).

The Padres opened the 1947 season on March 29 against Oakland, managed by Casey Stengel. By April 9, the Padres team was in sixth. Two weeks after that Johnnie suspended Eaves for breaking training rules. Eaves was released shortly after.

More problems: The team was unable to get to Seattle due to transport problems and needed bats didn't arrive. Two weeks after that Martin, furious, was thrown out of a game, causing pop bottles to be thrown on the field at a time when the team was six and a half games behind San Francisco.

Some help for the team arrived in the person of Pete Coscarart, an infielder with nine years' major league experience. But there was no pitching. And even when the team was able to move into fourth place by winning fifteen of twenty-two games, they were still eight and a half games back of Oakland.

Martin was clearly frustrated and on July 15 he suspended pitcher Boots Poffenberger. Martin's dissatisfaction may have resided also in the talk of a Pacific Coast League players union, something that Martin absolutely opposed. Yet "players blamed Martin for constant lineup changes and his failure to maintain a high team spirit" (Swank, 365). At this point, as usual, what was called for was a vote of confidence from the team president. Martin got it: "He is the finest man I ever have been associated with in baseball, and a fellow who is entitled to and deserves the support of everyone" (Swank, 365). Starr may have thought so but the players didn't. Whether the failure of the team and the unhappiness of the players were Martin's fault or not is probably impossible to judge.

What can be said is that by mid-August the team with a recent record of 10–34 was thirty-five games behind the San Francisco Seals. At that point Martin fined and suspended pitcher Tom Seats and fined infielder Jack Angle. Angle accepted the fine; Seats left. Pepper explained, "We don't have hard and fast training rules but there are common sense regulations understood by players and fans alike. Violations are not fair to the public and every player knows it" (Swank, 369).

Two weeks later, Carl Dumler, who had won twenty games for the Padres in 1945, did not get his first win until September 3. Martin did not have the twenty-one wins of Eaves that he had in 1945 either.

A change had to be made and Pepper was told that his contract would not be renewed in 1947. When he stepped down, on September 10, Johnnie was replaced by pitching coach Jim Brillheart.

In October, Pepper's pal Ripper Collins signed as manager with Bill Starr.

Was there a job for Pepper in baseball? He had to do what all baseball people do: wait for a call. Go to the winter meetings.

But meanwhile, the house back in Quinton, his two year project, had to be finished.

And Pepper could play with the Quinton Baptists football team against the McAlester State Prison team in the fall.

26

1947–1948: Jack of All Trades

After his early exit from San Diego, Pepper immediately went to work on the 960 acre ranch in Quinton, Oklahoma, that he had bought in 1944 soon after receiving his World Series money. The house on the property was a wreck, Pepper's daughter Alice told me. Pepper had to rebuild the house, which was without electricity or running water, even after they moved in. Then it became time for the girls to go to school for the 1946–47 school year. A generator, used only at night, was jury-rigged and the family had electricity.

Pepper had many dreams for the property, cattle ranching for one, which he would follow in later years.

But the call came again from Branch Rickey, now with the Dodgers, as spring training approached, and Pepper went to Florida. There he met with other specialists: George Sisler on batting and first base play, Ray Blades on outfield play and Burt Shotton on managerial strategy. (Shotton was Pepper's manager in 1926 and would soon be the Dodger manager.) The New York *World-Telegram* let it be known that, beginning in mid–February, "Pepper Martin will be in charge of base running at the Brooklyn instruction camp at Pensacola. Some 400 hopefuls will pass through this baseball indoctrination center, which is to be in charge of [scout] Wid Matthews and Fresco Thompson, Rickey's chief field agents" (Jan. 24, 1947).

Johnnie was also hired to be "the eyes and ears of Rickey" in the Dodger farm system during the season replacing Clyde Sukeforth, whom Leo Durocher hired as a coach (Roscoe McGowen, *New York Times*, Jan. 24, 1947). Certainly Pepper would be familiar with the manager of the Dodger farm team there, a fellow Mississippi Mudcat, Frenchy Bordagaray the Greenville manager.

Pepper performed his duties traveling to the various farm teams. In July of 1947, he was sent by Rickey to Frenchy's Greenville to replace Bordagaray as manager of the Spinners.

On July 14, Umpire Dallas Blackiston was working the game between the Augusta Tigers and Greenville, as Frenchy's team was trying to get into second place with a win. But the Tigers scored six in the first inning; then the Spinners rallied so that by the seventh inning the score was 6–5. Bordagaray, playing left field, grabbed a liner in left, and threw to first to double off Brown — except Blackiston called Brown safe at first. "The fiery Greenville manager was ordered from the field after striking the umpire and had to be escorted from the diamond by the police" (Greenville *News*, July 14, 1947). Frenchy also spat on the offending umpire.

After Bordagaray was told there was a fine, the usual penalty, and a sixty-day suspension, he said that the suspension "was more than he expectorated" (Greenville *News*, July 20, 1947: 6). Until Pepper arrived, relief pitcher Merle Strachan was the temporary field leader.

Bordagaray, 37, used up all his appeals and went back home to Brooklyn. The Greenville *News*' Carter Latimer's sendoff was that "Frenchy played to win and kept the team running and hustling all the way" (Greenville *News*, July 27, 1947: 6). On the Spinners, the manager was one of the eighteen players whose salary limit was $4,750.

Martin reported to President Gaston at 27 Mayberry Street. The *News* announced shortly after that July 29 would be "tagged 'Howda Partner' night in greeting to the Wild Horse of the Osage. Johnnie Price, the well-known comedy man of the diamonds, will be on hand to keep 'em laughing with his humorous baseball antics" (Greenville *News*, July 28, 1947: 6). Greenville, in second, remained well back, ten and a half games behind the Columbus Cardinals.

The rest of the games, both in the home Meadowbrook Park and away, kept the team just about where it was when Pepper took over. Johnnie played in fourteen games, including some pitching, until September 10, season's end. (On August 4, Pep pitched for Greenville and was credited with a win in a curfewed game of five innings against Jacksonville.)

At 77–77, the team was eleven and a half games behind, but had averaged almost 1,700 fans per game.

At home once more, Johnnie and Ruby would take the whole family on a camping trip on the ranch. Pepper might bring a friend along and one time, his daughter Jennie Lee remembered, Martin and the friend found a rattlesnake and were toying with it within the camping space. Ruby told him to get the snake away from her children and when he ignored her, Ruby took out her rifle and blew the head off of the snake.

1948

The next time Pepper's name appeared in the papers was for the seven Hall of Fame votes he received in the 1948 balloting. His oldest daughter was almost nineteen now and she spent a great deal of time on the party line phone when not away at college. With her sisters, she also tended to the ranch's cows. The children had a horse named Frosty to ride with friends, particularly on Sundays after church in Blocker. Pepper's daughter Alice described her father as "quietly religious." Though he was influenced by Ruby, he was never enthusiastic about church at this time.

That may have fit the stay-at-home pattern of Martin's life. Alice said that the only place he went was to church, but only on Sunday in the morning, not in the afternoon, and he never went out to dinner. Though he had many friends in baseball, one of them being Don Gutteridge, ball players other than Dizzy Dean rarely came to the house in the off-season. Pepper might visit with Carl Hubbell or Warren Spahn who lived nearby.

Pepper told baseball stories to his children and stories of hunting as well. To people in Quinton, Pepper wasn't so much as a celebrity as he was the source of good times and good talk. Many times people would come to visit and Johnnie would ask Ruby to cook something for the visitors. They would all sit around and eat and talk. Ruby seemed to like all the activity as much as Pepper did.

Pepper was still traveling around the country, as in 1947, and some of his time was spent on running tryout camps for the Dodgers. Sometimes, for fun, Johnnie would leap from a standing start to the top of a dugout roof.

In mid summer, he was contacted by former pitcher for Rickey and the Dodgers (1937–1943) Freddie Fitzsimmons, who left Brooklyn to manage the Phillies for owner William D. Cox. Cox also owned the All-America Conference Brooklyn Dodgers, a football team which played in Ebbets Field, renting the space from Rickey. Cox hired Fitzsimmons to be the team's general manager. Fitzsimmons, Cox and Rickey agreed to try out Pepper as the team's place kicker and part-time halfback.

Pepper accepted the opportunity. Now forty-four, Martin left for Canton, New York, for place-kicking lessons. A schoolboy player in Oklahoma City, Martin had also played football with the Oklahoma City Chiefs as well as the Hominy Indians in 1931 and 1932. On July 19, the Syracuse *Post-Standard* reported on Pepper's schooling during the weekend of July 17–19, 1948 at Week's Field with Roy Clogston and Paul Patten, two St. Lawrence University football coaches (10).

When that workout was finished, he visited with Ronald Burkman with whom he was directing the Brooklyn Dodgers' baseball tryout camps throughout the East during the summer months. Then Pepper reported to the Dodger football camp at Champlain College in Plattsburg, New York, to begin his first workouts with the team on July 21.

Pepper, listed as a halfback and wearing number 94, played in the team's first scrimmage on July 27. He kicked four-for-four extra points against the Alouettes in Montreal and also ran back a punt for ten yards in that exhibition game.

On August 17, in exhibition against the Buffalo Bills at Buffalo's Civic Stadium, 27,630 watched as Martin "kicked the first extra point ... but shanked the second into the charging line. Hardy Brown, entrusted with the third, was low" (AP, *New York Times*, Aug. 17, 1948). The Dodgers lost 21–19. Eight days later, on August 21, at Braves Field in Boston against the football New York Yankees before 14,101, Pepper kicked an extra point in a 14–7 loss (AP, *New York Times*, Aug. 21, 1948).

It was a ripped muscle in his kicking leg before the season started that kept Martin out of the first game on August 27, 1948, at Ebbets Field; he was never to play professional football again. When the final thirty-five player roster was published, Hardy Brown, another back, was listed as the place kicker on the team.

He finished out the baseball year and went home to his Quinton ranch on a rural route. Quinton is a town near to Blocker and seventeen miles northeast of McAlester. He began to raise top quality Hereford beef cattle, without making a lot of money from it, while all the time remaining an avid quail hunter. He developed the reputation of a fine judge of bird dogs and was often called upon to be the final arbiter in field trial competitions.

Still he had an acceptable record as a manager in baseball, finishing second, first, fifth and sixth in his full seasons, and on Christmas Day, 1948, Martin signed to manage his fourth team.

27

1949–1952:
A Florida League

Pepper Martin's agreeing to manage in the Florida International League (FIL) meant that he was accepting a demotion. Only recently a "B" level league, the four-year-old league's "international" aspect was the presence of a team from Havana; otherwise it was a Florida league, with half of the eight teams having major league affiliations. Pepper's team, the Miami Sun Sox, was a Dodger farm team. Rickey was still with Brooklyn. The job was certainly steps down from the very high minors of the Pacific Coast and International Leagues. But it still was a job in professional baseball and that was what mattered to Johnnie. The city was large enough, 450,000, and plans were complete for a new ballpark.

Pepper and family arrived in Miami March for a season that ran from April 4 to September 5. The president of the club, H.B. Taber, had seen Havana repeatedly win the title, thanks to the fact that many of the Cuban team's players worked at baseball practically the year round; winter leagues in the Caribbean always were very competitive.

One of Pep's players, Knobby Rosa, remembered, "When the rookies came in ... Pepper would race them — and beat them. He'd just say to them 'Let's go' and he'd outrun them. He made you hustle. We used to have ping pong tables in the clubhouse and when you beat Pepper at Ping Pong he'd get mad at you. That's the kind of man he was. He wanted to win" (John Crittenden, Miami *News*, Jan. 28, 1976).

The last of the Gashouse Gang to play in the major leagues, Joe Medwick, left the majors in 1948. In 1949, Pepper saw his old teammate across the diamond as the manager of the Miami Beach Flamingos. Travis Jackson, interviewed before the 1949 season, commented on baseball in the Miami area and the excitement liable to be caused by two old Gashousers in the

This photograph may have been taken when former Cardinal teammates Joe Medwick and Pepper Martin were opposing managers in the Florida International League during the 1949 season. (National Baseball Hall of Fame Library, Cooperstown, N.Y.)

same league. "Medwick won't go after Martin, but Pepper will go after Joe. Don't think he won't. He loves a scrap," said the former Giants infielder (*The Sporting News*).

But the Gashouse Gang was gone: the youngest of the gang, Joe Medwick, was thirty-seven and the oldest, Pop Haines, was fifty-six. And then Sam Breadon, Cardinal owner for twenty-eight years, died of cancer in 1949 at the age of seventy-two.

Martin's Sun Sox team was 8–2 in the beginning of the season, while Medwick's team was off to a slow start.

By the end of June, Havana was once again leading the league with Miami and Tampa two and a half games back and Miami Beach six back. Before the all-star game, Martin's team opposed Medwick's on July fourth, with the first game of the doubleheader played at 2:30 in Miami and game two played at 8:30 in Miami Beach.

The FIL's All-Star Game a week later featured Medwick in left and Martin in right field. Pepper drove in the only run for his team. Medwick's play in the game prompted Martin to say, "I could use a few of those old Redbirds like Rip Collins, Joe Medwick, Leo Durocher, the Dean Boys, Frankie Frisch, and the late Bill Delancey. And you don't find men like that on trees. Those were Rickey-type players. They hustled all the way, had spirit, and speed. They won more games by taking the extra base than any other team I've seen" (Miami *News*, July 12, 1949).

Perhaps the competitive fire of those Cardinal teams came back to Pepper. His players remembered Martin making a rule that anybody who stayed on the bench while there was a fight going would be sure to be fined. And Johnnie said, "When you fight, fight to kill" (Crittenden, *Miami News*, January 28, 1976).

Martin must have taken his own advice during a series in Cuba. These were games seen by his family, who flew down from Miami in late August with the team. On the way to Havana Pepper told them that games in Cuba were not always fairly umpired. The officials, he said, worked in fear of the fans and did not want to displease them.

When a call went against the Sun Sox, a call Pepper was convinced went unfairly against his team, Pepper reacted and, as he told the papers, "I looked at my two hands and darned if I didn't have an umpire's throat between them."

Pepper and his family had to be escorted off the field and back to their Cuban hotel. Jennie watched this at age 15 and her younger sister Alice was frightened that her Daddy could do such a thing. Jennie told me, "I never saw Daddy mad at home."

The *Spaulding Guide* in 1950 said Pepper was "charged with using his hands to choke Umpire Clem Camia at Havana August 26 ... suspended and fined $100.... Miami player didn't leave the field fast enough to suit the umpire ... suspension invoked September 1 ... suspension limited because of Martin's fine record in the game" (227).

At season's end, after finishing second of eight at 87–62, Pepper's team lost in the semi-final to Tampa to end the season.

At the gate, the Sun Sox did well, averaging 2,139 at home, including the 13,007 who came to the first game in the new Miami Stadium on August 31.

1950

In 1950, the All-Time Rochester all-stars were selected and Johnnie, along with six others from the 1930 Red Wings, attended a January banquet at the Rochester Press-Radio-TV Club to commemorate the all-star group.

A month after the banquet, Pepper returned to Miami but now to the new offices at 2301 N.W. 10th St., and to the new ballpark. His Hall of Fame votes, which were never very high, dropped from sixteen in 1949 to just seven in 1950.

> April 26, 1950. Mrs. G. W. Martin, NW corner 24th and Okla. Avenue, Okla. City, Okla. Wednesday, Miami, Fla. Dearest Mother and all, Thought perhaps an letter would please you. I was reading (as I do quite a lot) and decided I wasn't writing the only Mother I'll ever have enough. God bless you and keep you well. Did George get to come down from Pueblo? this year. Our family has dwindled we all ought to get together

at least once a year. I'd support at our place near McAlester.(17,000 pop) ? why don't [PAGE Missing] so far we're doing fairly well. We are in fourth place 2 1/2 games out of first place. It's a worrisome job but still fascinates me. This section of the country was hot in the summer but if one gets out of the sun it's cool, quite a breeze nearly all the time so cool at night. Well Mama Letha Ray and all I say God bless you. Your son and brother.

With a league salary limit of $4000, and a seventeen man roster, Pepper did well enough in the five month 1950 FIL season, finishing second at 98–55, four a half games back of the powerful Havana team, winner now of five straight pennants. Martin guided his team through round one of the playoffs and was victorious. Against Havana in the finals, Martin's team took the championship four games to one over the Cuban team.

It was a rare victory over the powerful Cubanos.

1951

Pepper's third year with the Florida International League in 1951 was made shorter by about two weeks and fifteen games. Forty-seven years old now, Martin smoked his pipe in the dugout in view of the fans and drank four cups of coffee per game. He played very rarely now. But he could still jump up five rows of the stadium in one leap.

And he was still sometimes volatile. He punched a fan during the season and was fined $25 by a Municipal Court and $50 by the league. Johnnie was suspended another time for hitting a fan whom he thought had become too abusive. "I don't like to hurt people ... but by God I bet he kept his mouth shut after that" (Broeg, *The Sporting News*, March 26, 1965). None of these things had happened when he was in the majors, when he was playing.

It may have been that Pepper, who did so well for himself on a minimum of talent, was growing restive with the mediocrity he saw around him. And, worst of all, he must have had a hard time with abusive fans because, after all, why would anyone want to hurt Pepper?

But then Pepper arranged to have a day given for himself. It was part of a scheme Pepper himself invented. After Martin bought a bulldozer that he wanted for his ranch in Quinton, he then had the fans present it to him before a game. He figured that way he could tell Ruby it was a gift. And Ruby didn't know the plans Martin had for the bulldozer (Milton Gross, St. Petersburg *Independent*, March 8, 1965: 15a).

The team was not doing well. In one game when Knobby Rosa ("our little second baseman") was thrown out trying to stretch a double, "the fans really gave it to me for what they thought was a misfire in my strategy. At that moment I pulled up stakes. I just strolled out of the ball park and went on home to think things over..." (*The Sporting News*, November 3, 1951).

He did come back to manage. Though the team finished third of eight teams at 77–61, in the playoffs, the Sun Sox beat the Tampa Smokers by three games to one. In the finals they lost to the St. Petersburg Saints 4–0. For whatever reason, and by whatever authority, Pepper was released on November 15, 1951, after almost winning two consecutive championships. This firing may have had something to do with the change in ownership in Brooklyn: O'Malley shoved Branch Rickey out the door.

1952

To begin 1952, the number of minor leagues had become fewer by sixteen, just since Pepper began to manage in the FIL in 1949. Havana, the biggest city in class "B" baseball, in 1951 sold off most off its stars. In 1952, Oscar Rodriguez, who had won five pennants as manager of the Havana Cubans, became the coach for the new Tampa Smokers manager, Joe Medwick. Max Macon, another Cardinal player from the 1930s, had been hired to manage Pepper's former team, the Sun Sox, and Martin was hired by Medwick's old team, the Miami Beach Flamingos.

Pepper still had his fun, as Bob Broeg told:

> Gil Torres, thirty-nine and Cuban-born, a former pitcher for the Senators, went fishing off the Keys with Pepper. Martin, being playful, stood up and began rocking the boat, but Torres admonished him to sit, telling Martin about the sharks known to frequent these waters. And in fact a shark's fin soon appeared. "Ha, as soon as he gets close enough, I'm going to get him." As the shark sidled next to the boat Pepper mounted the thin gunwale and jumped at the fish with both feet. The intelligent shark fled and Martin climbed back into the boat, a happy man [*The Sporting News*, March, 1965: 29].

Martin was happy too when, after a win on May 16, Pepper's Flamingos were in front by two and a half games.

And Martin did well enough getting his players to work hard. The team came very close to winning the regular season pennant as it finished just one game back with an excellent record of 103–49. The record encouraged sports editors in the league to vote Pepper most popular manager.

The team did well in the playoffs. After beating St. Petersburg, the finals against Max Macon's Sun Sox were lost. The league, as many others, found itself in trouble: average attendance at games had slipped to 750 per game, a loss of almost 1400 fans per game for 76 games or a loss of more than 106,000 attendees in the 1952 season, two-thirds of the gate, even for Pepper's team, one which had had a successful season.

How successful that season was can be seen in the ranking by minor league baseball in 2001 of Pepper's 1952 Miami Sun Sox team as its number 40 best of all time.

28

1953–1956: Five Teams in the Minors; One in the Majors

At age forty-nine, Pepper did not know if there would be a job for him in the Florida International League in 1953. Indeed, he did not know if there would be a league. One team, the Ft. Lauderdale Braves, went out of business in 1952. Their goods were auctioned off on the steps of the county court house. Public support had been there for the team, but apparently not enough to keep the team solvent.

Still, Martin's life in Oklahoma went on. In the autumn of 1952 he was asked and agreed to help coach the Quinton High School football team. At one point during the season, there was a game arranged which would match an alumni team and the high school team. When the older team found itself without enough players, forty-eight year old Johnnie played end.

His athletic daughter Jennie was now playing softball and Pepper coached his second daughter as the third daughter, Alice, caught her pitches. Jennie, in addition, fished with her father and she recalls catching, or almost catching, her first bass, which "would have weighed five pounds," she says, calling herself "Daddy's fishing buddy."

In the beginning of 1953, Martin became a Pittsburg County deputy sheriff under Dee Sanders, who had played some major league baseball and a lot of semi-pro ball and minor league baseball including a stint with the local McAlester Rockets, a "D" class Sooner State league team. According to Clyde Woolridge, "Martin said his being against whiskey and vice prompted his aspirations for law enforcement. 'I don't drink and can't stand to be around those who are drunk.'"

"They gave him a gun with his badge, but carrying it made his hip sore," W. C. Heinz wrote, "and he says he could never get it out of the holster quick enough anyway, so he always left it at home" (100).

Dee Sanders told me in a telephone interview that, for whatever his reasons, Pepper wanted to be a deputy. A paycheck, of course, was a big reason. And once the deputy job was his, Johnnie "worked real hard … went whole hog." Perhaps, Mr. Sanders suggested, this attitude was because "down deep he was very honest, very hard working" and Martin didn't know how to behave any other way. Johnnie did take the opportunity to speak out against drinking. He would "make speeches at the drop of a hat about alcohol."

Sanders also told me about the frequent visits by Dizzy Dean to Pepper and his family. Dean wanted Johnnie to come with him to work doing the television game of the week. (Dean had established himself as a popular announcer famous for his mangling of standard English.) Because a beer company, Falstaff, sponsored the broadcasts, Pepper refused.

Pepper wasn't the most efficient deputy, Sanders told me. Frequently, Johnnie "wouldn't arrest a guy" because this new deputy would listen very carefully to a suspect. Martin's fine flaw was that he "was too sympathetic," saying, "I don't blame the guy; I probably would have done the same."

Pepper received twelve more votes than in 1952 in the Hall of Fame elections, his total now numbering forty-three. Burleigh Grimes, Chick Hafey and Mike Gonzalez also received votes, though not as many as Pepper's Gashouse teammate Dizzy Dean, who was elected with 209 votes.

News arrived that the Miami Beach Flamingos president, Paul D. Rust, Jr., was about to move his team and become the Ft. Lauderdale Lions, but that Rust intended to retain Pepper and several players. Surely, the offer from the city of Ft. Lauderdale must have been lucrative for the team. Certainly, too, the new affiliation with the just moved Milwaukee Braves was a convincing point. So there was to be a seventh FIL season.

Another job offer, from John Holland, arrived in the mail, this one to manage the Des Moines Bruins in 1953. But by then Pepper had already signed on with Ft. Lauderdale. That city had but 45,000 people and the ballyard, Westside Park on West Broward Boulevard, seated only 2,500. But it was a job in baseball and there were fewer teams and fewer jobs. In this league alone there were now just six teams since Lakeland folded and Key West had to leave the league to make the teams an even number.

In mid–March, Pepper began his work with general manager Joe Ryan. They put the team together through the next month. Martin got a sense of the team in exhibitions against the North Miami Police and the Key West Navy team.

Martin also performed his duties in public relations. On April 3, he went to a Roy Rogers Headquarters party at Sears that "brought out scores of boys in their western finery to enjoy ice cream, balloons and motion pictures" (Fort Lauderdale *Daily News*, April 3, 1953). Martin was one of the judges for the boy who was to be acclaimed as the best dressed cowboy.

The team began its season by playing Havana at the Key West Stadium, the Cubanos without a stadium lease at home. Then, for the first home game on April 17, a 3:30 parade led by the Ft. Lauderdale and high school bands ended at city hall where political and sports leaders welcomed the team to the city. There, "Martin introduced his players in almost fatherly fashion" (Fort Lauderdale *Daily News*, April 3, 1953). One of Martin's player was Ed Charles, 20, who, like Pepper, would be an older rookie when he made it to the majors.

The team dressed in a uniform that featured "Lions" in script on the blue nylon shirt's front; the cap had a raised "L" in script. The pin-striped pants were shorts.

Dressed in this fashion, by May 1, the team was 8–8, three-and-a-half games behind Miami, because, as Dick Meyer said in the Fort Lauderdale *Daily News*, the Lions were "still inclined to fall apart at the seams in the late going." It was true, the paper added, that "Pepper Martin has an unpredictable crew" who were 3–5 after winning the first five games. FIL President Phil O'Connell said, "Pepper is a colorful manager all right ... but at times it'll be necessary to dim some of his color" (Fort Lauderdale *Daily News*, April 3, 1953).

Part of Pepper's inventiveness was the way he dealt with the absence of a batting cage. Martin solved the problem by building one himself, of his own design. From netting and wheels, from pipes and tarpaulins, and with the help of a catcher from Nicaragua and a pitcher from Panama, Pep finished the batting cage, a marvel of welding, in three weeks (Heinz, 101).

There were times now when Pep would appear with a beard, because he would skip shaving for a day "if my wife isn't around to remind me.... She has to keep after me about haircuts too" (Des Moines *Register*, July 27, 1955).

He was fortunate to have had on his pitching staff a former major leaguer named Hooks Iott, who once struck out twenty-five batters in a nine inning game and thirty in a seventeen inning game. Iott helped the team to the first half championship and added an extra inning win in the July 18 All-Star Game, which matched the Lions team against an all-star team made up of players from the other five teams.

Near the end of the season in Fort Lauderdale, delight with the team was apparent at a banquet on August 31. Lion players were given toiletry kits by FIL President O'Connell as mementos of their participation in the All-Star Game in July. The next day Dick Meyer of the Ft. Lauderdale *Daily News* wrote, "The season's last game attracted 1,254 fans, most of whom came to pay tribute to the color-rich Lion skipper as well as to say farewell to a cornucopian diamond campaign.... The 49-year-old part-time rancher was choked with emotion after receiving gifts estimated to be worth $2,000. Included were a lathe, grinder, sander, spray gun and compressor, cigars and fruit. Tears welled in Pepper's eyes" when he was given a scrapbook of the team's season by an eleven-year-old girl. Then, "Speaking simply but effectively, like a latter-day Will Rogers, Martin's words came slowly and pointedly from a full heart" (August 22, 1953: 2b).

The newspaper's sports editor, Fred Pettijohn, took over the next day: "It's difficult to imagine anyone having more success that Pepper's had this season winning both the first and second halves ... piloting the club that is leading the league in attendance and furnishing a big percentage of the individual leaders in the various batting and pitching departments in the circuit. And it's even more difficult to imagine any manager capturing the hearts and respect of the paying public any more than the now pastured Wild Hoss of the Osage has lassoed Lauderdale this season.... He did the job like the book says it should be done.... I don't claim he's a genius. I just say he's a ball player's manager" (Fort Lauderdale *Daily News*, Sept. 1: 2b).

Razor Williams, the third baseman, won the titles in batting average, runs, RBI and home runs. Another hitter for Pepper, Jesse Levan, led the league in hits. Of the eight hitters on the team with the most at bats, their averages were .334, .327, .323, .313, .306, .290, .263 and .255. Winston Brown led all pitchers in wins and strikeouts. With a record of 39–19 in the second half, the Lions swept the league, a dominance so complete the second place team finished fourteen games behind. The record of 92–46 showed a drop of fourteen fewer games played than in 1952. Attendance averaged 888 per game.

At the victory dinner at the Downtown Lions Club clubhouse on SW 11th St., one of his players praised Martin "as the greatest teacher, manager and leader he knew in baseball." Then "steak was served and each player received a money clip engraved with his name and team position" (Meyer, Fort Lauderdale *Daily News*, Sept. 1: 2b).

The semi-finals against Havana were played without any radio coverage so that attendance might be raised and thus the players' shares increased. But in the 3–1 series won by the Lions, the crowd averaged only 546. Attendance was better in the Shaunessey playoffs final series though a steady drizzle in both games five and six forced fans to huddle under the grandstand for much of the games. When the Ft. Lauderdale Lions beat St. Petersburg 7–4 in game six, the championship was theirs. This was the second FIL championship since 1949 for Pepper.

The players hoped to take home some more money through a player appreciation game. A clowning game with "Martin, George Handy and Sylvester Sneed, local Negro player just back from a whirl at pro ball in Canada, put on a slick, sleight-of-hand warm-up act ... in a Pepper game which saw the trip fake most of its throws to the hitter and toss the ball amongst themselves. Four rousing rounds of clowning followed with as many as five baseballs flying around the diamond at one time ... base runners were tackled, umpires fielded the ball" (Meyer, Fort Lauderdale *Daily News*, Sept. 9). The crowd was 498 paid; fans threw an additional $165 into a hat.

Pepper made the mistake of playing third in that game for five innings. The next day he laughed about his stint, saying, "When your arm hurts so bad after five innings that you can't lift a spoonful of cereal from a bowl to your lips you are definitely a bench manager. Boys, I have retired again" (Pettijohn, Fort Lauderdale *Daily News*, Sept. 17).

That same day a proposed series between the FIL champion Lions and the Caribbean champion was called off when the championship of the Caribbean was taking so long to play that the Lions players could not wait around to see it end.

1954

The next year saw even more changes in the Florida International League as both Havana and Ft. Lauderdale withdrew. Tallahassee's team replaced one and Miami Beach replaced the other. Tampa, Miami, West Palm Beach and St. Petersburg remained in the six team league for 1954. Once again Pepper was working with G. M. Joe Ryan, but now at Miami Beach and having yet another home, Flamingo Park, which seated 3000. Martin was now in his thirtieth year in professional baseball and with his tenth professional team.

But the 3000 seats were never filled and the team averaged only 282 paid per game, which could not produce the revenue to pay the $4,600 for the higher salaried players and the lower salaries for the rest of the sixteen players per team.

Pep earned his pay. Seeing that the pitching mound was a mess, and hearing that there was particularly good red clay just north of Tallahassee, the manager drove up there, shoveled a load of clay into a truck and drove back. There he built a fine area from which to pitch (Heinz, 101).

But to whom?

By May 5, Tampa and Miami disbanded. To try to salvage something from the season, Miami Beach moved to Miami (and its bigger stadium), changing the team name to the Greater Miami Flamingos. The four team league tried to play the rest of the 150 game schedule.

Pepper had his team play hard as usual. His team won the first half championship of the 1954 season. However, the FIL did not extend the season much beyond that time and the whole league folded on July 27.

Five days later, Martin was in a new job and so were many of his FIL players, as they moved to the Piedmont League and the Portsmouth, Virginia, Merrimacs. For the only unaffiliated team in the league, adding the Miami Beach manager and some of his players was an infusion of talent. Their home park was Portsmouth Stadium, seating 6,000, but the Merrimacs were without a major league team sending them players. Portsmouth, under former manager Alex Monchak, was 50–48 and ten and a half games behind before Pepper's first game on August 1. Pepper arrived late on July 31 after a long drive from Florida.

The Piedmont League's leading team was the Norfolk Tars, at 61–38, while in second were the York White Roses at 57–42. After a first game loss by 15–5 to fourth place Newport News, Martin sized up the team.

Photographed in first base coaching box, his black horn-rimmed glasses by now obvious to all, Martin knew that three fourths of the infield had come from his own Flamingos team. Here, after one hundred games played, there was one hitter on the team with more than 400 at bats, one with 377 and one with 307. No one else was above 200. There were two pitchers with more than 100 innings pitched and three who had appeared in 22, 17 and 14 games. The four other throwers averaged three games pitched.

Bill Jackson of the Portsmouth *Pilot* believed that "no clutch hitting [was] the same ol' problem which plagued Al Monchak, [and] is causing Pepper Martin to get off to a rough start" (Aug. 3, 1954). Rough start indeed with a 3–6 record to begin August. But the team stayed in fourth place, a playoff spot, even though they were under .500 at 53–54.

In a close game in an important series, the story went, fifty-year-old Martin came to bat, lined a hit to center and stretched the hit as the runner scored the wining run, Martin sliding once again head first into second base. The sliding grandfather.

By the end of August, the team was still under .500 but at least they were four and a half games ahead of the Hagerstown Packets for fourth.

And fourth was where the team finished a week later, but with a record of 71–69, two games over .500.

In the 1954 playoffs, the Merrimacs beat Norfolk four games to two to make it into the finals against the Newport News Dodgers. The Merrimacs pushed the series to seven games, but lost the last game. Clearly, Martin got the most out of that team.

Meanwhile, lost from baseball were the Philadelphia Athletics from that Pennsylvania city and the Browns from St. Louis, these two teams joining the Braves in moving out of their fifty year homes. Even the Piedmont League had little time left to live.

1955

In the off-season, Wid Matthews, who had been one of "Branch Rickey's chief field agents," was now the Cubs' personnel director; that is, the director of the farm system. Matthews and Pepper had worked together in the late forties. In 1955 Pepper was hired to be the manager of a Cubs minor league affiliate, the Macon, Georgia, Peaches.

Before he left home, though, he helped to finish a project started during the winter. The Baptist church in McAlester, called Victory, decided to put a mission church in Blocker and so representatives of the church came to Pepper to help get it started, as he was influential in the area. His two older daughters were married now and Alice, his very youngest child, was nineteen. By now Pepper and wife would drive every Sunday to church by themselves. Before services began, Ruby taught married ladies Sunday School.

When Pepper reported to Luther Williams Field in Macon in March of 1955, he was instructed to put together a Sally League team of eighteen, himself included, for a season about a month shorter than the majors. The team included the first black players to play for Macon and it turned out that "this squad was a young one and a very fast one, but it was deficient in both power and pitching" (Wilson, 170).

Martin "exhibited certain eccentricities that the fans picked up on right away," Carl Wilson wrote in his book on Macon baseball. "First, he did not hit ground balls for infield practice ... ," something that managers do up until the present day, "but assigned this duty to a pitcher, saying that he just didn't do it very well himself" (169). While this may seem odd, it was typical of Martin not to try to do something if it could not be done well and not to embarrass himself on the field. With a bad toe that season, Martin always coached in the coach's box nearest the dugout; in

Macon that meant first base. He didn't mind being odd; he just did what felt right.

The team was in trouble. Attendance dropped from 1300 from the year before to 600 per game and the American Legion had to underwrite a game for $1500 so the payroll could be met.

On May 28, according to the book *Macon Plays at Home Tonight*, "Shortstop Ted ... Lewandowski ... missed a squeeze signal and also had failed to run the bases in the manner his manager had directed." Shortly after, in the team dugout, Martin yelled at Lewandowski and Lewandowski said something to Pepper to infuriate the manager enough to make him punch his player. Lewandowski attacked as well, the fight in full view of 1500 fans. When the brawl was broken up, Lewandowski left the club and "since then the Peaches have been playing sandlot ball in the field" and their pitching, which had never been too strong, collapsed (Wilson, 171).

But Pepper used what he had to work with — speed, not power. So Martin had the team hit and run many times, and used the sacrifice bunt whenever he could. If there was no power on the team, the runners had to be moved up in order for singles hitters to do their jobs. Those strategies did not help the team much or they helped only to keep the Peaches out of eighth place. Wilson tells us that "he used an abundance of pinch hitters, relief pitchers and more pinch runners than any other manager ... [using] about 15 of his ... men in each game" (171). Trying to do his best with what he had did not work out through two months of the 1955 season.

A decision was made, the idea of Wid Matthews, to make three shifts: first, to bring in Ivy Griffin to replace Pepper in Macon; second, to replace Les Peden, the Des Moines manager; third, to shift Pepper to the managership of the Des Moines Bruins. Macon would finish the season at 67–73, suggesting that the problem was with the team, not the managers.

Martin left Macon by car on July 5 with his wife and drove home to Oklahoma. From Quinton, Pepper arrived in Des Moines on July 9, after a series of rainstorms delayed him. (Martin had been offered the Des Moines job once before, in 1953.)

The Western League class "A" team had "a distressing inability to win on the road," said the Des Moines *Register*, "[which] ruined the Bruins as contenders this season." In fact the team's record was 24–15 at home but 11–31 on the road. The Bruins, a Cubs farm team, were hitting .250, and were sixth in a seven team league. They were also eleven games behind when Pepper joined the team.

The *Register* reported that Martin "believes in having players take advantage of their speed when they have it, and employs the steal and hit-and-run much more than most managers of today. [His theory of managing includes building] morale and hustle. They are the important things. 'I have always given everything I had every second of every game. I expect the same thing from my players'" (July 7, 1955).

Yet Pepper knew about grand statements. To Bill Bryson of the *Register* he said, "It's inconceivable that an experienced baseball man would hazard an opinion after witnessing so few innings. If I told you I had come here with a magic formula for winning, you would classify me as a simplified simpleton" (July 7, 1955).

Against the Lincoln Chiefs, Martin's first games as Des Moines' manager was a doubleheader. When Pepper came out for the pre-game discussion with the umpires, the turnout of 1570 at Pioneer Memorial Stadium gave him affectionate applause. In the crowd, as it was then the major league All-Star break, was Dutch Leonard, 49, pitching coach of the Cubs, who had come to look over the Bruins' pitching.

After the doubleheader, the team left by train for games in Colorado. First they went to Pueblo to play the Dodgers at Runyon Field and then to Colorado Springs to play the Sky Sox. While in Colorado Springs on Sunday, July 17, Pepper was called on to hit in the press versus the radio broadcasters game. "He drilled a hit past third [but the crowd] was unprepared for the furious burst of speed from those old bow-legs.... Martin did not let up until he was on second ... but fearing possible physical harm to Martin, the manager of the press team sent a pinch-runner for him at second" (Des Moines *Register*, July 20, 1955).

Two weeks later, by the end of July, Pepper had helped move the team from sixth to third place. By season's end on September 5 the team finished tied for the third spot at 77–74. When he took the team over it was 35–46, so this managing job was yet another remarkable turn-around performance by Pepper.

In the playoffs, the Bruins played second place Colorado Springs and won the semi-finals, three games to one. Des Moines met Wichita in the finals but was swept in the three games.

Pepper had done his job in overseeing the team's performance and the attendance of 1,175 per game was an acceptable number.

1956

In fact, he had done so well that in 1956 he was promoted to the big club in Chicago. There Pepper had many friends. Wid Matthews was, of course, now the de facto general manager of the team; Ray Blades, Pepper's teammate and former manager with the Cardinals in the 1930s was

By TOM M. OLSON

This cartoon and accompanying tract illustrated Pepper's growing religious faith, inspired by his wife Ruby.

now, like Martin, a Cubs coach; Pants Rowland, who was the Pacific Coast League president when Johnnie managed the San Diego Padres, had been appointed the executive vice-president of the Cubs. Pepper would be working directly under manager Smiling Stan Hack, who was in his third year as field leader.

Martin seemed to be a changed man. Under Ruby Martin's good influence, Martin became a vocal Christian, teaching Sunday school at the First Baptist church in Quinton. *Guideposts* magazine quoted Pepper saying "I have been a backslider many times.... Ruby will go the bedroom and get down on her knees.... Only the Lord knows how much she has done to make a Christian out of me.... Jesus was aggressive with the money changers yet he took the knocks and the bruises without whining.... Christ was kindly and gentle, but this was not weakness. It takes more guts to be kind than mean" (February, 1955: 16).

How complete Martin's reformation was is hard to tell. He hadn't lost his delightful sense of play but he certainly was less aggressive than he had been. When he joined the Cubs as a coach in 1956, he was reported as saying, "There was a time when if I was insulted or had just taken too much, I simply would double up my fists and start swinging in. But now I have learned to walk away.... I have never hurt anyone intentionally. I always played hard, but never dirty or viciously" (*The Sporting News*, March 26, 1965).

His career from 1928 on brought him a few writers' votes in the Hall of Fame election that year, fewer votes than he had been getting in the previous few years. Martin had not been at work in the major leagues since 1944.

The Chicago team was awful, worse than 1955, when they finished sixth. The 1956 team featured Ernie Banks, then 25, in his fourth year, and Monte Irvin. But Irvin was thirty-seven. The combination of a team batting average of .244, a team ERA of 3.96 and a pitching staff that also handed out 613 walks did not help the Cubs succeed. In addition, not one batter on the squad hit .300.

When the Cubs finished last at 60–94, thirty-three games behind Brooklyn, the owners released many employees, including Hack, Blades, Dutch Leonard, Wid Matthews and Pepper.

29

1957–1964: At Home in Oklahoma

It wasn't lack of regard for his abilities that kept Martin out of baseball in 1957; baseball jobs were disappearing. When Johnnie started managing in the Florida International League in 1949, there were fifty-nine minor leagues. Now there were twenty-eight. That number would go down. In more specific terms, where there were 461 managing jobs to be filled in 1949, by 1957 there were 209.

The greed of the owners was made manifest that year. *Total Baseball* explained, "After the 1957 season, the baseball industry was thoroughly introduced to ... the decisions by Giants owner Horace Stoneham and Dodgers owner Walter O'Malley to go west; [it] sent shock waves through the baseball community. It was one thing to sell a wilting franchise to an enthusiastic new owner and a hungry new town.... In the eyes of many ... mainly from the East, baseball had broken a social contract by allowing the moves to take place."

The youngest of the Martin children, Alice, finished her nursing degree at Oklahoma Baptist University. Martin and Ruby had seen to it that all of their children went to college.

When Johnnie said in 1931 that he wanted to get back to Oklahoma and go hunting and fishing, he was very serious. He was still very serious about it in 1957. Alice said that he "usually gets him a deer every year and a deer head was mounted in his home and on the front of his barn." Martin was able to hunt with his bird dogs as well and to work year round on his ranch in Quinton, along with his helper, Ham.

Pepper roamed his property, content to be there. Having the full-time opportunity to use the bulldozer he gave himself in 1951, as his daughter Alice told me, her father created fifteen ponds or lakes on the 960 acres and planned to sell minnows that he grew there. "My dad could do anything with tools, but my dad wasn't a businessman." Johnnie paid for geese and paid again to have their wings clipped and then settled the birds on one of the ponds; those geese brought other geese in. "I don't like to kill the ducks" he told the McAlester paper. Martin did not have signs saying "Private" or "No Hunting" on his land and, typically, made sure that everyone knew they were welcome as long as they behaved properly. The other ponds he stocked with fish and "anybody in the world could come in and fish." His daughters marveled at his generosity and all from a man who never seemed to have "an extra dime to his name," Jennie Lee Martin told me. "He was poor as Joe's turkey."

His Hereford cattle business brought him income. His pipe brought him pleasure. He was serene, it seemed, as his religion brought him comfort. Sometimes there would be visitors to the ranch; Patricia and Dizzy Dean were two frequent guests. Dizzy's use of spirits and his gambling were frowned on by the Martins but their twenty-five year friendship held solid.

His Baptist faith and ability as a speaker made him well-known in Blocker, and the story is told of Pepper called on to speak after the main preacher had his say. Pepper had in his mind the home-made ice cream that awaited the congregation and his prayer was but nine words long: "Dear God, may the ice cream not be melted."

Meanwhile Johnnie continued to speak to area groups. Martin was one of those men who, when he entered into a room, made sure he talked to everyone in the room and shook each hand. People could see how soft and gentle his eyes were. The wide grin and plainness of the man made him well-liked wherever he went.

Pepper genuinely liked people and they liked him, particularly in his home state of Oklahoma. Aleyne Martin's husband, Alan Cherry, who was Pepper's frequent companion, told me:

> Pepper had a fantastically large vocabulary because he made it a practice to learn ten new words each week and with that many new words learned he sometimes used them wrong, which Pepper soon learned has the effect of loud laughter on his audience. Soon, he could use that trick so that sometimes Pepper used words wrong on purpose so that audience would feel sorry for him and at that point he would cut loose using the words correctly. And it made the audience pay attention.

Another story about Pepper was told to me by Tom Crowl in an e-mail:

> My Dad was the driving force in establishing Minor League Baseball in McAlester, later to become the first President of the McAlester Rockets, one of the clubs that made up the Sooner State League. The league got

Daughter Aleyne and her husband, Alan Cherry, Mrs. George Martin (Pepper's mother), Pepper and wife Ruby. (Courtesy the Pepper Martin Family.)

its start in 1947 closing out 10 years later after the invention of air conditioning and television.

We were affiliated with the New York Yankees and had some tremendous ballplayers come through here. The family business was built around a hardware store. It is through this store and the association with baseball that we came to know Pepper Martin. After baseball, Pepper settled in an area of Pittsburg County near Featherston, Okla. and began to farm and ranch. He was as common as one can get and very easy to get to know.

The rest of the story is: One day a young ball player came to town having recently been assigned to the Rockets by the Yankee organization and immediately went to the business office. Then it was customary to go to the Diamond hardware (my Dad's business), [go to the] president of the club and get yourself settled in.

Upon his arrival at the store, the new player was asked if he could be helped, only to find out that he was there to meet Mr. Crowl. He was busy at the time but to hang around and he would be with him shortly.

Well, this didn't sit too well with the youngster for he thought he was a cut above the normal guy, having just signed to play Class D professional baseball with the Yankees. You could tell that he felt he was pretty special and should not have to wait so long; however what the young man did not know was Dad was visiting and he would just have to wait.

Well, to make a long story short, after 30 minutes or so their conversation wound down and Pepper comes walking up the aisle, sticking out his paw to the young man congratulating him on his accomplishments and wishing him well with his professional career. You have to know Pepper to appreciate him for when he came to town he always wore his work boots, an old baseball cap and his overalls and looked just like a country bumpkin.

After he left, cousin Tom went up to the rookie and told him he had just shaken hands with Pepper Martin and the kid now realized that he needed to come down from his high and mighty ways.

This a story I remember from the mid-'50s which proves to me that there are things in life you never forget.

Arthur Daley of the *Times* agreed. He was "... a simple, genuine man," Daley wrote, remembering Pepper (*New York Times*, October 8, 1958). Other sportswriters, liking him as well, gave Pepper his highest vote total yet, forty-six, in the Hall of Fame election that year. That year no one was elected and Martin, fifteenth in the election, had more votes than one hundred others. Johnnie had only four fewer votes than Joe Medwick, his old teammate.

Pepper began yet another job, this time as a baseball broadcaster. He was hired by station KVOO-TV, channel two in Tulsa, an NBC affiliate, to co-host the pre-game World Series show. The veteran Len Morton guided him through the thirty minute show which sometimes had guests, and sometimes featured Pepper on harmonica. Of course, Pepper had first hand experience with four World Series, so he could talk about those as well.

Then the Tulsa Oilers needed a coach and they called on Pepper in 1958. The last of his daughters at home, Alice, now a nurse, married that year, and with house empty, Pepper was looking around for something to do. Pepper called the owner's number, Tulsa 6-2104, to accept the offer. The Oilers then were a Phillies farm team with a 7626 seat facility named Texas League Park. The "AA" Texas League team, managed by Albert Widmar, had a season of 154 games from April 18 to September 7.

The season's work really began when players reported on March 21 to the Oiler Spring camp at Austin, Texas. The team had to end up with nineteen on the squad, with the highest salaried players being paid $13,500. (One of those players was twenty-seven year old Bobby Winkles, who would be a major league manager.) One-a-day workouts lasted until March 28. During that pre-exhibition time, Albert Widmar said, "Coach Pepper Martin injected a lot of life into the players today, and we had a fine workout" (John Turner, *Tulsa World*). The exhibition schedule started with a game against the Austin Senators at Disch Field.

Seventeen exhibition games later, the season opened at Fort Worth on April 18; the home opener was played on April 20 again against the Fort Worth Cats. Though the team was affiliated with the Phillies, they also depended on Miami for players. Whoever they had, the team did not play well, causing the firing of Widmar on July 19, 1958, and the hiring of Jim Fanning, 31, a catcher on the 1956 Cubs that Pepper had coached.

It may have been the team's poor performance that caused Martin to play in one game and although the team drew 110,759, it finished seventeen and a half games back with a 71–81 record.

By now, baseball teams fifty years and more in one city had moved far from their original homes. The Braves, in Boston in 1940, were in Milwaukee in 1957 and were the champions for that year. While producing almost exactly the same number of runs as the 1940 Cardinals, the Braves produced them with 67 percent more home runs and 65 percent fewer steals. On March 24, the Associated Press carried a story about one of the Braves players and a Cardinal player:

> Eddie Mathews and Al Dark, a pair of hustle guys, contend "hustle is the most overrated gimmick in baseball.... It might look good from the stands but all that hustle doesn't get you a base hit" [Mathews]. "What gets me," added Dark, "... are the guys who run like crazy after hitting a pop-up to the infield. It doesn't get them anywhere but somebody always says, 'that guy's got hustle.' 'I've never heard of a guy yet," said Mathews, "who got $40,000 for 'hustle'" [The New York *Times*].

The era of mocking hustle, even by those who are known for hustle, had arrived.

1959

Change in baseball continued. There was the threat of a strike by the Players Association in the International League. Baseball, now just seven years from Marvin Miller and ten from the Curt Flood case, was clearly more and more an industry, a bottom line business.

Memories of other times remained. There was the twenty-fifth anniversary banquet for the Gas House Gang on January 20, 1959. Branch Rickey was recorded as calling Martin "that fellow who would kill you in a game and then sit up all night with you to get well..." (Heinz, 101). Branch Rickey, reflecting next on the current trends in major league baseball, said, "Why, they loved the game so much by Judas Priest I believe these boys would have played for nothing!"

Martin's loud whispered reply was: "By John Brown, Mr. Rickey, we almost did!"

The affection between many of these teammates was in evidence throughout the years.

One minor league team of the AAA International League, the Miami Marlins, a Baltimore Orioles affiliate, was being run by Pepper's friend from the Florida International League, Joe Ryan. Ryan hired Pepper to manage the team while saying that the team needed to draw 250,000 paid admissions to break even.

Numbers which used to be well-kept secrets in Martin's playing days were now the stuff of daily newspaper stories. Ryan said that he paid out $175,000 for salaries of players and front office staff, $45,000 for road expenses—travel, lodging and meals—for the season, $20,000 for spring training, $40,000 for the use of Miami Stadium (including utilities) and an additional $300,000 (or more) for the rest of the Marlins' expenses. The team's revenue to cover all these expenses—$580,000—had to come from major league spring exhibition games and ticket sales with prices which ranged from seventy five cents to $2. If the 13,500 seat stadium was half filled on average for each game, that would about break even.

How would Pepper react to all of this? Would he now begin to worry about filling the park? Pepper always went along with owners. He understood as a player that he was not a Dean or a Medwick or a Mize or a Frisch. He would have to take what he was offered, but luckily his needs were modest. He knew that his talents were as well. As he believed and behaved, he thought others must, too.

He believed playing baseball for money was a thrill and a privilege. A union must have struck him as a threat to his basic feeling about the game. Maybe he thought that each man needed to bargain for himself. He must have wondered how Mr. Rickey, now finishing up his time with the Pittsburgh Pirates, felt about all of this.

But Pepper was now fifty-five and he had become less intense about the game. He cooperated with owner George Storer as much as he could; he worked with general manager Joe Ryan to get the roster down to twenty players. But it was a league that would wear on Pepper because of the travel. The trips to Toronto and Columbus would be difficult enough as would the short plane flights to Cuba, not to mention the political climate in Cuba with Castro coming into power on January 1, 1959.

Yet on April 11, 1959, in a town in Cuba, Pepper had another happy experience in that country, his experiences now covering almost a quarter of a century.

> Most of Moron's 25,000 inhabitants lined the narrow gravel main street for the Marlin entrance to the city and on to the stadium. A ten piece band blaring forth with the *Washington Post* March led the five car motorcade to the city hall. There 'Peppie' Martin (as he was known in Cuba) was presented with a golf key to the city by the mayor of the town. The ceremony brought a tear to the sentimental Martin's eye [*Miami Herald*, April 11, 1959].

Then it was on to play the Havana Sugar Kings.

Back at Miami Stadium on April 15, Edwin Pope's column in the Miami *Herald* told this story:

> It was almost time for Manager Pepper Martin to step out and be introduced with his Marlins. He knocked the tobacco from his pipe and explained that his wife insisted on him giving up "seegars." That reminded me of a time when Pepper was managing the Sun Sox of the now defunct class B Florida International League. One night Pepper invited me to go under the wooden stands with him. Pepper kept running his hands over the rafters and finally grunted in satisfaction. He'd found the stub of a cigar which he had parked there for future reference. Pepper nodded negatively when asked if he was nervous about the opener. "No," Pepper replied enthusiastically. "It's my 36th opening in baseball ... but I'm thrilled about it. I told my players I hoped they were."

His players included former major league players Virgil Trucks, 42, Mickey McDermott, 31, and Johnnie Bucha, 34. The team started off well, staying in first place for sixteen games, but faded to 71–83 by season's end, eighteen-and-a-half games behind.

The team drew 110,000 fans, fewer than the owner needed, even with concessions sales, and with an average of 1,829 fans per games, that 13,500 seat stadium must have sounded very empty.

Pepper also got the news that a former player, Jesse Levan, then of the Chattanooga Lookouts, was accused along with Hooper Triplett of conspiring with gamblers to foul off a set number of pitches to match the number gamblers had arranged to put bets on. Both players were permanently banned from professional baseball.

Even with the changes, with the awful aspects of the sport being brought forward, some wonderful things remained. Sportswriter Joe King reported that Botts Crowley saw Martin reading a book on the bench and remembered, "To my surprise, I saw it was the Bible...." Jimmy Burns of the Miami *Herald* recalls an evening when Pepper said that his ambition was to get to heaven. Somebody inquired whether he wanted to play the harp, too. "Mister," Burns reports Martin replied, "I don't think that's funny" (King, New York *World Telegram*, March 8, 1965).

W. C. Heinz interviewed Pepper in 1959 for *True* magazine and Johnnie's baseball's creativity could sometimes clash with his honesty as in this exercise of his imagination:

> I had an idea once and it would have worked. My idea was to get somebody to make a baseball out of pastry, like a pie crust.... I talked about it in St. Louis with Doc Weaver. He was for it, and he knew a guy who could make a pie crust ball.
>
> Let's say the other team has a guy on third with the tyin' run and two out in the ninth inning. You're playin' third and you got the ball and the pie-crust ball. You throw the pie-crust ball to the pitcher. The runner sees it and steps off the bag. You tag him with the real ball, and meantime the pitcher eats the pie crust so there's no evidence.... There's no rule against it and it woulda worked. You see, in the excitement and the confusion nobody notices the pitcher eatin' the pie-crust ball. Diz coulda eaten it easily [Heinz, 107].

In 1960 and 1961, Pepper withdrew from organized baseball. He had managed at the B, A, AA and AAA levels. He had worked in professional baseball almost without pause since 1924. The ownership of the Tulsa team shifted from A. Ray Smith, an admirer of Pepper's, to Grayle Howlett.

Martin remained an interesting man in his home state of Oklahoma in a number of unexpected ways.

In October of 1960, he agreed to become the Athletic Director at the Oklahoma State Penitentiary in McAlester. The appointment may have had something to do with Pepper's evangelical attitude and the job choice may have had something to do with his religious convictions about reforming. Besides the pay check, it may have filled Pepper's need to be active. It may have had something to do with wanting to be actively involved in baseball.

He couldn't do that during the winter, but since he had experience in football and basketball he could work on those sports with the inmates. And in that winter, on January 10, 1961, Martin petitioned to be legally named Pepper, which action "would facilitate his business transactions consistent with his acquaintanceship and reputation" (AP, New York *World-Telegram*, Dec. 29, 1961). The name change may have also been a preparation for running for office as commissioner of corrections and charities.

And, in fact, he resigned his job at the penitentiary. Before he left, some prisoners made a sign for Pepper, "Wild Horse Ranch," which for years sat unhung in the Martin barn, since the ranch had never been named.

The reason for the resignation was that Martin was asked to be a deputy sheriff under Clarence Hurt, a job not unlike the one he held in

1953. Pepper, too, found time to visit with Warren Spahn who also lived in Pittsburg County, near Hartshorne, just twenty-two miles from Quinton.

Still receiving Hall of Fame votes in 1962, Pepper was called by A. Ray Smith, again the Tulsa Oilers team owner, a man who idolized old stars, and Johnnie was asked if he would like to coach the Oilers again as he had in 1958. Martin, now fifty-eight, had to consider the distance from home, more than a hundred miles, and the commitment he had been asked for by radio station KVOO.

When Pepper called back Ray Smith in early February at WE 6-2104 to accept, it must have been with great joy. Pepper would work under old teammate Whitey Kurowski, forty-four, whom Pepper had played with in 1944. Pepper would again be in the Cardinal chain as he had been almost from the very start of his career.

But the coaching seemed to be in large part honorary. For one, Pepper was expected only to work home games. Chances are, Martin was considered more of a gate draw and his work might be restricted to working out with the club on the field before games and working at team sponsored kids' clinics. He was included in the team picture in 1962.

Martin was also broadcasting games at this time. He was famous for bringing a fishing net to the game and trying to snare foul balls that came his way while broadcasting. Pepper liked the radio job, and liked spending time in Tulsa during the season where he would attend Emmanuel Baptist Church. Few of his Cardinal teammates had jobs in baseball anymore.

The Tulsa field manager was changed in 1963, with Grover Resinger taking over. Again, A. Ray Smith hired Pepper to be a part-time coach and Pepper again appeared in the team picture as he had as coach in 1962. Again, Martin's co-broadcaster was Len Morton. By now Martin was such a popular broadcaster that he was given assignments other than baseball. Viewers remember, for example, Pepper covering the Oklahoma state fair. The choice was logical. Martin has been a favorite in Oklahoma ever since the 1931 World Series. His knowledge of cattle and bird dogs also served him well at the fair in Tulsa.

At age sixty, Martin continued to receive some support for his election to the Hall of Fame. One of his supporters was columnist Joe King of the New York *World-Telegram* staff. "For years," King wrote, "I campaigned to put Pepper Martin in baseball's Hall of Fame at Cooperstown but my colleagues would recoil in horror and point to the statistics.... Statistics ... Bah! Baseball is choked with statistics. To a whole generation John Leonard Martin was the red blood of baseball, the sprit of the game.... He was the ordinary guy who thumbed his nose at the VIP's and made them all seem stuffed shirts. He was a guy who could bounce fallen spirits sky high" (King, New York *World-Telegram*, March 8, 1965).

But after receiving some votes in fourteen different years, 1964 was his last year to receive any votes, and the votes only totaled five. Still, he had been getting votes since 1942.

But his old team, the St. Louis Cardinals, after being quite a way behind in the pennant race to the Phillies, won the pennant on the last day of the 1964 season. St. Louis went into the World Series against the Yankees.

As Pepper co-hosted the pre-game shows, he saw the hit total mount for Yankee second baseman Bobby Richardson. For game six of the 1964 World Series, with pilot Alan Seal, Alan Cherry and Pepper flew in a small plane to St. Louis. There Pepper could see Branch Rickey, now a consultant to the team, and Bob Broeg, the sportswriter he liked so much. Pepper, though slighter now than in his playing days, and with much of his fine hair lost from his head's top, was still popular, fans swarming around him so thickly that ushers had to be sent to clear the aisles. At that point, the Cardinals' owner and the namesake for the renamed Sportsman's Park since 1953, August Busch, spotted Johnnie in the stands and called him out to the field for a pre-game ceremony. Pepper balked at first, but then was convinced to go out and show himself to all the fans.

Despite the ceremony, Pepper was not to be a lucky charm for his team that day; the Cardinals lost and the series was tied 3–3, Richardson making his eleventh hit in the game. The trio flew back to Oklahoma and, by the end of the seventh game, Yankee infielder Bobby Richardson had made thirteen hits, breaking the record that Pepper had tied in 1931. Pepper owned the highest batting average for World Series play with a .418 average. He still does.

As 1964 wound down, Pepper still had his arrangement with the Oilers and with KVOO in place for 1965.

30

1965: Death of a Baseball Man

> He'd run to first base real hard, and instead of running through the play and slowing down, he'd stop [Golenbock, 145].

In February, 1965, Martin, now a member of Oklahoma's Hall of Baseball Fame, again attended again Tulsa's annual Diamond Dinner. In addition to Allie Reynolds, Warren Spahn, Leo Durocher and Mickey Mantle, also attending was Branch Rickey, now eighty-three, and no doubt he and Johnnie discussed Pepper's renewed position as Oilers coach and KVOO work. In addition to being asked to speak, Pepper also presented the first Pepper Martin Award to Ken Boyer. It was just the "biggest thrill for Pepper. He always liked to see Mr. Rickey, who just loved him so much," Mr. Cherry told me.

Saying goodbye to all, Pepper and Alan returned the one hundred miles to his ranch. Their youngest, Alice, was now almost thirty and so Johnnie and Ruby now had the ranch to themselves. They were grandparents eight times.

Less than a month later Johnnie complained to Ruby about chest pains. Ruby called McAlester General Hospital at nine o'clock that March 4 night and was told an ambulance would be sent. Then she called her daughter Alice who lived not too far up the road. By the time Alice came down to the family house, the ambulance had come and gone. Mother and daughter left for McAlester. As they drove, Alice, a nurse, and her mother decided that Pepper's illness was probably his heart. When Pepper's condition looked like it would not change for a while, Alice left her mother to get home to her babies.

When Alice awoke the next morning she readied herself for the trip to the hospital. But before she was out the door, the phone call came: her

1965: *Death of a Baseball Man*

Pepper, wearing his Tulsa hat, fooling with his daughter Aleyne two months before his death. (Courtesy the Pepper Martin Family.)

mother saying Daddy was dead. At 8:25 AM on March 5, 1965, Dr. Cauley had pronounced Martin dead. The physician wrote as the cause on the death certificate: "ruptured dissecting aortic aneurysm due to arteriosclerosis." The name Pepper appeared on the certificate in quotes.

Alice then made arrangements for her children and drove back to

An older Pepper Martin is seen here, enjoying himself as he so often did. (National Baseball Hall of Fame Library, Cooperstown, N.Y.)

McAlester. She and her mother made arrangements for the funeral and all those decisions that have to be made in the event of sudden death. "He had the body of a twenty-year-old," even then, said Alice.

When the news went out, the Daily *Oklahoman* reported that "more than one hundred messages expressing sympathy were received by his family from the great and near great of the baseball world." Teammate Dizzy Dean said, "We have lost a good friend. There ain't nobody who gave it more on the ball field. He gave it all. Baseball and society has lost a great player and a great man." Teammate Medwick called Martin "one of the most colorful players I've known. He was an inspiration."

Arthur Daley wrote that when news of Pepper's death reached outside of Oklahoma "an ineffable sadness descended on the baseball world." And some delight had left the world with Johnnie's death. "He played with such zest that he was a joy to watch and a joy to be with. If he fell short of greatness as a ballplayer, he did not fall short of it as a man" (*New York Times*, March 8, 1965).

Funeral services held in McAlester at the First Baptist Church were conducted by Bill Presnell and Dr. Eugene Enloe. Four hundred heard the pastor say that Johnnie was a deeply religious man who gave "all the credit ... to God.... Pepper Martin is safe at home. He did not have to steal home as he did so many times. Boys for many years will look back and remember that Pepper Martin taught them how to bat, how to field and how to slide. But many will remember he gave the right kind of example. All the credit that was to be given he gave to God. He said, 'God made it possible by giving me the ability.' A man without God is not at his best" (AP).

The pallbearers included officials of the Oilers, who had insisted on providing their services to the family. Honorary pallbearers were teammate Mickey Owen, friend Allie Reynolds, and Branch Rickey. After the service in Blocker, the procession traveled to Oklahoma City for burial at Memorial Park cemetery.

Two weeks later, both houses of the Oklahoma legislature passed a resolution praising Martin and expressing their sorrow for his death.

On October 30, 1966, the Blocker Baptist church announced an addition to the sanctuary of a space sixty by thirty feet to add "The Pepper Martin Memorial Auditorium." Martin had been on the governing board of the church and the expansion was his idea. Now, a plaque inside the front door of the church marks his contribution to that church.

Bibliography

Blake, Mike. *Baseball Chronicles*. St. Louis: Betterway, 1994.
Brashler, William. *Josh Gibson*. New York: Harper and Row, 1978.
Broeg, Bob. *Baseball from a Different Angle*. South Bend, IN: Diamond Communications, 1988.
_____.*The Pilot Light and the Gas House Gang*. St. Louis: Bethany, 1980.
_____, and Jerry Vickery. *The St. Louis Cardinals Encyclopedia*. Indianapolis: Masters, 1998.
Carmichael, John P., ed. *My Greatest Day in Baseball*. New York: Barnes, 1945.
Chieger, Bob, ed. *Voices of Baseball*. New York: Signet, 1983.
Craft, David, and Tom Owens. *Redbirds Revisited: Great Memories and Stories from St. Louis Cardinals*. Chicago: Bonus Books, 1990.
Eskenazi, Gerald. *The Lip: A Biography of Leo Durocher*. New York: Morrow, 1993.
Frisch, Frank, as told to J. Roy Stockton. *Frank Frisch: The Fordham Flash*. Garden City, NY: Doubleday, 1962.
Gilbert, Bill. *They Also Served: Baseball and the Home Front, 1941–1945*. New York: Crown, 1992.
Giles, George. *Black Diamonds*. Westport, CT: Meckler, 1989.
Goldstein, Richard. *Spartan Seasons: How Baseball Survived the Second World War*. New York: Macmillan, 1980.
Golenbock, Peter. *Spirit of St. Louis*. New York: Morrow, 2000.
Gregory, Robert. *Diz*. New York: Viking, 1992.
Heinz, W. C. "The Happiest Hooligan of Them All." *True* (October, 1959): 66.
Holway, John. *Voices from the Great Black Baseball Leagues, Revised*. New York: Da Capo, 1992.
Honig, Donald. *Baseball Between the Lines*. New York: Coward, McCann, Geoghegan, 1974.
_____. *Baseball When the Grass Was Real*. New York: Coward, McCann, Geoghegan, 1976.
Hood, Robert. *The Gashouse Gang*. New York: Morrow, 1976.
Johnson, Lloyd, and Miles Wolff, eds. *The Encyclopedia of Minor League Baseball (2nd Edition)*. Durham, NC: Baseball America, 1997.
Karst, Gene, and Martin J. Jones. *Who's Who in Professional Baseball*. New Rochelle, NY: Arlington House, 1973.

Kashatus, William C. *One-Armed Wonder: Pete Gray, Wartime Baseball, and the American Dream*. Jefferson, NC: McFarland, 1995.
Light, Jonathan. *Cultural Encyclopedia of Baseball*. Jefferson, NC: McFarland, 2000.
Mandelaro, Jim, and Scott Potoniak. *Silver Seasons*. Syracuse, NY: Syracuse University Press, 1996.
McCombs, Wayne. *The History of Professional Baseball in Tulsa, Oklahoma*. Tulsa: Tulsa Drillers, 1990.
Murdock, Eugene. *Baseball Players and Their Times: A History of the Major Leagues, 1920–1940*. Westport, CT: Meckler, 1991.
Okkonen, Marc. *Baseball Memories, 1930–1939: A Complete Pictorial History of the "Hall of Fame" Decade*. New York: Sterling, 1994.
_____. *Baseball Uniforms of the 20th Century: The Official Major League Guide*. New York: Sterling, 1991.
O'Neal, Bill. *The Texas League*. Austin: Eakin, 1987.
Paige, LeRoy. *Maybe I'll Pitch Forever*. Garden City, NY: Doubleday, 1962.
_____. *Pitchin' Man*. Westport, CT: Meckler, 1982.
Peary, Danny. *We Played the Game*. New York: Hyperion, 1994.
Peterson, Robert. *Only the Ball Was White*. New York: McGraw-Hill, 1984.
Pietrusza, David. *Judge & Jury: The Life and Times of Judge Kenesaw Mountain Landis*. South Bend, IN: Diamond Communications, 1998.
Polner, Murray. *Branch Rickey*. New York: Atheneum, 1982.
Rains, Rob. *The St. Louis Cardinals: The Official 100th Anniversary History*. New York: St. Martin's, 1992.
Robinson, Ray. *Greatest World Series Thrillers*. New York: Random House, 1965.
Schoendienst, Red. *Red, a Baseball Life*. Champaign, IL: Sports Publishing, 1998.
Slaughter, Enos, with Kevin Reid. *Country Hardball: The Autobiography of Enos "Country" Slaughter*. New York: Tudor, 1991.
Smith, Curt. *America's Dizzy Dean*. St. Louis: Bethany, 1978.
Smith, Ira L., and Harvey Allen. *Three Men on Third*. Garden City, NY: Doubleday, 1951.
Spalding, John E. *Sacramento Senators and Solons*. Manhattan, KS: Ag Press, 1995.
Spalding's Official Baseball Guide. New York: American Sports Publishing, 1907–1941.
Stang, Mark, and Linda Harkness. *Baseball by the Numbers: A Guide to the Uniform Numbers of Major League Teams*. American Sports History Series, No. 4. Lanham, MD: Scarecrow, 1997.
Stockton, J. Roy. *The Gashouse Gang and a Couple of Other Guys*. New York: Barnes, 1945.
Swank, Bill. *Echoes from Lane Field*. Paducah, KY: Turner, 1997.
Thorn, John, and Pete Palmer. *Total Baseball*. Portland, OR: Creative Multimedia Corporation, 1994.
Thurmond, Ray. *Journal of Sport History*. Vol. 2, No. 1 (1975): 51-78.
Turner, Fredrick. *When the Boys Come Back*. New York: Holt, 1996.
Vricella, Mario T. *The St. Louis Cardinals — The First Century: A Short History of the National League's Greatest Team*. New York: Vantage, 1992.
Ward, Geoffrey C., and Ken Burns. *Baseball: An Illustrated History*. New York: Knopf, 1994.
Wilson, Carl. *Macon Plays at Home Tonight*. Chapel Hill, NC: Professional Press, 1996.

Index

Academy of Music (Philadelphia, PA) 57
Adams, Buster 171
Adams, Joseph H. 23
Adams, Joseph T. 37, 38
Adams, Sparky 53, 78, 88, 109, 110, 167
Adams, Wilbur 8, 169
Alexander, Pete 33
Ali Baba 131
All-American Conference 187
All-Star Game: *(1933)* 111; *(1934)* 114–115; *(1935)* 124; *(1938)* 150
Allen, Lee 1
Altrock, Nick 61
Ambassador Theater (St. Louis, MO) 92, 99
American Association 39
American League 54, 124
American Legion (Macon, GA) 202
American Legion (Post 61, Sacramento, CA) 166
American Legion Stadium 128
Andrews Field 20
Angle, Jack 184
Ankenman, Fred 26
Arcade Building (St. Louis, MO) 54
Archibold Stadium (Syracuse, NY) 23
Ardmore Boomers 20
Armstrong, Louis 93
Associated Press (AP) 71, 88, 92, 99, 102, 176, 210
Atlanta, GA 129
Atlanta Crackers 129
Augusta Tigers 186
Austin, TX 209
Austin Senators 210
Averill, Earl 102, 141

Bailey, Eugene 34
Baker Bowl 69, 123, 139
Ballinger, Snuffy 182
Baltimore Orioles 36, 211
Banks, Ernie 205
Barrett, Charley 19, 23, 41, 153
Bartelme, Phil 23, 165, 167
Baseball Between the Lines 123
Baseball Hall of Fame 148, 171, 173, 178, 187, 191, 196, 204, 209, 214
Batchtown 16, 148
Baumgartner, Stan 50, 63, 80, 86
Beech-Nut (tobacco) 152
"The Beer Barrel Polka" 168
Bellevue-Stratford Hotel (Philadelphia) 48, 130, 149, 153
Benjamin Franklin Hotel 69
Bergarno, Augie 177
Berger, Wally 111, 112
Berra, Yogi 121
Birmingham, AL 129
Bishop, Max 62, 92, 96
Black Sox Scandal 74
Blackiston, Dallas 186
Blackwell, OK 135
Blades, Ray 31, 32, 34, 41, 151, 157, 158, 185, 203, 205
Blattner, Buddy 171
Blocker Baptist Church 219
Bordagaray, Frenchy 136, 137, 138, 140, 142, 143, 147, 149, 185, 186
Boston Braves (Bees) 54, 115, 131, 133, 147, 210
Boston Red Sox 8, 32
Bottomley, Jim 33, 48, 53, 59, 62, 80, 83
Bowman, Bub 151, 153, 159
Boyer, Ken 216
Boys' Club 130

Index

Brandt, William E. 66, 91
Branscome Hotel (St. Louis, MO) 110
Braves Field 188
Breadon, Sam 25, 36, 43, 44, 72, 99, 119, 143, 148, 165, 172, 176, 177, 190
Bremer, Herb 147
Brillheart, Jim 183, 184
Broeg, Bob 40–41, 48, 108, 109, 114, 122, 130, 134, 143, 174, 215
Brooklyn Dodgers (baseball) 132, 146, 153, 156, 159, 172, 179, 185, 187, 188, 189, 193, 205, 206
Brooklyn Dodgers (football) 187, 188
Brooks Hardware Co. 12
Brown, Hardy 188
Brown, Jimmy 138, 147
Brown, K.O. 126
Brown, Winston 198
Brundidge, Harry T. 41
Bryson, Bill 203
Bucha, Johnnie 212
Buckman, Ronald 187
Buffalo Bills 188
"Buff'lo Gal" 137
Buffalo Stadium (Houston, TX) 34
Burgess, Jack 38
Burns, Jimmy 212
Busch, August 215

Calhoun, George 47
Camel cigarettes 119
Camia, Clem 191
Camilli, Dolf 179
Camp Matthews (SD) 178
Camp Pendleton (SD) 178
Campbell, Cliff 16
Canton, NY 187
Cardinal Field (Sacramento, CA) 166
Cardinal Girls 140
Carey, Max 178
Carl's Baseball Inn (San Diego, CA) 179
Carlton, Tex 26, 34, 37, 39, 113, 115
Carmichael, John P. 57, 72, 78, 100, 138
Carteret, NJ 147
Casey, Hugh 160
Castro, Fidel 211
"Caught on the Fly" (*The Sporting News*) 144
Cauley, Dr. 217
Champlain College 188
Charles, Ed 197
Chattanooga Lookouts 212
Cherry, Alan 143, 207, 215, 216
Chicago Board of Trade Band 150

Chicago Cubs 124, 126, 131, 132, 133, 135, 136, 146, 183, 201, 203, 204, 205, 210
Chicago White Sox 183
Cincinnati Reds 43, 110, 142, 179
Citizen's Baseball Committee 24
City Stadium (Newark, NJ) 23
Civic Stadium (Buffalo, NY) 188
Classen High School 10
Clogston, Roy 187
Cobb, Ty 63, 69
Cochrane, Mickey 47, 56, 62, 63, 65, 76, 79, 80, 90, 95, 96, 118
Collins, Eddie 48, 62, 63
Collins, Rip 37, 38, 101, 107, 109, 113, 117, 118, 120, 126, 129, 131, 132, 133, 136, 149, 184, 190
Colorado Springs Sky Sox 203
Columbus Cardinals 186
Consumer Building (NY World's Fair) 152
Coogan's Bluff 115
Cooney, Jimmy 23
Cooper, Mort 151, 153
Copiah County League 15
Cory, Virgil 136
Coscarat, Pete 184
Court of Sport (NY World's Fair) 152
"Cowboy Waltz" 137
Cox, William D. 187
Cramer, Doc 51
Crawford, Sam 171
Criscola, Tony 179, 180, 182
Cronin, Joe 115
Crosley Field 152
Crowder, Aluin "General" 111
Crowl, Tom 207
Crowley, Boots 212
Cuyler, Kiki 25, 34

Dago Hill (St. Louis, MO) 121
Daily Oklahoman 7, 105, 218
Daley, Arthur 209, 218
Daniel, Dan 120, 128, 160
Dark, Alvin 210
Davis, Curt 154, 159
Davis, George 125, 142
Davis, L.C. 96
Davis, Virgil "Spud" 113, 129, 131, 132
Dean, Dizzy 106, 107, 112, 113, 114, 115, 117, 118, 122, 125, 126, 129, 130, 131, 132, 133, 135, 136, 139, 141, 142, 146, 150, 157, 168, 173, 187, 190, 196, 207, 211, 213, 218
Dean, Pat (wife of Dizzy) 106, 107, 207

Index

Dean, Paul 113, 115, 117, 126, 131, 146, 169, 190
DeLancey, Bill 113, 117, 158, 190
Derringer, Paul 37, 38, 39, 50, 53, 59, 92, 101, 110, 117, 152
Des Moines Bruins 196, 202, 203
Des Moines Register 202, 203
DeWitt, Bill, Sr. 100
DiMaggio, Joe 178
Disch Field (Austin, TX) 210
Dixie Grande Hotel (Bradenton, FL) 40, 113
Dixie Series 26, 29
Dizzy Dean All-Stars 157
Dodier St. 92
Dooly, Bill 73
Douthit, Taylor 31, 32, 33, 36, 42, 43, 44
Downtown Lion's Club (Ft. Lauderdale, FL) 198
Drebinger, John 44, 61, 63, 69, 76, 92, 98, 100, 153, 154
Dressen, Charlie 160
Dumler, Carl 184
Durocher, Leo 110, 119, 123, 126, 127, 131, 134, 135, 143, 146, 152, 159, 160, 185, 190, 216
Dyer, Eddie 24
Dykes, Jimmy 61, 62, 168

Earnshaw, George "Moose" 53, 56, 57, 60, 61, 62, 75, 76, 90, 94, 95, 98, 99
East Texas League 18
Eaves, Vallie 179, 180, 181, 183
Ebbets Field 147, 152, 187, 188
Echoes from Lane Field 178
Ecker, William 60
Edgemere School (Oklahoma City, OK) 6, 8
Ehmke, Howard 78
Eighth Avenue El (New York, NY) 115
El Centro, CA 179
Elks Ballroom (Philadelphia, PA) 57
Emmanuel Baptist Church (Tulsa, OK) 214
Empire State Building 80
Enloe, Dr. Eugene 218
Ens, Jewel 54
Estes, Virginia 149
Evans, Red 147

Falstaff (beer) 196
Fanning, Jim 210
Featherston, OK 208
Federal League 26

First Baptist Church (McAlester, OK) 218
First Baptist Church (Quinton, OK) 204
Fisher, George 36
Fitzsimmons, Freddie 187
Flamingo Park (Miami Beach, FL) 199
Fletcher, Elbie 124, 133
Flood, Curt 210
Florida International League 189, 192, 193, 195, 196, 197, 198, 199, 200, 206, 211, 212
Flowers, Jake 62, 88
"The Flying Redbird Flychasers" 119
Forbes Field 122, 160
Forest Park Hotel (St. Louis, MO) 50
Ft. Lauderdale Braves 195
Ft. Lauderdale *Daily News* 197, 198
Ft. Lauderdale Lions 196, 197, 198, 199
Ft. Lee, NJ 66
Ft. Meyers, FL 114
Ft. Smith *Southwest American* 20
Ft. Smith Twins 20, 22
Ft. Worth Cats 210
Foxx, Jimmie 47, 53, 59, 62, 78, 83, 88, 92, 111, 115
Franks, Herman 151
French, Oliver 173
Frick, Ford 66, 129, 153, 173
Friday 160
Frisch, Frankie 31, 32, 33, 44, 48, 53, 59, 76, 78, 79, 81, 88, 94, 98, 102, 107, 109, 111, 113, 114, 115, 120, 122, 123, 125, 126, 128, 129, 131, 132, 133, 134, 135, 137, 139, 140, 141, 143, 146, 147, 148, 150, 167, 168, 211
Froman, Guy 24
Frosty (horse) 187
Frye, Mrs. Dora 9
Fullis, Chuck 117

Gallico, Paul 83
Garagiola, Joe 121
Garms, Deb 167, 171
The Gas House Gang 114, 121, 124, 126, 128, 131, 137, 141, 146, 147, 150, 152, 159, 165, 189, 190, 196, 210
Gehrig, Lou 34, 66, 111, 115, 128
Gelbert, Charles 61, 62, 72, 73, 109, 123, 129, 131
Geyselman, Dick 182
Gibson, "Hoot" 66
Gibson, Sam 108
Giles, Warren 23, 36
Gillespie, Ray 148, 149
Goldstein, Richard 180

Golenbock, Peter 57, 99, 109, 134, 147
Goliad, TX 179
Gonzalez, Mike 129, 151, 158, 196
"Goodnight, Sweetheart", 102
Graham, Frank 122, 129
Grand Blvd. (St. Louis, MO) 54
The Great Depression 56
Greater Miami Flamingos 200
Greenlese-Moore Cadillac Co. 12
Greenville, TX 138
Greenville Hunters 18
Greenville *News* 186
Greenville Spinners 23, 185, 186
Gregory, Robert 130, 137, 143, 150
Griesedieck Beer 140
Griffin, Ivy 202
Grilik, Jim 167, 172
Grimes, Burleigh 48, 50, 51, 73, 74, 76, 94, 96, 98, 196
Grimm, Charlie 129
Gross, Milton 151
Grove, Lefty 47, 50, 51, 53, 56, 57, 59, 69, 70, 72, 84, 90, 92, 98, 99, 111
Gudat, Marvin 179
Guideposts 204
Gutteridge, Don 122, 128, 131, 134, 138, 139, 141, 142, 146, 147, 148, 153, 159, 160, 167, 169, 171, 187

Haas, Mule 51, 61
Hack, Stan 115, 204, 205
Hafey, Chick 31, 32, 33, 36, 41, 42, 43, 48, 53, 59, 72, 73, 76, 83, 94, 107, 111, 196
Hagerstown Packets 200
"Hail, Hail, the Gang's All Here" 91
Haines, Jesse 32, 48, 50, 115, 129, 132, 141, 153, 190
Hall of Fame *see* Baseball Hall of Fame
Hallahan, "Wild Bill" 60, 61, 62, 63, 64, 70, 80, 81, 96, 98, 111, 113, 126
Ham 206
Handley, Gene 167
Handy, George 199
Hanna (mayor, Syracuse, NY) 24
Hanny 47
"Happy Days Are Here Again" 54
Harper, Blake 19, 20
Harper, George 31
Hartnett, "Gabby" 111, 150
Havana, Cuba 189, 191, 192, 193
Havana Cubanos 193, 197, 198
Havana Sugar Kings 212
Hayworth, Ray 173
Heinz, W.C. 72, 132, 167, 170, 196, 213

Herman, Babe 167
Herzog, Buck 80
Heusser, Ed "Strangler" 122, 125
Heydler, John 57
High, Andy 44, 78, 79, 94, 95, 96, 98
Hinkle, Gordon 37
Holland, John 196
Hollingsworth, Al 171
Hollywood Stars 171, 179
Holm, Wattie 31
Homing Indians 12, 101, 109, 187
Honig, Donald 124
Hoover, Herbert 54, 56, 71, 72
Hoover, Mrs. Herbert 54, 71
Hornsby, Rogers 47, 109, 171
Hotel Bainbridge (St. Petersburg, FL) 157
Hotel Jefferson (St. Louis, MO) 129, 151
Hotel Manatee River (Bradenton, FL) 120, 128
Hotel Oregon (Syracuse, NY) 22
Hotel Osceola (Daytona Beach, FL) 136
Howlett, Grayle 213
Howley, Dan 43
Hoyt, Waite 78, 79
Hubbell, Carl 17, 111, 112, 113, 115, 153, 160, 187
Huntington, WV 114
Hurt, Clarence 213
Hyland, Dr. Robert F. 119, 132

"I Want a Girl" 117
"In Birmingham Jail" 137, 138
International League 22, 23, 25, 34, 38, 39, 173, 189, 210, 211
Iott, Hooks 197
Irvin, Monte 205
Irving Junior High School 10
Isaminger 72, 92

Jackson, Bill 200
Jackson, Joe 80
Jackson, Travis 189
Jersey City Black Cats 36
Jersey City Skeeters 23
Johnson, Si 141
Johnson, Walter 49
Junior World Series 39
Jurges, Billy 124

Kansas City Monarchs 136
Karst, Gene 99, 100
Keane, Johnny 1
Kelley Jewelry 12
Kelly, King 24, 60

Kenmore Hotel (Boston, MA) 134
Kessler Brothers (Bull and Eddie) 69
Key West Stadium 197
KFBK (radio) 166
Kiernan, John 51, 62, 66, 80
King, Joe 1, 212, 214
King, Lynn 131, 134, 167, 169
Kitty League 49
Klein, Chuck 41, 111, 112
Kleinke, Nub 171
Klem, Bill 123, 140, 154
Kluttz, Clyde 169, 171
Knothole Boys 140
Koester, Tony 166
Koy, Ernie 156
KSD (radio) 140
Kurowski, Whitey 214
KVOO (radio) 214, 215, 216
KVOO (television) 209
KWK (radio) 88

Laclede Gas Light Co. 143
LaGuardia, Fiorello 152
Laird, Tom 170
Lake Overholser, OK 106, 172
Lamman, Prof. VW 90
Lanahan, Dick 160
Landis, Commissioner Kenesaw Mountain 50, 71, 88
Lane Field (SD) 178, 183
Lanier, Max 135, 142, 149, 156
Largoe, OE 112
Latimer, Carter 186
Lazzieri, Tony 111
Lee, Harold "Burr" 16
Lehigh Valley System 36
Leonard, "Dutch" 8, 203, 205
Levan, Jesse 198, 212
Lewandowski, Ted 202
Lewis, Clarence 99
Lexington Park (St. Paul, MN) 133
Lincoln Chiefs 203
Lincoln Hotel (New York, NY) 142
Lindstrom, Fred 108
Lions Club at Brea 166
Literary Digest 101
Litwhiler, Danny 176, 177
Lloyd, Clarence 40, 41, 141
Los Angeles Angels 172, 183
Luque, Dolf 139
Lurie, Dora 68
Luther Williams Field (Macon, GA) 201
Lyric Theatre (Dayton, OH) 143

Mack, Connie 47, 48, 50, 53, 54, 65, 67, 68, 70, 76, 78, 79, 81, 84, 168, 178
Mackay, Gordon 63, 68, 70, 72, 74
Mackay, Harry 54
Macon, Max 193
Macon Peaches 201, 202
Macon Plays at Home Tonight 202
MacPhail, Larry 159
Madison St. (St. Louis, MO) 60
Magerkurth, George 158
Mancuso, Gus 125, 138
Mantle, Mickey 216
"Many Happy Returns of the Day" 91
Maranville, Rabbit 33
Martin, Alice Jane (third daughter) 133, 147, 185, 187, 191, 195, 201, 206
Martin, Celia Spears (mother) 5, 51, 52, 110, 117, 191
Martin, Charley 5, 110, 180
Martin, Cora (sister) 5
Martin, George 5, 52, 191
Martin, George Washington (father) 5, 29
Martin, John Leonard "Pepper": aggressiveness of 44, 124; and alcohol 110, 180, 195, 196; barnstorming 112, 135, 157, 165; basketball 113; born 5; as center fielder 44, 50; contract negotiation 105–16, 113; death 217; descriptions of 1, 63, 66, 68, 83–84, 108, 132, 140, 142, 154, 156; football 10, 12, 100, 109, 111, 187–88, 195; and guns 50–51, 115, 128; hits for the cycle 110; on hitting 53, 157; and hunting 8; and ice cream 74, 88, 115, 135, 207; midget racing 122; and money 100; as musician 108, 109, 128, 137, 150, 168–69, 209; origin of nickname "Pepper" 19–20; as outfielder 29; as pitcher 18, 115, 133, 156, 181, 186; poetry about 67, 76–77, 102; pranks 107, 134–35, 159; and religion 204; sandlot baseball 10–11; as shortstop 17, 21; as third baseman 25, 209, 123–24, 125; and umpires 140; and vaudeville 90, 92–93, 99, 143–44, 150; "The Wild Horse at the Osage" 38
Martin, Letha 5
Martin, Mable (sister) 5
Martin, Mary (sister) 5, 29
Martin, Mary Aleyne (first daughter) 34, 38, 168, 177, 201, 207
Martin, Ruby (wife) *see* Pope, Ruby
Martin, Stu 127, 128, 131, 133, 146, 147, 152

Index

Martin, Virginia Lee (Jennie Lee, second daughter) 119, 156, 157, 177, 186, 191, 195, 201, 207
Mathes, Joe 26, 29
Mathews, Eddie 210
Matthews, Wid 185, 201, 202, 203, 205
McAlester General Hospital 216
McAlester Rockets 195, 207, 208
McCarthy, Johnny 138
McCullough, John C. 80
McDermott, Mickey 212
McGee, Bill 137, 138, 149
McGee, Max 148
McGowan, Bill 59
McGraw, John 51, 54, 57, 75, 111
McKechnie, Bill 33, 54, 57
McNair, "Boob" 80
McNamee, Graham 75
Meany, Tom 121, 131
Medwick, Joe "Ducky" 109, 113, 114, 117, 118, 119, 122, 123, 124, 126, 131, 132, 133, 135, 138, 141, 143, 146, 147, 148, 149, 150, 151, 152, 156, 157, 158, 159, 160, 189, 190, 193, 209, 211, 218
Memorial Park Cemetery (Oklahoma City, OK) 219
Merrick, Mr. 38
Merrick, Monty 110
Merrick, Sanders 110
Mexicali All Stars 183
Mexican League 183
Meyer, Dick 197, 198
Miami Beach Flamingos 189, 193, 196
Miami *Herald* 212
Miami Marlins 211, 212
Miami Stadium 191, 211, 212
Miami Sun Sox 189, 190, 191, 193, 194, 212
Miles, Roscoe 15
Miley, Jack 142
Miller, Bing 72
Miller, Marvin 210
Miller, Victor 54
Milwaukee Braves 196
Mississippi Mudcats *see* Mudcats
Missouri Mudcats *see* Mudcats
Mistletoe Shoe Co. 10
Mize, Johnny 131, 132, 133, 139, 141, 147, 148, 150, 156, 160, 211
Monchak, Alex 200
Montreal Alouettes 188
Mooney, 115
Moore, Jimmy 62
Moore, Johnny 123
Moore, Roy 41

Moore, Terry 120, 127, 129, 131, 134, 138, 147, 158
Morrison, Morrie 181
Morton, Len 209, 214
Most Valuable Player (MVP) award 112, 127
Mudcats 135, 138, 140, 141, 142, 143, 144, 145, 147, 148, 150, 151, 185
Mueller, Ray 171
Mullin, Willard 121
Municipal Stadium (Cleveland, OH) 124
Munger, Red 167
Mungo, Van 117, 146
Munsell, Junior 138, 145
Murphy, S.A. 114, 126, 150
Muskogee Mets 20

Nason, Chief 24
"National Emblem March" 90–91
National League 34, 51, 54, 101, 102, 111, 114, 124
National Youth Association 152
Naval Training Center (SD) 178
Navin Field 117
NBC 209
Nelson Bros. 11
Nevill, C.P. 18
New York *Daily News* 142
New York Giants (baseball) 33, 51, 54, 108, 111, 113, 114, 115, 117, 125, 131, 132, 138, 139, 147, 206
New York Giants (football) 12
New York State Fair 25
New York *Sun* 122
New York *Times* 44, 51, 61, 62, 63, 66, 79, 80, 91, 209
New York *World-Telegram* 1, 120, 121, 154, 185, 214
New York World's Fair 152
New York Yankees (baseball) 128, 150, 179, 208, 209, 215
New York Yankees (football) 188
Newport News Dodgers 201
The News (Oklahoma City, OK) 7
Norfolk Tars 200, 201
North Philadelphia station 50

O'Connell, Phil 197, 198
O'Dea, Ken 124
O'Doul, Lefty 179, 183
Oestermueller, Fritz 39
O'Farrell, Bob 126
Ogradowski, Brusie 127, 131, 140, 141, 167

Oklahoma Baptist University 206
Oklahoma Chiefs 100, 187
Oklahoma City, OK 6,7, 10, 11, 12, 15, 30, 52, 100, 109, 113, 136, 145, 147, 157, 171, 176, 187, 191, 219
Oklahoma City Warriors 136
Oklahoma Gas & Electric Co. 12
Oklahoma Hall of Baseball Fame 216
Oklahoma National Guard 12
Oklahoma State League 16, 17, 18
Oklahoma State Penitentiary 213
Okmulgee Drillers 20
Orengo, Joe 151
Orsatti, Ernie 26, 31, 33, 41, 42, 51, 94, 96, 117, 119, 120, 124, 127, 129
Ott, Mel 125
Ouimet, Francis 102
Owen, Marv 119, 167, 179, 183
Owen, Mickey 137, 138, 141, 147, 219

Pacific Coast League 165, 169, 177, 179, 183, 184, 189, 204
Padgett, Don 138, 142, 146, 147, 160
Paige, "Satchel" 112
Parker, Charles E. 108
Parmelee, Roy 117
Peden, Les 202
Pennsylvania Railroad 50, 65
Pennsylvania State Association 156
Pepper, Ray 37
Pepper Martin Award 216
"Pepper Martin Day" 133, 149, 153
"Pepper Martin Night" 169
Peters, Nick 24
Pettijohn, Fred 198
Phelps, Babe 160
Philadelphia Athletics 47, 48, 56, 59, 60, 62, 64, 65, 66, 69, 71, 80, 86, 88, 91, 111, 201
Philadelphia *Inquirer* 6, 15, 48, 57, 59, 61, 63, 67, 68, 75, 80, 85, 92, 99
Philadelphia Phillies 54, 69, 139, 187, 209, 210, 215
Philadelphia *Record* 63, 72
Piedmont League 200, 201
Pioneer Memorial Stadium 203
Pittsburgh County 195, 208, 214
Pittsburgh Pirates 54, 171, 211
Plattsburg, NY 188
Players Association (International League) 210
Poffenberger, Boots 184
Polner, Murray 41
Polo Grounds 114, 115, 117, 125, 149

Pope, Edwin 212
Pope, Ruby (Mrs. Pepper Martin) 30, 32, 34, 38, 65, 74, 84, 85, 87, 99, 106, 107, 110, 120, 132, 133, 136, 139, 142, 169, 170, 173, 177, 180, 186, 187, 192, 201, 204, 206, 216
Portsmouth (VA) Merrimacs 200, 201
Portsmouth *Pilot* 200
Portsmouth Stadium 200
"Possum Up a Gum Tree" 137
President's Cup 170
Presnell, Bill 218
Price, Johnnie 186
Puccinelli, George 108

Quinton, OK 177, 184, 185, 187, 188, 192, 202, 206
Quinton Baptists 184
Quinton High School 195

Radio City Music Hall 142
Raffenberger, Ken 151
Reading Keys 23
Reardon, "Beans" 140
Red, A Baseball Life 174
Red Wing Stadium (Rochester, NY) 37, 173
Reiser, Pete 134
Remington, Cray 38
Resinger, Grover 214
Reynolds, Allie 216, 219
Rhem, Flint 34
Rice, Grantland 161
Rice, Sam 80
Richardson, Bobby 215
Rickey, Branch 19, 25, 26, 36, 41, 42, 43, 57, 70, 100, 105, 113, 127, 145, 146, 147, 148, 151, 158, 159, 160, 165, 172, 185, 186, 187, 189, 190, 193, 201, 210, 211, 215, 216, 219
Rigney, Bill 170
"Ripley's Believe it or Not" 142
Ripple, Jimmy 139
Robertson, M.H. 16
Rochester Press-Radio-TV Club 191
Rochester Red Wings 173, 175, 176, 191
Rodriguez, Oscar 193
Roettger, Wally 31, 32, 51, 92
Rogell, Billy 117
Rohr Aircraft 178
Rommel, Eddie 91
Rosa, Knobby 189, 192
Rotary Club 48, 130
Rothrock, Jack 117, 119, 120, 127, 129

Index

Rowland, Pants 183, 204
Ruffing, Red 173
Runyon Field (Pueblo, CO) 203
Russell, Jack 157
Rust, Paul D., Jr. 196
Ruth, Babe 1, 8, 34, 62, 66, 69, 74, 76, 84, 85, 88, 91, 101, 111, 115, 128, 173
Ryan, Joe 196, 199, 211
Ryba, Mike 147

Sacramento *Bee* 8, 169
Sacramento Chamber of Commerce 169
Sacaramento Lions Club 166
Sacramento Senators and Solons 169
Sacramento Solons 165, 166, 169, 170, 172, 173
St. John's Hospital (St. Louis, MO) 119
St. Lawrence University 187
St. Louis Ave. (St. Louis, MO) 54
St. Louis Browns 129, 171, 201
St. Louis Cardinals 19, 41, 43, 48, 50, 59, 63, 64, 66, 76, 79, 80, 83, 85, 88, 90, 91, 94, 96, 99, 105, 108, 109, 110, 111, 114, 115, 117, 118, 122, 124, 125, 126, 129, 131, 132, 133, 135, 136, 138, 140, 143, 145, 148, 149, 150, 151, 152, 156, 158, 161, 166, 168, 172, 173, 176, 177, 179, 190, 193, 203, 210, 214, 215
St. Louis Chamber of Commerce 129
St. Louis *Globe Democrat* 166
St. Louis Optimist Club 147
St. Louis *Post-Dispatch* 32, 40, 41, 48, 53, 61, 66, 79, 86, 90, 105, 112, 119, 136, 143, 153, 166
St. Louis *Star* 41, 99
St. Louis *Star-Times* 148
St. Paul Saints 133
St. Petersburg Saints 193
Sally League 201
San Diego Club 178
San Diego Padres 170, 177, 178, 179, 180, 181, 182, 183, 184, 204
San Francisco *News* 170
San Francisco Seals 169, 184
Sanders, Dee 195. 196
Saturday Evening Post 131
Schneider, Lou 122
Schoendienst, Al "Red" 174, 175
Schuble, Heine 130
Seal, Alan 215
Seals Stadium 180
Sears, John "Ziggy" 140
Seats, Tom 184
Seattle Rainiers 170, 171, 172

Second Presbyterian Church 10
Selkirk, George "Twinkletoes" 37
Shibe Park 47, 69, 70, 75, 83
Shotton, Burt 23, 24, 25, 26, 54, 185
Shriver, Tom 72
Silver Seasons 174
Simmons, Al 47, 54, 61, 78, 83, 92, 115
Sisler, George 185
Slaughter, Enos 146, 149, 153, 160
Slocum, Bill 102
Smith, A. Ray 213, 214
Smith, Red 133
Smith, Walter W. 99
Sneed, Sylvestri 199
Snyder, Frank 34
Sooner State League 195, 207
Sothoron, Alan 39
South Atlantic League 23
South Ends St. Louis semi-pro team 135
Southern Association 20, 29
Southworth, Billy 36, 38, 176, 177
Spahn, Warren 187, 214, 216
Spalding, John E. 166, 170, 171
Spalding Guide 1932 102
Spalding Guide 1950 191
Spartan Seasons 180
Spears, Mr. 38
The Spirit of St. Louis 134
"Sport Salad" 96
The Sporting News 43, 100, 101, 115, 120, 136, 144, 176, 178
Sportsman's Park 19, 47, 53, 57, 60, 69, 84, 90, 98, 117, 131, 147, 149, 160, 166, 215
Spring Ave. (St. Louis, MO) 54
Springfield Midgets 20
Stainback, Tuck 147
Star Park (Syr.) 23
Stark, Dolly 80
Starr, Bill 177, 178, 179, 184
Stengel, Casey 124, 139, 183
Stewart, Bill 158
Stockton, Roy 32, 48, 51, 59, 84, 86, 88, 105, 106, 132, 136, 140
Stoneham, Horace 206
Storer, George 211
Stout, Allan 50
Strachan, Merle 186
Street, Gabby 42, 44, 48, 49, 50, 56, 57, 61, 65, 66, 69, 72, 78, 85, 88, 91, 92, 94, 96, 98, 107, 133
Stripp, Joe 147
Sturdy, Maurice 151

Sukeforth, Clyde 185
Sullivan Ave. (St. Louis, MO) 54
Sumter County (KS) 126, 150
Sunkel, Tom 151
Suwannee Hotel (St. Petersburg, FL) 150
Sweet Pea 151
Syracuse *Post-Standard* 22, 23, 187
Syracuse Stars 25, 165

Taber, H. B. 189
Tampa Smokers 193
Temple, OK 172
Terry, Bill 112, 124, 141
Texas League 26, 29, 34, 209
Texas League Park (Tulsa, OK) 209
Texas State League 17
"They Cut Down the Old Pine Tree" 138
Thompson, Fresco 185
Three-I League 38
Todd, Al 123
Torporcer, Specs 37, 39
Torres, Gil 193
Total Baseball 19, 128, 175, 206
Traynor, Pie 102, 111
Triplett, Hooper 212
Trolley Car Series *see* World Series: 1944
Trucks, Virgil 212
True 132, 213
Tuberculosis Day 153
Tulsa, OK 209
Tulsa Oilers 209, 214, 215, 216, 218
Twentieth Century Club (St. Louis, MO) 126
20th Street (Philadelphia, PA) 69, 72, 75

United Nations 180
United Press International (UPI) 90, 180
Urbanski, Bill 25

Vance, Dazzy 48
Vaughan, Arky 124
V-E Day 178
Vezilich, Lou 178
Victory Baptist Church (McAlester, OK) 201
Vines, Ellsworth 102
V-J Day 182

Walker, Bill 51, 113
Walsh Stadium (St. Louis, MO) 122
Waner, Paul 111
Ward, Leo 143, 151

Wares, Buzzy 117, 149
Warneke, Ernie 124
Warneke, Lon 136, 137, 138, 140, 147, 149, 153
Warren, Pat 122
Washington, PA 156
Washington Grammar School (Oklahoma City, OK) 6
Washington Senators 193
Waterfront Park 150, 151
Watkins, George 26, 30, 36, 42, 56, 57, 80, 91, 94, 95, 96, 98, 113
"We, the People" *see* Mudcats
Weaver, Harrison "Doc" 108, 136, 167, 213
Webb, Jimmie 126
Webster Grove (St. Louis, MO) 122, 154
Wecke, Herman 60, 101
Week's Field 187
Weil, Sidney 43
Weiland, Bob "Lefty" 137, 147, 149
Wensloff, Butch 179
Werber, Billy 152
"We're In the Money" 117
West Arkansas League 20
West Coast Negro Baseball Association 183
West End Park (Houston, TX) 26
West New York, NJ 66
West New York Stadium 66
Westbeach, FL 151
Western League 202
Westside Park (Ft. Lauderdale, FL) 196
Wheaties 142
White, Jo-Jo 183
Whitehead, Burgess "Whitey" 115, 123, 132
Wichita, KS 114, 135
Widmar, Albert 209, 210
Wiegand, Harold J. 75
Williams, Dib 54
Williams, Joe 66, 76, 125, 151, 154
Williams, Razor 198
Wilson, Carl 201
Wilson, Charlie 124
Wilson, Jimmy "Ace" 61, 62, 70, 72, 73, 88, 93, 123
Winkles, Bobby 209
Wise, L.K. 19
Wofford College 23
Woolridge, Clyde 195
World Series 44, 51, 56, 59, 62, 67, 70, 71, 76, 78, 79, 80, 84, 90, 98, 99, 100, 105, 106, 127, 143, 146, 173, 177, 185, 209,

215; *(1928)* 34; *1929* 48; *1930* 48; *(1931)* 1, 47, 60, 75, 78, 84, 90, 98, 102, 106, 107, 117, 165, 178, 214; *(1934)* 117, 118; *1938* 150; *(1944; Trolley Car Series)* 177
World War I 49
World War II 175
Worthington, Red 36, 38, 39

Wrigley, Phil 146
Wrigley Field 115

Yatkeman, Butch 71
Yo-Yo 128, 136, 151
York White Roses 200

Ziegler, Joe 166

www.ingramcontent.com/pod-product-compliance
Ingram Content Group UK Ltd.
Pitfield, Milton Keynes, MK11 3LW, UK
UKHW041943140426
5217IPUK00014B/629